Word 2002 For Windows® For Dummies®

Cheat Sheet

W9-CEL-919

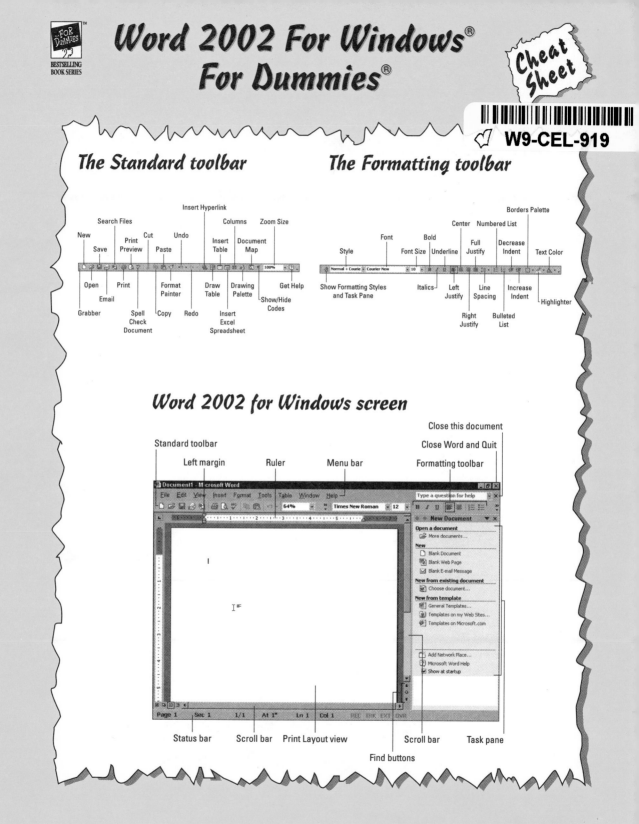

The Standard toolbar

- New
- Save
- Search Files
- Print Preview
- Print
- Cut
- Paste
- Undo
- Insert Hyperlink
- Insert Table
- Columns
- Document Map
- Zoom Size
- Open
- Email
- Grabber
- Spell Check Document
- Format Painter
- Copy
- Draw Table
- Redo
- Insert Excel Spreadsheet
- Drawing Palette
- Show/Hide Codes
- Get Help

The Formatting toolbar

- Style
- Font
- Font Size
- Bold
- Underline
- Center
- Numbered List
- Full Justify
- Decrease Indent
- Borders Palette
- Text Color
- Show Formatting Styles and Task Pane
- Italics
- Left Justify
- Line Spacing
- Increase Indent
- Highlighter
- Right Justify
- Bulleted List

Word 2002 for Windows screen

- Close this document
- Close Word and Quit
- Standard toolbar
- Left margin
- Ruler
- Menu bar
- Formatting toolbar

Document1 - Microsoft Word

File   Edit   View   Insert   Format   Tools   Table   Window   Help

Type a question for help

64%   Times New Roman   12

New Document

Open a document
- More documents...

New
- Blank Document
- Blank Web Page
- Blank E-mail Message

New from existing document
- Choose document...

New from template
- General Templates...
- Templates on my Web Sites...
- Templates on Microsoft.com

- Add Network Place...
- Microsoft Word Help
- ☑ Show at startup

Page 1   Sec 1   1/1   At 1"   Ln 1   Col 1   REC TRK EXT OVR

- Status bar
- Scroll bar
- Print Layout view
- Scroll bar
- Task pane
- Find buttons

For Dummies: Bestselling Book Series for Beginners

Word 2002 For Windows For Dummies

Cheat Sheet

Common Word Key Commands

Cancel	Escape
Go back	Shift+F5
Help	F1
Mark block	F8
New document	Ctrl+N
Open	Ctrl+O
Print	Ctrl+P
Quick save	Ctrl+S
Repeat command	F4
Repeat find	Shift+F4

Common Word Formatting Key Commands

Bold	Ctrl+B
Italic	Ctrl+I
Underline	Ctrl+U
Center text	Ctrl+E
Left align	Ctrl+L
Right align	Ctrl+R
Justify	Ctrl+J

The Kindergarten Keys

Copy	Ctrl+C
Cut	Ctrl+X
Paste	Ctrl+V
Undo	Ctrl+Z

Getting around in a document

↑	Moves toothpick cursor up one line of text
↓	Moves toothpick cursor down one line of text
→	Moves toothpick cursor right to the next character
←	Moves toothpick cursor left to the next character
Ctrl + ↑	Moves toothpick cursor up one paragraph
Ctrl + ↓	Moves toothpick cursor down one paragraph
Ctrl + →	Moves toothpick cursor right one word
Ctrl + ←	Moves toothpick cursor left one word
PgUp	Moves toothpick cursor up one screen
PgDn	Moves toothpick cursor down one screen
End	Moves toothpick cursor to end of current line
Home	Moves toothpick cursor to start of current line
Ctrl+Home	Moves toothpick cursor to top of document
Ctrl+End	Moves toothpick cursor to bottom of document

For Dummies: Bestselling Book Series for Beginners

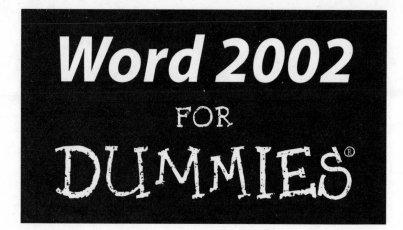

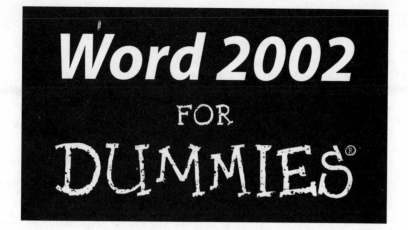

Word 2002 FOR DUMMIES®

by Dan Gookin

Wiley Publishing, Inc.

Word 2002 For Dummies®

Published by
Wiley Publishing, Inc.
909 Third Avenue
New York, NY 10022

www.wiley.com

Copyright © 2001 by Wiley Publishing, Inc., Indianapolis, Indiana

No part of this publication may be reproduced, stored in a retrieval system or transmitted in any form or by any means, electronic, mechanical, photocopying, recording, scanning or otherwise, except as permitted under Sections 107 or 108 of the 1976 United States Copyright Act, without either the prior written permission of the Publisher, or authorization through payment of the appropriate per-copy fee to the Copyright Clearance Center, 222 Rosewood Drive, Danvers, MA 01923, (978) 750-8400, fax (978) 750-4744. Requests to the Publisher for permission should be addressed to the Legal Department, Wiley Publishing, Inc., 10475 Crosspoint Blvd., Indianapolis, IN 46256, (317) 572-3447, fax (317) 572-4447, e-mail: permcoordinator@wiley.com.

Trademarks: Wiley, the Wiley Publishing logo, For Dummies, the Dummies Man logo, A Reference for the Rest of Us!, The Dummies Way, Dummies Daily, The Fun and Easy way, Dummies.com and related trade dress are trademarks or registered trademarks of Wiley Publishing, Inc., in the United States and other countries, and may not be used without written permission. Microsoft is a registered trademark of Microsoft Corporation. All other trademarks are the property of their respective owners. Wiley Publishing, Inc., is not associated with any product or vendor mentioned in this book.

For general information on our other products and services or to obtain technical support, please contact our Customer Care Department within the U.S. at 800-762-2974, outside the U.S. at 317-572-3993, or fax 317-572-4002.

Wiley also publishes its books in a variety of electronic formats. Some content that appears in print may not be available in electronic books.

Library of Congress Control Number: 2001089288

ISBN: 0-7645-0839-3

Manufactured in the United States of America

10 9 8 7 6 5

About the Author

Dan Gookin got started with computers back in the post-slide-rule age of computing: 1982. His first intention was to buy a computer to replace his aged and constantly breaking typewriter. Working as slave labor in a restaurant, however, Gookin was unable to afford the full "word processor" setup and settled on a computer that had a monitor, keyboard, and little else. Soon his writing career was under way with several submissions to (and lots of rejections from) fiction magazines.

The big break came in 1984 when he began writing about computers. Applying his flair for fiction with a self-taught knowledge of computers, Gookin was able to demystify the subject and explain technology in a relaxed and understandable voice. He even dared to add humor, which eventually won him a column in a local computer magazine.

Eventually, Gookin's talents came to roost as he became a ghostwriter at a computer book publishing house. That was followed by an editing position at a San Diego computer magazine, at which time he also regularly participated in a radio talk show about computers. In addition, Gookin kept writing books about computers, some of which became minor best sellers.

In 1990, Gookin came to Hungry Minds, Inc. (then named IDG Books Worldwide, Inc.), with a book proposal. From that initial meeting unfolded an idea for an outrageous book: a long overdue and original idea for the computer book for the rest of us. What became *DOS For Dummies* blossomed into an international bestseller with hundreds and thousands of copies in print and many foreign translations.

Today, Gookin still considers himself a writer and computer "guru" whose job it is to remind everyone that computers are not to be taken too seriously. His approach to computers is light and humorous yet very informative. He knows that the complex beasts are important and can help people become productive and successful. Yet Gookin mixes his knowledge of computers with a unique, dry sense of humor that keeps everyone informed — and awake. His favorite quote is "Computers are a notoriously dull subject, but that doesn't mean I have to write about them that way."

Gookin's titles for Hungry Minds include *DOS For Dummies,* Windows 95 Edition; *PCs For Dummies,* 6th Edition; and *Discovering Windows 95.* Gookin holds a degree in communications from the University of California, San Diego, and lives with his wife and four boys in the rare and gentle woods of Idaho.

Publisher's Acknowledgments

We're proud of this book; please send us your comments through our online registration form located at www.dummies.com/register/.

Some of the people who helped bring this book to market include the following:

Acquisitions, Editorial, and Media Development

Project Editor: Rebecca Whitney

Acquisitions Editor: Jill Byus Schorr

Technical Editor: Mark L. Chambers

Editorial Manager: Constance Carlisle

Media Development Supervisor: Richard Graves

Editorial Assistant: Amanda M. Foxworth

Production

Project Coordinator: Maridee Ennis

Layout and Graphics: Jackie Nicholas, Jacque Schneider, Brian Torwelle

Proofreaders: Laura Albert, John Greenough, Andy Hollandbeck, Susan Moritz, Angel Perez, Charles Spencer, TECHBOOKS Production Services

Indexer: Maro Riofrancos

General and Administrative

Wiley Technology Publishing Group: Richard Swadley, Vice President and Executive Group Publisher; Bob Ipsen, Vice President and Group Publisher; Joseph Wikert, Vice President and Publisher; Barry Pruett, Vice President and Publisher; Mary Bednarek, Editorial Director; Mary C. Corder, Editorial Director; Andy Cummings, Editorial Director

Wiley Manufacturing: Ivor Parker, Vice President, Manufacturing

Wiley Marketing: John Helmus, Assistant Vice President, Director of Marketing

Wiley Composition Services for Branded Press: Debbie Stailey, Composition Services Director

Contents at a Glance

Table of Contents

Introduction

Welcome to *Word 2002 For Dummies,* the book that explains the myths and madness of Microsoft's latest and greatest word processor, for the year 2001, 2002, 2003, or whatever year this may be.

Word is a massive program with an impressive history. It does much more than merely process words. Do you need to know all that? No! You don't need to know everything about Word to use it. A better question is: Do you *want* to know everything about Microsoft Word? Probably not. You don't want to know all the command options, all the typographical mumbo jumbo, or even all those special features that you know are in there but terrify you. No, all you want to know is the single answer to a tiny question. Then you can happily close the book and be on your way. If that's you, you've found your book.

This book informs and entertains. And it has a serious attitude problem. After all, I don't want to teach you to love Microsoft Word. Instead, be prepared to encounter some informative, down-to-earth explanations — in English — of how to get the job done by using Microsoft Word. You take your work seriously, but you definitely don't need to take Microsoft Word seriously.

About This Book

I don't intend for you to read this book from cover to cover. It's not a novel, and if it were, I'd kill off all the characters at the end, so it would be a bad read anyway. Instead, this book is a reference. Each chapter covers a specific topic or task that Word does. Within a chapter, you find self-contained sections, each of which describes how to perform a specific task or get something done. Sample sections you encounter in this book include

- ✔ Saving your stuff
- ✔ Cutting and pasting a block
- ✔ Quickly finding your place
- ✔ Aligning paragraphs
- ✔ Cobbling a table together quickly
- ✔ Configuring Word to listen to you
- ✔ Using a document template

There are no keys to memorize, no secret codes, no tricks, no pop-up dioramas, and no wall charts. Instead, each section explains a topic as though it's the first thing you read in this book. Nothing is assumed, and everything is cross-referenced. Technical terms and topics, when they come up, are neatly shoved to the side, where you can easily avoid reading them. The idea here isn't for you to learn anything. This book's philosophy is to help you look it up, figure it out, and get back to work.

How to Use This Book

This book helps you when you're at a loss over what to do in Word 2002. I think that this situation happens to everyone way too often. For example, if you press Ctrl+F9, Word displays a { } thing in your text. I have no idea what that means, nor do I want to know. What I do know, however, is that I can press Ctrl+Z to make the annoying thing go away. That's the kind of knowledge you find in this book.

Word uses the mouse and menus to get things done, which is what you would expect from Windows. Yet there are times when various *key combinations,* several keys you may press together or in sequence, are required. This book shows you two different kinds of key combinations.

This is a keyboard shortcut:

Ctrl+Shift+P

This shortcut means that you should press and hold Ctrl and Shift together, press the P key, and then release all three keys.

Menu commands are listed like this:

File⇨Open

This command means that you open the File menu (with the mouse or the keyboard — it's your choice) and then choose the Open command. The underlined letters represent "hot keys" used in Windows. You can press the Alt+F key combination to access the F in File and then the O (or Alt+O) to access the O in Open.

Note that in Windows 2002, you may have to press the Alt key first (by itself) to activate the menu hot keys. Then you can use the hot keys to access menu and dialog box commands.

If I describe a message or something you see onscreen, it looks like this:

```
Cannot find hard drive, save elsewhere?
```

If you need further help operating your computer or a good general reference, I can recommend my book *PCs For Dummies*, 7th Edition, published by Hungry Minds, Inc. The book contains lots of useful information to supplement what you'll find in this book.

What You're Not to Read

Special technical sections dot this book like chicken pox on an eight-year-old. They offer annoyingly endless and technical explanations, descriptions of advanced topics, or alternative commands that you really don't need to know about. Each one of them is flagged with a special icon or enclosed in an electrified, barbed wire and poison ivy box (an idea I stole from the Terwilliker Piano Method books). Reading this stuff is optional.

Foolish Assumptions

Here are my assumptions about you. You use a computer. You use Windows — either Windows 95, Windows 98, Windows Me, Windows 2000, or Windows NT. There is little difference between them as far as this book is concerned. If there's anything special going on between Word and Windows, I flag it in the text (which happens maybe twice in this entire book).

Your word processor is Microsoft Word 2002. I refer to it as "Word" throughout this book. Word may have come with your computer, you may have purchased it as a stand-alone program, or it may be a part of a larger suite of programs named Microsoft Office. Whatever. Same program, same Word.

I do not assume that you have Microsoft Office installed. This book does not cover using Office or any of the other Office applications.

How This Book Is Organized

This book contains seven major parts, each of which is divided into several chapters. The chapters themselves have been sliced into smaller, modular sections. You can pick up the book and read any section without necessarily knowing what has already been covered in the rest of the book. Start anywhere.

Here is a breakdown of the parts and what you can find in them:

Part I: Hello, Word!

This is baby Word stuff — the bare essentials. Here you discover how to giggle, teethe, crawl, walk, burp, and spit up. Then you can move up to the advanced topics of moving the cursor, editing text, searching and replacing, marking blocks, spell checking, and printing. (A pacifier is optional for this section.)

Part II: Letting Word Do the Formatting Work

Formatting is the art of beating your text into typographical submission. It's not the heady work of creating a document and getting the right words. No, it's "You will be italic!" "Indent, you moron!" and "Gimme a new page *here*." Often, formatting involves lots of yelling. This part of the book contains chapters that show you how to format characters, lines, paragraphs, pages, and entire documents without raising your voice (too much).

Part III: Sprucing Up Your Document

Beyond formatting is the realm of adding things to your document to make it look nice. This part of the book is a potpourri of esoteric doodads and thingies you can add to your text: borders, shading, tables, figures, columns, footnotes, and other interesting goobers.

Part IV: Land of the Fun and Strange

This part covers some general and miscellaneous topics, items that others might consider to be too borderline bizarre to be found in a "beginners" book on Word.

Part V: Creating Lotsa Stuff in Word

Word's very own cookbook of sorts. Though I didn't have the space to include *everything*, this part of the book gives you some hints and tips on creating various fun and interesting (and unexpected) things in Word.

Part VI: The Part of Tens

How about "The Ten Commandments of Word"? Or consider "Ten Truly Bizarre Things." Or the handy "Ten Things Worth Remembering." This section is a gold mine of tens.

What's Not Here

This book can be only so big. The book's author, on the other hand, can grow to immense sizes! To keep them both in check, I've created a companion Web page. This site covers issues that may arise after the book goes to press. It's not to contain anything "missing" from the book; no, you have everything you need right in your eager, ready-to-type hands. The Web page is just to keep up-to-date. That way, I can offer you supplemental information after the book goes to press.

If you have Internet access and a web browser, you can visit this book's Web page, at

```
http://www.wambooli.com/help/Word/
```

Icons Used in This Book

This icon flags useful, helpful tips or shortcuts.

This icon marks a friendly reminder to do something.

This icon marks a friendly reminder not to do something.

This icon alerts you to overly nerdy information and technical discussions of the topic at hand. The information is optional reading, but it may enhance your reputation at cocktail parties if you repeat it.

Where to Go from Here

Start reading! Observe the table of contents and find something that interests you. Or, look up your puzzle in the index.

If you're new to Word, start off with Chapter 1.

If you're an old hand at Word, consider checking out Part V for some inspiration.

Want to try out Word's new speech recognition? See Chapter 25.

Read! Write! Speak! Produce!

By the way, I am available on the Internet (dgookin@wambooli.com) for any questions you may have about this book or Microsoft Word 2002. Although I cannot answer every question (you should use the Microsoft technical support for that), I may be able to offer a suggestion. I'm open to input, and, in fact, several parts of this book have come from reader input.

I answer all my own e-mail and respond to everyone who writes. Enjoy the book. And enjoy Word 2002. Or at least tolerate it.

Part I
Hello, Word!

The 5th Wave   By Rich Tennant

@RICHTENNANT

Dear Margaret,
What I have to say to you is very personal...

In this part . . .

Word processing is as old as the personal computer itself. Back in the 1970s, when personal computers were called *microcomputers,* the first word processor made its debut. Named *Electric Pencil,* it was little more than a meek text editor by today's standards. But it did let you edit a full screen of text, which was more advanced than the simple "line editors" of the day. Electric Pencil was considered revolutionary.

Twenty-five years later, the revolution continues. Microsoft Word is now chairman of the word processing Politburo. Electric Pencil began the revolution, and then a program named WordStar took over. Eventually, WordStar was toppled by the WordPerfect insurrection. And about 12 years ago, Microsoft Word became the dominant word processor, riding on the back of the popularity of Microsoft Windows.

Word looks nothing like the Electric Pencil program of 25 years ago. Even so, many basic activities remain the same: You create text, edit, delete, search and replace, copy and move blocks, save, open, and print. This is all basic word processing, but imagine how an Electric Pencil user of 1976 would react to the way Word does things here in the 21st century!

This part of the book introduces you to Word, starting with a grand overview and then discussing each of the basic word processing functions in detail. Long live the word processor revolution! All hail Electric Pencil! All hail Word! Merry Computer Users Rejoice!

Chapter 1

The Big Picture

- -

In This Chapter

▶ Starting Word

▶ Reading the Word screen

▶ Understanding the Office Assistant

▶ Using your keyboard

▶ Exiting Word (or not)

- -

They laughed when I sat down at the computer to write. . . .

Oh, writing on a computer isn't such a big deal any more. In fact, it's the typewriter that gets the double take today. A computer? They're as common as cobwebs. Chances are that if you're writing anything, you're using a computer with word processing software. And the odds are very good that you'll be using a PC with some variation of Windows and Microsoft Word to help you process those words.

This chapter is your introduction to Microsoft Word. I swing open the door and you take a peek to see what you're in for. There's nothing scary. Nothing dangerous. Well, not that dangerous. No, it just may be unfamiliar to you. This chapter helps make it familiar.

The Good, Best, and Worst Ways to Start Word

How do I start thee, Word? Let me count the ways. . . .

If you've been using Windows for any length of time, you may have noticed that there is usually more than one way to do anything. For example, at last count, I tallied up 23 different ways to copy a file in Windows Me. The same type of multiple-choice logic occurs when you go to start a program.

All told, there are probably a dozen or so different ways to start Word. Rather than document them all, I thought I'd show you the good or obvious ways first, and then my favorite way, and, finally, lump the rest of the ways into the "worst" category, which you can read at your own peril.

First, some basic steps you need to take no matter what:

1. **Ensure that your computer is on and toasty.**

   Any computer that's on is, in fact, toasty. The only way to make it toastier is to actually insert bread, which is not recommended.

2. **Prepare yourself physically.**

   Make sure you're seated, with a nice, upright, firm posture. Inhale deeply. Crack your knuckles. Are your fingers ready to dance on the keyboard? Good!

3. **Prepare yourself mentally.**

   Close your eyes. Relax. Exhale. Think of calm, blue waters. Prepare to let your thoughts flow into the computer. Remember, you are the master. Mutter that over and over: *I am the master. . . .*

If you need help starting your computer, refer to my book *PCs For Dummies* (Hungry Minds, Inc.) for quick and accurate turning-on-the-computer instructions.

You can stop muttering "I am the master" now.

A good, reliable way to start Word

Time and time again, it's been proven that the most reliable way to start Word is to use the trusty Windows Start button. Heed these steps:

1. **Pop up the Start menu.**

   Click the Start button to pop up the menu. That button is often found on the left side of the taskbar, at the bottom of the screen.

   Another way to pop up the Start menu is to press the Ctrl+Esc key combination or, if your keyboard has one, press the Windows key (between the Ctrl and Alt keys).

2. **Choose Programs➪Microsoft Word 2002.**

   Look at Figure 1-1. Note that the menu item may say Word or Microsoft Word or possibly Microsoft Word 2002 or even Word 10.

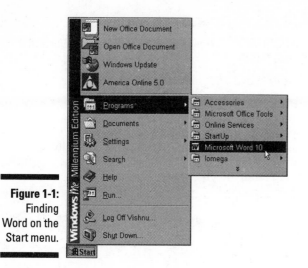

Figure 1-1:
Finding
Word on the
Start menu.

Watch in amazement as your computer whizzes and whirs. Before too long, Word appears on the computer's monitor, looking like a drunk relative showing up late to a family dinner bringing only a cheap bottle of scotch as a consolation.

Don't fret over Word's appearance just yet; I discuss what you're looking at in the section, "Word on the Screen," later in this chapter.

Your computer can be set up to run Word automatically every time you turn it on. Think of the time that can save! If you want your computer set up in this manner, grab someone more knowledgeable than yourself — an individual I call a computer guru. Tell your guru: "Make my computer always start in Word." If your guru is unavailable, frantically grab other people at random until you find someone bold enough to obey you.

The best way to start Word

My favorite way to run Word is by opening a shortcut icon pasted to the desktop or by clicking a button on the Quick Launch bar. Both ways are more direct than using the silly Start menu, and the Quick Launch bar method is the fastest because you need to click the button only once to start Word.

Whether you're pasting a Word shortcut icon to the desktop or to the Quick Launch bar, the first step is the same: to create the Word shortcut icon. This can be a little technical, so put on your Paying Attention cap as you follow these steps:

1. **Locate the Start menu's Microsoft Word 10 menu item.**

   Don't start Word now! Just point the mouse at the Microsoft Word menu item, as shown in Figure 1-1.

2. **Right-click the Microsoft Word 10 menu item.**

   A pop-up menu appears.

3. **Choose Copy.**

   There. You've just copied the Word menu item. Well, technically, you copied the command Windows uses to start Word. That's good because you can now paste that command elsewhere.

4. **Click the mouse on the desktop.**

   The desktop is the background you see when you use Windows. Clicking on the desktop hides the Start menu.

5. **Right-click the mouse on the desktop.**

   A pop-up menu appears.

6. **Chose Paste.**

   A shortcut icon (a type of copy) of Microsoft Word 10 appears on the desktop.

You can now use that icon to start Word without having to mess with the Start menu.

If you'd rather have Word on the Quick Launch bar, drag and drop the shortcut icon down there: Use your mouse to drag the Word icon to the Quick Launch bar, and then release the mouse button to "drop" the icon, as shown in Figure 1-2. (You may need to resize the Quick Launch bar to see the Word icon.) Now, Word is only one quick click away from in-your-face word processing.

Word shortcut icon on the desktop

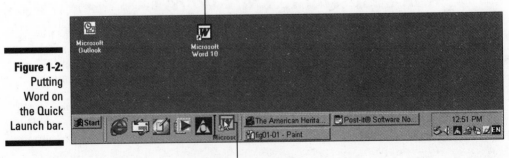

Figure 1-2:
Putting
Word on
the Quick
Launch bar.

Drag the Word icon here.

Other random, often awkward, ways to start Word

Here's my short list of the multitudinous ways to start Word:

- ✔ Choose Programs⇨Microsoft Word 10 from the Start menu.
- ✔ Open (double-click) a Word shortcut icon on the desktop.
- ✔ Open (single-click) a Word icon on the Quick Launch bar.
- ✔ Use any of the various Microsoft Office tools (at the top of the Start menu or from the Office toolbar) to start Word or create a new document.
- ✔ Choose a Word document from the Documents menu on the Start menu.
- ✔ Open (double-click) any Word document.

Those last two points are not really that random or awkward. If you're a Word maven, a quick way to get back into writing mode is to choose your currently hot document from the Start menu's Documents submenu:

1. **Click the Start button.**

   Up pops the Start menu.

2. **Point at the Documents menu item.**

   The Documents submenu appears. That menu lists the last 16-or-so files or documents you opened in Windows (though not every file is listed there because shiny objects easily distract Windows).

3. **Locate your document on the list and click it.**

   The document wakes up Word, and you're busy on your favorite document. Again.

Documents appear in the Documents window in alphabetical order. Newer documents you open bump the older ones off the list. So, if you just edited 16 graphics files, they push off any Word documents that were once there.

Honestly, any Word document icon you open starts Word. In fact, if you've been working on the Great American Novel for several years now, consider pasting that document icon on the desktop and just opening it to start your day.

At the top of the Documents menu is the My Documents folder, where Word automatically stores the documents you create. Choosing the My Documents folder opens a window in which you can locate other Word documents that may not be on the Documents menu.

Documents, documents, and documents. All of a sudden, the word *documents* has lost its meaning.

Word on the Screen

Right after starting Word, I prefer to maximize. That doesn't mean that I sit down and stuff myself with a swell meal. No, maximizing is a Windows trick you can pull to increase the amount of screen real estate Word uses.

 To run Word in full-screen mode, click the Maximize button (the middle one) in the upper-right corner of the window. This button maximizes Word to fill the entire screen. If Word is already maximized, two overlapping boxes appear on the button; you don't need to click anything in that case.

Now that you can see Word long and tall on the screen, follow along with this text and Figure 1-3 to locate the many fresh and exciting items on the typical blank Word screen.

Gizmos and gadgets

Writing is Word's primary job. Well, not "writing" in the Ernest Hemingway sense. Actually, it's processing words that Word does best. That's why the largest portion of the Word screen is for composing text (refer to Figure 1-3).

Surrounding the text-composing area are various bells, whistles, switches, and doodads that would be interesting only if they were edible. And the good news is that with Word, all that stuff is totally customizable by you (better know what it all means before you go changing everything):

- ✔ **The title bar,** which says `Document 1 - Microsoft Word` until you save your document to disk

- ✔ **The menu bar,** which contains a full list of Word's various and sundry commands

- ✔ **The Standard and Formatting toolbars,** which are shown side-by-side in Figure 1-3, although you can rearrange them at your whim

- ✔ **The ruler,** which helps you set margins and tabs

- ✔ **The task pane,** which lists commands relevant to whatever you're now doing in Word

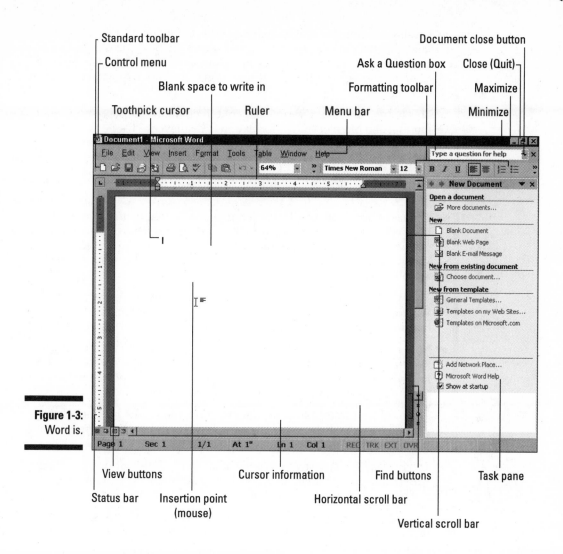

Figure 1-3:
Word is.

Standard toolbar
Control menu
Blank space to write in
Toothpick cursor
Ruler
Menu bar
Document close button
Ask a Question box
Close (Quit)
Formatting toolbar
Maximize
Minimize

View buttons
Cursor information
Find buttons
Task pane
Status bar
Insertion point
(mouse)
Horizontal scroll bar
Vertical scroll bar

Below the writing area are two items:

- **The View buttons,** located to the left of the horizontal scroll bar, control how your document is displayed.

- **The status bar** dishes up lots of trivia about your document, some of which is interesting.

What each of these various buttons, bars, and menus does and whether it's important is covered elsewhere in this book. Right now, you just need to know the names of things so that you don't get lost later:

- Missing from previous versions of Word is the infamous Office Assistant (an animated paper clip). As it comes out of the box, Word 10 does not automatically display the Office Assistant. Fear not — I tell you how to summon him (or is it her?) in the section, "The Office Assistant," later in this chapter.

- The status bar is not a yuppie hangout. It contains cubbyholes in which random and often cryptic information is displayed. This book explains when the information is useful to you.

- Figure 1-3 shows Word in Print Layout view. If it looks different on your screen, choose View➪Print Layout from the menu. (Some people prefer to use Word in Normal view.)

- The task pane (and, yes, I have fun toying with that name later in this book) is a new feature of Word 10. It can easily be removed, however, if you want to devote more room to the writing part of the screen: Choose View➪Task Pane to hide the task pane. Choose that same menu item again to show it.

- The Windows taskbar, located at the bottom of the screen, is a part of Windows itself and not Word. However, as you open documents in Word, buttons representing those documents appear on the Windows taskbar.

- Notice the mouse pointer in Figure 1-3? It's the *insertion* pointer, shaped like an I-beam. That's the way the mouse pointer appears when it's sliding over your document in Word. The I-beam means "I beam the insertion pointer to this spot when you click the mouse."

- The lines next to (or beneath) the insertion pointer are part of Word's click-and-type feature. Using click-and-type is covered in Chapter 18, in the section that discusses automatic formatting as it happens.

- You can use the mouse to see what some of the little buttons and things with pictures on them do in Word. Just hover the mouse pointer over the button and — voilà! — It's like Folger's Instant Information Crystals.

- If you don't actually see the Standard or Formatting toolbars or the ruler or you want to change the way the Word screen looks *right now,* hop on over to Chapter 29.

The blank place where you write

After Word starts, you're faced with the electronic version of The Blank Page, the same idea-crippling concept that induced writer's block in generations of writers. It makes you wonder if cavepeople ever had "stone block."

The key to writing in Word is to look for the blinking *insertion pointer* — a blinking toothpick in your text that shows you where your typing will appear on the screen:

Choose View➪Normal from the menu.

In Normal view, more of the screen is devoted to writing text. However, in this view, a horizontal line appears on the screen, just below the blinking toothpick cursor. That's that the *End-of-Text marker.* Consider it the steel beam that supports your text, keeping it from harm's way, in the evil nothingness that exists below your text:

Choose Underline View⇨Print Layout from the menu.

In Print Layout view, the End-of-Text marker disappears. Unlike in Normal view, the focus here is how the words look on the page. Personally, I prefer to write in Normal view and then switch to Print Layout for formatting and editing.

- Writing (or typing, depending on how good you are) is covered in the next chapter. That would be Chapter 2.

- Any weird stuff you see onscreen (a ¶, for example) is a Word secret symbol. Chapter 2 tells you why you may want to view those secret symbols and how to hide them if they annoy you.

- The *cursor* shows the exact spot where text appears. The cursor is also called an insertion pointer because traditional computer cursors are underlines that slide under what you type. I prefer the term *toothpick cursor* because *insertion pointer* is just too medically geometric for my tastes. Characters you type appear immediately to the left of where the toothpick cursor is flashing, and then the cursor moves forward and waits for the next character.

The Office Assistant

There are many ways to get help from Word, most of which are covered in Chapter 2. For now, on the screen, you may see two places to get help.

First, there's the Ask a Question box, where you can type a question and see a list of possible answers.

Second, and more interesting than the Ask a Question box, is the Office Assistant.

If the Office Assistant isn't visible on the screen, choose Help⇨Show the Office Assistant from the menu. What appears is a helpful character (you can change the character to something else if you like — I tell you how in Chapter 2). The Office Assistant is shown in Figure 1-4.

Figure 1-4:
The dog.

The Office Assistant is there to help you. Most of the time, however, it just sits there watching while you type or getting bored while you rummage for a thought.

Here are my Office Assistant musings:

✔ You can move the Office Assistant around by dragging it with the mouse. I put my assistant down in the lower-right corner of the screen, where he won't get into any trouble.

✔ Right-click the Office Assistant to see a list of its menu options. My favorite menu item is Animate, which makes the Office Assistant do something interesting.

✔ You can choose from among a host of Office Assistants: Right-click the Office Assistant and choose the Choose Assistant item from the pop-up menu. My favorite assistant is the dog, though I'm also fond of Merlin.

✔ If you detest the Office Assistant, right-click on his nose and choose the Hide menu option. Hey, the screen is crowded enough!

✔ The Office Assistant hides when you switch from Word to other applications.

✔ Using the Office Assistant to get help is covered in Chapter 2.

A Look at Your Keyboard

Yes, it's entirely possible to yank up a microphone and tell Word exactly what to do with itself. I discuss (and ridicule) this amazing speech-recognition feature in Chapter 25. Yet even though you can dictate to Word, the keyboard is still a handy thing to have — especially for editing (or, if you're one of those individuals, such as myself, who types faster and more accurately than I can speak).

Figure 1-5 shows the typical PC keyboard used during the turn of the century (the turn from the 20th to the 21st century, not from the 19th to the 20th century, when "keyboard" typically implied a piano.)

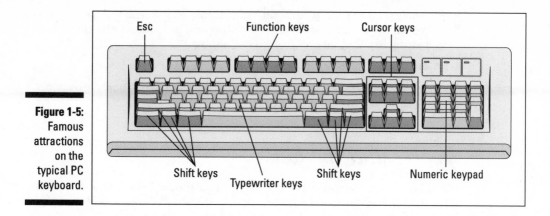

Esc   Function keys   Cursor keys

Figure 1-5:
Famous
attractions
on the
typical PC
keyboard.

Shift keys   Typewriter keys   Shift keys   Numeric keypad

Notice how the keyboard is divided into separate areas, each of which has a special function? In Word, you use the keys in these groups either alone or in combination with other keys:

- **Function keys:** These keys are located along the top row of the keyboard, labeled F1 through F12. You can use them alone or in cahoots with the Ctrl, Alt, and Shift keys.

- **Typewriter keys:** These are the standard alphanumeric keys you find on any typewriter: A through Z, 1 through 0, plus symbols and other exotic characters.

- **Cursor keys:** These arrow keys move the toothpick cursor around the screen. Also lumped in are the Home, End, PgUp (or Page Up), PgDn (or Page Down), Insert, and Delete keys. Oh, and the big plus and minus keys on the number pad are counted as well.

- **Don key:** A domesticated ass — like a little, stupid horse.

- **Numeric keypad:** These keys toggle (meaning that they can't make up their minds) between cursor keys and number keys. The split personality is evident on each key cap, which displays two symbols. The Num Lock key and its corresponding light are on if the numeric keypad (1, 2, 3) is active. If the cursor keys (arrows, Home) are active, Num Lock is off.

- **Shift keys:** These keys don't do anything by themselves. Instead, the Shift, Ctrl, and Alt keys work in combination with other keys.

Here are some individual keys worth noting:

- **Enter:** Marked with the word *Enter* and sometimes a cryptic, curved arrow-thing: (. You use the Enter key to end a paragraph of text.

- **Spacebar:** The only key with no mark; inserts spaces between the words.

- **Tab:** Inserts the tab "character," which shoves the next text you type over to the next tab stop. An interesting and potentially frustrating formatting key (but nicely covered in Chapter 13).
- **Backspace:** Your backing-up-and-erasing key. Very handy.
- **Delete:** Also labeled Del and works like Backspace but doesn't back up to erase. More on that in Chapter 4.

Depressing the keys

When I tell you to "depress the Enter key," you should look at your keyboard, stare the Enter key squarely in the eye, and say aloud, "You, you funny-looking key. You're worthless. All the other keys hate you. My right pinky hates you. You're despised! You should leave the keyboard right now and hide in shame, you worthless key, you!" There, now the Enter key is quite depressed.

Seriously, you don't "depress" any key on your keyboard. You press keys. Press them down, and then release them. Any swift tapping motion will do. And the better keyboards pleasingly click for you, making your typing as noisy as it would be on an old manual Olympia.

Typing key combinations

Aside from regular typing, you need to use various key combinations to tell Word how to carry out certain commands. For example:

Ctrl+P

Say, "control pee." That's the Control+P key combination. Or, if you can palm a basketball in one hand, you can try:

Ctrl+Shift+F12

That's "control shift F twelve." Both keyboard shortcuts open the Print dialog box — which isn't really important right now. What is important is what these key combinations tell you to do, namely: Press and hold the Ctrl key while you press P and then release both keys; or press and hold the Ctrl and Shift keys and then press the F12 key. Release all three keys.

Always press and hold the first key (or keys) and then press the last key: Press and release.

- This key combination method works just like pressing Shift+F to get a capital F. It's the same thing, but with the odd Ctrl (Control) and Alt (Alternate) keys.

✔ Yeah, you have to really reach to get some of those key combinations.

✔ You don't need to press hard. If you're having trouble working a keyboard shortcut, pressing harder doesn't make the computer think, "Oh, Lordy, she's pressing really hard now. I think she means it. Wake up, wake up!" A light touch is all that's required.

✔ Remember to release the keys: With Ctrl+P, for example, press and hold the Ctrl key, press P, and then release both keys. If you don't know which one to release first, release the second key and then the Shift key (Shift, Ctrl, Alt) last.

✔ Click the Cancel or Close button if you accidentally open the Print dialog box; you can also press the Esc key on the keyboard. See Chapter 9 for more information on canceling printing.

Quitting Word When You're All Done

Knowing when to leave is the height of proper etiquette. And sometimes it pays to not even show up. But Word cares not for social things. When the writing is done, or you're done writing, it's time to quit Word:

1. **Choose File⇨Exit from the menu.**

   This is the standard way to quit any Windows program.

2. **Save any files, if Word prompts you to do so.**

   Word always warns you before it leaves; if you have any unsaved work, you're prompted to save it to disk. You see a warning displayed on the screen. If the Office Assistant is visible, it explains the warning in a cartoon bubble, as shown in Figure 1-6.

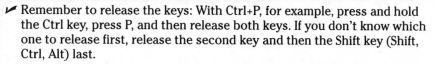

Figure 1-6:
Arf! Arf!
Arf!

Click Yes to save your file. You may be asked to give the file a name if you haven't yet done so. (Chapter 2 tells you how this is done.)

If the slop you typed isn't worth saving, click No.

You can click Cancel to "quit" the Exit command and return to Word for more word processing delight.

If you elect to quit, Word leaves the screen and you return to the Windows desktop, where you can busy yourself with yet another game of FreeCell.

Do not reset or turn off your computer to quit Word! Doing so can potentially scramble files on your computer's hard disk. Computers are troublesome enough by themselves. No point in your contributing to that madness by doing something sloppy.

How to Quit What You're Doing
without Quitting Word

If you're finished with a document, you can make it vanish from your screen and start on something new without quitting Word. You do this by "closing" a document, which is similar to ripping a sheet of paper out of your typewriter — without the satisfying *SSHHHHHTHWP!* sound it makes.

To close a document, choose File➪Close. This step closes the document window and makes it vanish from the screen. The "white space" in the window disappears.

To start a new document, choose File➪New, which summons the New Document task pane, and then click the Blank Document item. (An easier way is to click the New Document icon on the toolbar.)

You can open a document on disk using the File➪Open command, which I introduce in the next chapter.

✔ Why close a document? Because you're done working on it! Maybe you want to work on something else or quit Word after closing. The choices are yours, and I explain them in the next chapter.

✔ There is no need to close a document, really. In fact, I work on a document over a period of days and keep it open (and my PC on) the entire time. Doesn't hurt a thing. (I do save it to disk, which *is* important.)

✔ If you try to close a document before it has been saved, Word displays a warning dialog box. Click the Yes button to save your document. If you want to continue editing, click the Cancel button and get back to work.

✔ If you're working on several documents at once, closing one makes another one appear onscreen in place of the document you just closed.

✔ You don't have to quit Word when you just want to start working on a new document.

Chapter 2

How Most Folks Use Word

I'm not out to crush your feelings. You may be a poet who insists on putting a sole word on a page. Or you may be under duress at some bureaucratic agency, struggling to find a paragraph break in five pages of solid text. Or you may be a student, pushing three pages out of a two-page paper. No matter what your word processing duties entail, chances are that you're going to use Word pretty much the same as everyone else. This isn't an attack on your individuality. It's just the naked truth.

This chapter gives you the basic steps to take as you use Word every day. In fact, if this book were a pamphlet, this chapter would be it. (The rest of the book just offers more details and highly useful information, as well as justification for the hefty cover price.)

Overview (for the Impatient)

The Word word processing process goes like this:

1. **Start a new document in Word.**
2. **Type.**
3. **Format.**

4. Save.

5. Preview.

6. Print.

7. Close.

Everyone follows these steps in one way or another. A good Word user repeats Steps 2, 3, and 4, sometimes varying the order. (Most of the time, you're typing in Word. Toward the end of the process, you should start formatting, though many people format as they type.)

I suppose that Step 2 could also be "dictate," as long as the new dictation feature works well for you (see Chapter 25).

If you saved a document earlier and want to work on it again, replace Step 1 with "Open a document on disk." (See Chapter 8 for more information on the Open command.)

Steps 5 and 6 are necessary only when you're done and plan on printing your work. (Chapter 9 discusses Preview and Print.)

The rest of this chapter elaborates on these steps.

Starting a New Document

When Word starts, it presents you with a blank document, suitable for typing. Your next step, logically, is to type. Or, illogically, you can try dictating (see Chapter 25 for information on setting up that feature). If you're just starting out, I recommend going the typing route for now — until you're familiar with Word.

If you need to start a new document while you're already editing something in Word (such as when you're writing a letter to a friend and realize that you forgot to type up that urgent business letter), choose File➪New from the menu. The new document appears in another window right inside Word's main window, blank and ready for typing.

✔ Clicking the New button on the toolbar also starts up a new document in case you need one in a hurry.

✔ If the task pane is visible (refer to Figure 1-3), look for the New area (second from the top) and click the Blank Document item.

✔ See Chapter 10 for more information on working with more than one document in Word.

✔ Another way to start your work is to open a document on disk (see Chapter 8 for more information). After the document is open, it appears in a window just like any other document you've created. Work away!

Typing (Or Hunting and Pecking)

Forget all the gizmos and fancy features! Most of your time in Word is spent typing.

Clackity-clack-clack-clack.

Go ahead, type away; let your fingers dance upon the keycaps! What you type appears onscreen, letter for letter — even derogatory stuff about the computer. (Your PC doesn't care, but that doesn't mean that Word lacks feelings.)

New text is inserted right in front of the blinking toothpick cursor. For example, you can type this line:

```
Farming is the world's oldest profession.
```

To change this sentence, move the toothpick cursor to just after the *s* in "world's." Type a space and the following text:

```
second
```

The new text is inserted as you type, with any existing text marching off to the right (and even to the next line), happily making room.

The whole sentence should now read:

```
Farming is the world's second oldest profession.
```

TIP

"Do I need to learn to type?"

No one needs to learn to type to use a word processor, but you'll do yourself a favor if you learn. My advice is to get a computer program that teaches you to type. I can recommend the Mavis Beacon Teaches Typing program, even though I don't get any money from her. I just like the name Mavis, I suppose.

Knowing how to type makes a painful experience like Word a wee bit more enjoyable.

- Every character key you press on the keyboard produces a character onscreen. This fact holds true for all letter, number, and symbol keys. The other keys, mostly gray on your keyboard, do strange and wonderful things, which the rest of this book tries hard to explain.

- If you're a former typewriter user, you're probably pushing 40! Man, you're old! Seriously, don't use the L or I key for a number one or the O (oh) key for a zero in a word processor. This is wrong. Please type **1** for the number one and **0** for the number zero.

- Don't be afraid to use your keyboard! Word always offers ample warning before anything serious happens. A handy Undo feature recovers anything you accidentally delete; see Chapter 4.

- The Shift key produces capital letters, just like on a typewriter (if you've ever used one).

- The Caps Lock key works like the Shift Lock key on a typewriter. After you press that key, the Caps Lock light on your keyboard comes on and everything you type is in ALL CAPS.

- Sorry for all the typewriter analogies.

- The number keys on the right side of the keyboard are on the numeric keypad. To use those keys, you must press the Num Lock key, and you see the Num Luck light on the keyboard turn on. When the Num Lock light is off, the number keys serve as duplicate cursor-control, or "arrow," keys.

- The world's oldest profession is most likely herding.

When to press that Enter key

Press the Enter key only when you reach the end of a paragraph.

No, that was too easy. Let me ramble on about this for a few more paragraphs:

The Enter key on your computer's keyboard does not work the same way as the Return key on a typewriter. Back in those days (when TV was black-and-white and Dad wore a hat to work), you pressed the Return key at the end of each line, usually after a "ding!" With a word processor, however, you don't need to press Enter at the end of each line, nor are you required to say "ding!" at any time.

For example, type the following text. Just type it all and don't bother pressing the Enter key, nope, not at all:

> In an effort to find the best typists in the universe, the
>   Federation enlisted the help of 7th grade typing
>   instructor Maxine Kornhieser. Traveling the
>   galaxy, Ms. Kornhieser almost found the perfect
>   match; the Dolesori of Plantax 9 could type
>   rapidly with their 12 double-jointed fingers on
>   each hand. Alas, the Dolesori lacked any backbone
>   whatsoever and, thus, Ms. Kornhieser disapproved
>   of their posture.

Notice how the text *wraps*? The last part of the text on the end of one line moves down to the start of the next line. It's automatic! There's no "ding!" — nor is there any need to press Enter at the end of the line.

Press Enter only at the end of a paragraph.

✔ This feature (wrapping text from one line to the next), is called *word wrap*.

✔ Some people end a paragraph with two presses of the Enter key; others use only one press. If it's extra space you want between paragraphs, you should use Word's paragraph formatting commands, as I describe in Chapter 12 of this book.

✔ Double-spacing your lines is *also* done with a paragraph-formatting command. Do not press Enter if you want double spacing! See Chapter 12 for more information.

✔ If you want to indent the next paragraph, press the Tab key after pressing Enter.

✔ If Kornhieser appears with a red, zigzag underline, that means Word believes it to be a misspelled word. Ditto for Plantax and Dolesori. See Chapter 7 for more information.

✔ If Maxine Kornhieser has a dotted purple line beneath it (as well as the red zigzag, though this is specifically a purple dot issue), that's Word's way of telling you that she has survived the chicken pox. Seriously, the purple dotted line is a *smart tag*, a feature covered in Chapter 34.

✔ If you press the Enter key in the middle of an existing paragraph, Word makes a new paragraph. The text above the toothpick cursor becomes its own paragraph, and the text following the toothpick cursor becomes the next paragraph.

✔ You can delete the Enter character by using the Backspace or Delete keys. Removing the Enter character joins two paragraphs.

The lure of the soft return

Another way to end a paragraph — but not really end it — is to use the Shift+Enter key combination, also called a *soft return* or *line break*. This allows you to end one line of text and start a new line, but without creating a new paragraph. Type this line:

```
Old Mr. Peabody
```

Now press Shift+Enter. A new line starts. Continue typing:

```
This character must be played by your most versatile actor.
            He must be tall and short, fat and skinny, able to
            laugh or cry on cue, and be 75% graceful, 30%
            enthusiastic, and 10% repulsive.
```

All that text is one paragraph, yet the `Old Mr. Peabody` part appears on a line by itself. That's the essence of a soft return or line break. Mostly they're used in tables, though you may find a purpose for them if you're creating forms, Web pages, or other documents where such formatting is necessary.

✔ No, you probably won't use soft returns as much as you use real returns (also called *hard* returns, coincidentally).

✔ See Chapter 20 for moron tables — I mean *more on* tables.

When to whack the Spacebar

You use the Spacebar to insert spaces between words or sentences. Withoutityourtextwouldbehardtoread.

In Word, as in all typing you do on a computer, you put only one space between sentences. (If you're a touch-typist, this habit is tough to break, but it's possible.)

The only peeve I have about the Spacebar is that too often folks use spaces to line up columns of information or to indent. This is terribly wrong, and, as those folks discover, the output on paper looks tawdry. Yes, cheap and tawdry.

Rather than use the Spacebar to indent or line up text, use the Tab key. The Tab key is the best way to organize information on the screen. Unlike the Spacebar, the Tab key indents text to an exact position so that when you print, everything lines up nice and neatly. (See Chapter 13 for more Tabby information.)

✔ Use that Spacebar to put spaces between words and sentences.

✔ One space between sentences is all you need. Whenever you feel like using more than one space, such as arranging text in columns or lining things up, use a Tab instead (see Chapter 13).

✔ I hear that typing teachers still tell students to put two spaces between sentences. Hey: You're wrong. Get over it. The typewriter is dead. Okay? Move on. . . .

✔ The Romans couldn't put spaces between words on buildings because the Chiselers Union didn't know how to charge for it.

Things to notice whilst you type

Lots of interesting things go on while you type, some of which may puzzle you, others of which may annoy you, and a few that may cause you undue consternation.

The status bar

The first thing to notice while you type is the status bar at the bottom of the screen. The information there tells you something about your document and where you're typing in it. Figure 2-1 explains everything, although the only items I refer to are the Page (current page you're editing) and the total pages in the document (the last number in item C in Figure 2-1).

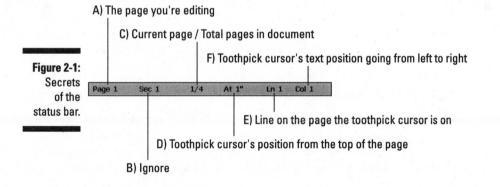

Figure 2-1: Secrets of the status bar.

A) The page you're editing

C) Current page / Total pages in document

F) Toothpick cursor's text position going from left to right

E) Line on the page the toothpick cursor is on

D) Toothpick cursor's position from the top of the page

B) Ignore

Life between pages

Word likes to show you where one page ends and another begins. This is a good thing to know because most of what you create ends up on a sheet of paper — or maybe two sheets, but you wanted only one. In that case, you can always use the status bar (refer to Figure 2-1) to see how many pages you have or which page you're on. But Word has visual methods as well.

Word uses two visual clues to show you where a new page happens, depending on which *view* you're using to see your document.

If you choose View⇨Print Layout (the way Word naturally looks), the break between pages shows up on the screen in a virtual manner. Figure 2-2 shows the details. The pages are white and the space between them is gray.

The preceding page   Insidious void between pages

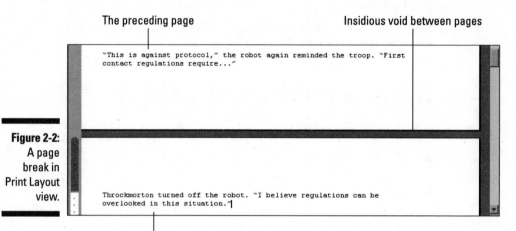

"This is against protocol," the robot again reminded the troop. "First contact regulations require..."

Throckmorton turned off the robot. "I believe regulations can be overlooked in this situation."

Figure 2-2:
A page
break in
Print Layout
view.

The next page

If you choose View⇨Normal, which is how I use Word, the break between pages shows up as a line of ants marching across the screen. *Don't spray 'em with bug killer!*

That thing (shown above) is a Normal view page break. The text you see above the ants, er, dots, is on the preceding page; text below the dots is on the next page.

✔ You cannot delete a page break. You can change where they happen, but if your text is too long for the page, Word automatically places it on the next page.

✔ A row of dots close together — very friendly ants — marks a hard page break. The words Page Break even appear right in the middle of the line. This on-purpose page break is covered in Chapter 14.

Spots between words!

There is no cause for alarm if you see spots — or dots — onscreen when you press the Spacebar or Enter key — like this:

```
This·can·be·very·annoying.¶
```

What's happening is that Word is showing you the *nonprinting characters*. Word uses various symbols to represent things you normally wouldn't see: spaces, tabs, and the Enter key.

Why bother? By displaying the nonprinting characters, you can easily find things that may be screwing up your text formatting but otherwise would be hard to see. For example, two tabs in a row may suddenly jerk your text around as you're editing. The only way to know that there are two tabs in a row would be to view the nonprinting characters.

✔ To turn the nonprinting characters off, press the Ctrl+Shift+8 key combination. (Press it again to turn them on, if you're curious.) Use the 8 on the keyboard, not on the numeric keypad.

✔ You can also click the Show/Hide button on the Standard toolbar to display or hide the nonprinting characters.

✔ The symbols show up onscreen but — fortunately — not in a printed document.

Underline squiggly wigglies

Adding underline to your text in Word is cinchy; Chapter 11 tells you all about it. Yet, there are times when Word may do some underlining by itself, with red, green, and purple underlines of zigzag and dotted styles. What Word is doing is alerting you to certain things about that text.

Spelling errors in Word are underlined with a red zigzag. That's Word's annoying real-time spelling checker in action.

Grammatical errors in Word are underlined with a green zigzag. Word is telling you (but it's usually wrong) that some English-language sin has been committed.

Refer to Chapter 7 for more information on fixing spelling and grammar errors in Word — and for turning the zigzag line feature off, if you're so inclined.

The dotted purple underline is used in Word to ID a potential contact person. Word's ultrasmart brain divines various names in your document and underlines them for you. Chapter 34 has more information on this feature, including how to turn it off.

Generally speaking, ignore all squiggly lines until you move into the editing phase for your document. (Well, unless you become obsessive, but that tends to slow down the writing process.)

Watch the Office Assistant!

As you type, the Office Assistant does various interesting things, which you may find amusing. In fact, if you wait too long while reading or composing your thoughts, you may notice the Office Assistant going to sleep (see the dog in the margin). That's a good clue that you should stop staring off into space and get back to work!

"Oops! I made a boo-boo!"

If you make a mistake, press the Backspace key to back up and erase. This key is named Backspace on your keyboard, or it may have a long, left-pointing arrow on it: ←.

Pressing and holding down the Backspace key puts you in Rapid Consumption mode — a whole lotta characters to the left of the blinking toothpick cursor are erased — until you release the Backspace key.

The Delete key also gobbles characters, though it deletes the character to the *right* of the blinking toothpick cursor.

For even larger boo-boos *(booboous maximus),* Word has an Undo key. It doesn't erase text, but it helps you yank back text you accidentally erase. See Chapter 4 for more Undo information.

Formatting Your Document

Formatting is what makes your document look professional and not like it came from a 1972 Smith Corona in need of a new ribbon. There are several things you can format in your document:

- ✔ Characters
- ✔ Paragraphs
- ✔ Tabs
- ✔ The entire document
- ✔ Pages
- ✔ Columns
- ✔ Headers and footers

Your primary duty in word processing is to get down the text. After that, you typically go back and format, changing the text style or adjusting the margins. This is all covered in Part II of this book.

 ✔ Word can format your document for you. I describe how in Chapter 18.

 ✔ Most folks format text as they type, adding italics or bold or whatever. You can also format paragraphs as you write, although some major formatting chores are best done *after* you write your text. (Examples of both techniques are shown in Part II.)

 ✔ Word also lets you format your document by adding drawings, pictures, lines, tables, columns, or other elements that can really make things look snazzy. Parts III and V cover those topics.

Getting Help

Help is available all over Word:

You can get help for just about anything by pressing the F1 key. Generally, this key summons the Office Assistant (even if he's not visible now). A cartoon bubble appears over the dog's head, asking "What would you like to do?" Type in your question, as shown in Figure 2-3. Press the Enter key and the dog answers your question:

Bark! Woof! Woof! Woooooooff!

Figure 2-3:
The Office Assistant is ready to help.

Seriously, a list of potential answers appears in the dog's cartoon bubble. For example, if you type "How do I save this document in WordPerfect format?" the dog shows you a list of possible answers. Clicking a particular answer tells you how to accomplish the task.

If you prefer not to use the Office Assistant, you can type a question in the Ask a Question box in the upper-right corner of Word's window. Type a question and press Enter. Answers are then displayed, but without the Office Assistant popping into view (which some folks find annoying).

- My experience is that choosing the help option "None of the above, look for more help on the Web" is a colossal waste of time.

- Hopefully, you'll end up using this book more than you'll use the dog.

- Oh, and I know that there are other Office Assistant characters. I'm just partial to the dog.

Save Your Stuff!

The computer is dumb. The computer is forgetful. And it loses things. To help the computer remember, you must tell it to save your stuff. Everything you create in Word should be saved to disk, stored there as a document.

To save a document to disk, choose the File⇨Save command, Alt+F, S. (You can also click the Save button, which looks like a wee li'l disk, on the Standard toolbar.)

If you're saving your document for the first time, the Save As dialog box appears, as shown in Figure 2-4.

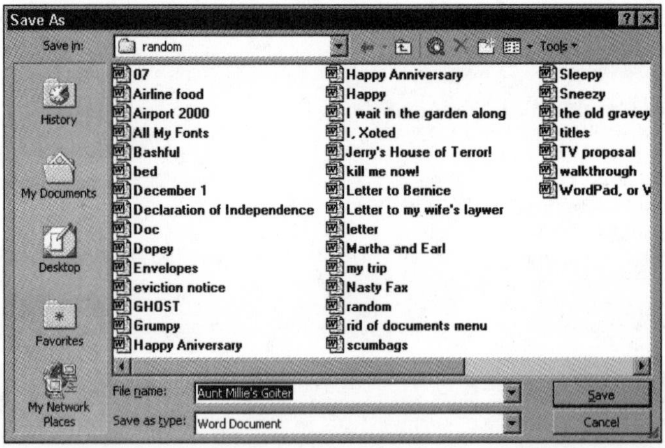

Figure 2-4:
The Save As
dialog box.

Type a name for your document in the File Name area. The name Aunt Millie's Goiter is shown in Figure 2-4. If you make a mistake typing, use the Backspace key to back up and erase.

Click the Save button to save your document.

✔ Chapter 8 offers more details about saving your document.

✔ The filename is how you recognize the file later, when you want to edit or print it again. It's important to think up and use a good, descriptive filename.

✔ The fastest way to save a file is to use the keyboard. The Save File key combination is Ctrl+S. Press and hold the Ctrl (Control) key and press the S key. If you can pick up a basketball with one hand, you can also use the Shift+F12 key combo.

✔ When you save a document, watch the status bar — it temporarily displays a message telling you that Word is saving your document (or fast saving, for our Frequent Fliers).

✔ The Office Assistant tells you when you enter a forbidden filename. Click OK and try again, heeding the dog's advice.

✔ After the document is saved to disk, you see its name displayed on the window's title bar. That name is your clue that your document has been saved to disk.

✔ If you're not in a clever mood, you may decide to name your file with the name of a file already on disk. This decision is a boo-boo because the newer file overwrites the other file with the same name already on disk. For example, if you decide to save your new letter by using the LETTER filename and LETTER already exists on disk, the new file overwrites the old one. There is no way to get the original back, so use another, more clever name instead. The dog warns you with this message:

```
Do you want to replace the existing whatever?
```

Click the No button. Use another name.

Getting It Down on Paper (Printing)

The great authors didn't worry about printing. Shakespeare never had to save his document or use print preview. Poe wrote *The Raven* on paper, so "printing" was what he did as he wrote. And Mark Twain, who wrote *The Adventures of Tom Sawyer* on that newfangled typewriter, well, he was pretty high tech. And you?

Printing is the result of your word processing labors. Hercules? He had to retrieve some gal's girdle. You? You have to print your document. Everything looks nice and tidy on paper — almost professional.

First, preview your printing

 To see what your document will look like without wasting valuable paper, use the Print Preview command. Choose File⇨Print Preview or click the handy Print Preview button on the toolbar.

Figure 2-5 shows you what Print Preview mode looks like. Your document is shown exactly as it will print, including any pictures, headers, or footers or other items that may not show up properly when you're editing.

Okay. It looks good. Click the Close button to return to your document for editing or printing.

Time to print

To print your document in Word — the document you see onscreen, all of it — do the following:

1. **Make sure that your printer is on and ready to print.**

   See Chapter 9 for additional information about preparing the printer if you need to.

Figure 2-5:
Print
Preview
mode.

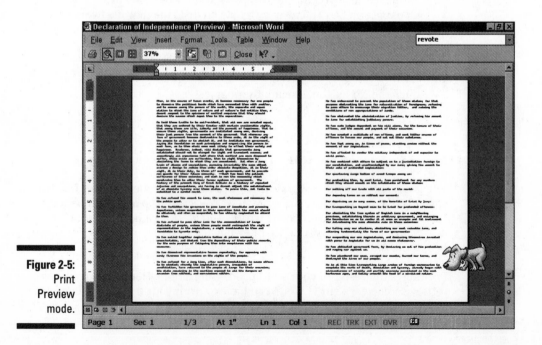

2. **Choose the File⇨Print command.**

   The Print dialog box opens. This is a busy place where printing and related activities happen.

3. **Click the OK button.**

   The document comes out of your printer.

✔ You can also summon the Print dialog box by pressing Alt+F, P, or Ctrl+P. This method is more desirable if you have long fingers or do needlepoint or if the mouse is off eating the cheese again.

✔ Chapter 9 provides detailed information about printing, including information about making sure that your printer is ready to print.

✔ Notice that saving comes before printing. It doesn't have to, but I'm a stickler for saving, saving, saving your document.

Close 'Er Up

To close a document when you're done, choose the File⇨Close command (Ctrl+W). This step closes the document window and makes it vanish from the screen. Zzzipp! (You have to say "Zzipp!" when you do this; Word is strangely mute on the point.) This step is covered succinctly in Chapter 1; for all the details, see the section about how to quit what you're doing without quitting Word.

✔ Why close a document? Because you're done working on it! Maybe you want to work on something else or quit Word after closing. The choices are yours.

✔ If you try to close a document before it has been saved, Word displays a warning dialog box. Click the Yes button to save your document. If you want to continue editing, click the Cancel button and get back to work.

✔ If you're working on only one document and you close it, Word looks like it has vacated the premises: Toolbars and menus disappear, as do scroll bars and other screen debris. Don't panic; you've just closed a document and Word has little else to do. Word sits patiently and waits for your next command.

✔ If you're done with Word, quit. Otherwise, you can start working on another document. Refer to "Starting a New Document," earlier in this chapter.

Chapter 3

Basic Movement

● ●

In This Chapter

▶ Moving the toothpick cursor

▶ Using key combinations to move up, down, to the top, to the bottom — you get the idea

▶ Using the Go To command

▶ Bookmarking memorable bits o' text

▶ Using the secret scroll bar buttons

● ●

I think that I shall never see, a poem lovely as a tree. Especially since a large branch has just impacted my occipital lobe and impaired my vision.

*W*riting means rewriting, which means that there will be times when you're just perusing your document. If you need a mental image, picture a typewriter with only one long sheet of paper. To reread your document, you would have to rewind it back through the platen until you found the part you wanted. Ugh. What a chore!

Fortunately, Word has some basic toothpick cursor movement commands that let you scroll, read, or edit through your document much easier than cranking a knob. It's all about movement! Exercise! Be active! Avoid falling branches!

Moving around Your Document

When you scribble on a pad of paper, it's hard to lose your place. And in the old typewriter days, a page of paper was only so big. But with Word, your documents can be downright humongous. Unfortunately, only a small part of that humongousness appears on your computer screen at a time. To get from one place to another, you need to do more than just press the arrow keys. You need to find out about Word's navigation keys and other special commands you can use to get around in your document.

Going hither, thither, and yon (basic arrow keys)

The most common way to move about in your document is to press the arrow keys, which are also called the *cursor-control keys* because they control the toothpick cursor onscreen. These keys can be used alone or with other keys on your keyboard to zippity-zap the toothpick cursor all over your document.

If you use the arrow keys on the numeric keypad, make sure that the Num Lock light is off. Do this by pressing the Num Lock key. If you don't do this, you see numbers in your text rather than the toothpick cursor dancing all over — like444this.

The four basic arrow keys move the toothpick cursor up, down, right, and left:

Key	What It Does
↑	Moves the cursor up to the preceding line of text
↓	Moves the cursor down to the next line of text
→	Moves the cursor right to the next character
←	Moves the cursor left to the preceding character

If you press and hold the Ctrl (Control) key and then press an arrow key, you enter afterburner mode. The supercharged toothpick cursor jumps in desperately quick leaps in all four directions:

Press These Keys	To Do This
Ctrl+↑	Moves the cursor up to the start of the previous paragraph
Ctrl+↓	Moves the cursor down to the start of the next paragraph
Ctrl+→	Moves the cursor right to the start (first letter) of the previous word
Ctrl+←	Moves the cursor left to the start (first letter) of the next word

Use the Ctrl key with the arrow key in the same way that you use the Shift key with the *s* key to get a capital *S:* Press and hold the Ctrl key and then press an arrow key. Release both keys. You don't have to press hard.

✔ You cannot move the toothpick cursor beyond the limits of your document: You cannot scroll "higher" than the first line or "lower" than the last line of a document, nor can you attempt to place the cursor in the nether regions between pages by clicking your mouse.

✔ If you like, you can direct Word to beep at you when you try to move the cursor beyond the limits of a document: Choose Tools⇨Options from the menu. Click on the General tab in the Options dialog box, and put a check mark by the item Provide feedback with sound. Click OK and Word cacophanously beeps when you attempt to force the toothpick cursor off the page.

✔ Moving the cursor does not erase characters; using the Backspace and Delete keys erases characters (among other things discussed in Chapter 4).

✔ The word *yon* was used in English as another form of the word *there.* Here is here, there is there, and yon is like *there,* but farther off. It's short for *yonder.*

Making that toothpick cursor skedaddle (moving by great leaps and bounds)

Not all your fingers are the same length. Look at them right now! See how some are shorter and some are longer? The short ones are probably that way because you press the arrow keys on your keyboard in an improper manner. For shame. There are better ways to jump around a document.

Instead of woodpeckering your keyboard, try using some of the arrow key (and non-arrow key) combinations in the following sections to really make that toothpick cursor fly around your document.

Paging Mr. PgUp and Mr. PgDn!

PgUp is keyboard language for Page Up. And PgDn is keyboard language for Page Down. Your keyboard has both sets of keys: keyboard language PgUp and PgDn on the numeric keypad and Page Up and Page Down on the cursor area (to the left of the keypad). Isn't that nice?

One would think, logically, that the Page Up set of keys moves a document up one page and that the Page Down set of keys moves a document down. 'Tain't so, though. Rather than slide your document around a page at a time, these keys move things one *screen* at a time:

PgUp   The PgUp key moves the toothpick cursor up one screen. Or, if you're at the tippy-top of your document, this key moves you to the top of the screen.

PgDn	Moves the cursor down one screen or to the end of the document, if you happen to be there, or to the end of the document if you happen to be less than a screen away.
	If you're just interested in moving to the top or bottom of the screen (the text displayed in Word's window), use these weirdoes:
Ctrl+Alt+PgUp	Moves the cursor to the top of the current screen.
Ctrl+Alt+PgDn	Moves the cursor to the bottom of the current screen.

Personally, I've never used those keys because it's just easier to click the mouse wherever I want to put the toothpick cursor.

The final two PgUp and PgDn key combinations are tougher to explain. When used in combination with the Ctrl key, PgUp and PgDn are used to browse through your document according to settings made by the Secret Scroll Bar Buttons. This information is covered later in this chapter.

There is no logic in the computer industry.

Beginnings and endings

Up/down, top/bottom, begin/end — sometimes you just need to get right there. These are the keys that do it — and they're named surprisingly well:

Key or Combination	Where It Puts Your Cursor
End	This key sends the toothpick cursor to the end of a line of text.
Home	This key sends the toothpick cursor to the start of a line of text.
Ctrl+End	This key combination whisks the toothpick cursor to the very, very end of your document.
Ctrl+Home	This key combination takes you to the tippy-top of your document. Zoom!

Ctrl+End is an easy key combination to mistakenly press. It throws you — literally — to the end of your document. If you do this and feel that you have boo-booed, press Shift+F5, the Go Back keyboard shortcut, to return from whence you came (that is, back to your previous edit). Also see "Going Back," later in this chapter.

Using the mouse to move yerself around

The mouse provides a quick and easy way to move the toothpick cursor: First, spy a new location for the cursor onscreen. Then move the mouse pointer to where you want the cursor to be and click. The cursor relocates there instantly. It's point and click.

You can also use your mouse to manipulate the vertical scroll bar (to the right of the document window). The scroll bar is a standard Windows toy, working in Word like it does in all of Windows. The only bonus you get here is that if you drag the elevator button with the mouse, you see a pop-up balloon telling you approximately which page you're dragging to in your document, as shown in Figure 3-1. You might even see the current part heading or chapter title as you drag the elevator button.

Figure 3-1:
Vital page-
numbering
information.

Finally, if your PC sports one of the new "wheel" mice, such as the Microsoft Intellimouse, you can scroll through your document using the center wheel button:

> Roll the wheel up or down to scroll your document up or down. (The number of lines the document scrolls is set by using the Mouse icon in the Windows Control Panel.)
>
> Click the wheel to exert super-mousian control over the vertical scroll bar to quickly scroll your document up and down.
>
> Press the wheel like a button and drag the mouse to smoothly scroll up and down or "pan" your document from left to right.

Oh, I just love those mouse toys!

> ✔ Watch out when you're using the vertical scroll bar to move around your document! Scrolling the screen does not make the cursor flippity-jibbit all over. You must *click the mouse* in the text to actually move the cursor to a given spot. So, for example, you may scroll to view page 5 but the toothpick cursor is still a-blinkin' on page 3. When you start to type, the new text appears on page 3 where the toothpick cursor is, not on page 5 where you're looking.

> ✔ You must click the mouse to move the cursor to that spot. If you don't click the mouse, you're just messing with the computer's mind.

Going Here or There with the Go To Command

Ah, one more timesaving tip: Suppose that you need to get to page 14. Well, if you're on page 1, you can A) use the scroll bar's elevator button to find it B) press the → key 14,000 times C) press PgDn to get there in 28-or-so strokes or D) use the Go To command.

Yes, Go To fits the bill.

Go To, as in the Shakespearean "Getteth thee outta hereth," enables you to go directly to just about wherever in the document you want to be. The Go To command lets you find a specific page number, line, or what-have-you in your document.

To use the Go To command, choose Edit⇨Go To (or press Alt, E, G), and the Go To tab in the Find and Replace dialog box appeareth before thine eyes (see Figure 3-2).

Figure 3-2:
Tell 'em
where to go
in the Go To
dialog box.

There are lots of places you can go to, as the confusing items in the Go To What list in Figure 3-2 demonstrate. Usually, though, you want to go to a specific page number.

Type a page number into the Enter Page Number box.

For example, type **14** in the box and press Enter, and you go to page 14. That's supposing you have a page 14 to go to.

> ✔ You can also press the F5 key to open the Go To tab in the Find and Replace dialog box.

> ✔ Heck, you can also press the Ctrl+G keyboard shortcut. (Makes more sense than F5, anyway.)

✔ If you click twice on the page number on the status bar (muttering "Change, you idiot — change, change," while you do this helps), the Go To dialog box appears like a genie out of a lamp.

✔ To be even more specific in your Go To commands, see "Don't Dog-Ear Your Monitor! Use the Bookmark Command," just ahead in this chapter.

Going Back

They say that once you commit, there's no going back. That is, unless you're running for office or using Word. If you go anywhere you don't want to be, press Shift+F5, and Word carries you back to where you started.

The Shift+F5 keyboard shortcut works only in Word; you can't use this command in real life.

 Pressing Shift+F5 returns you to where you were before; pressing it again takes you back to where you were before that. This keyboard shortcut works about three times before it starts repeating itself. Repeating itself. Repeating itself.

Don't Dog-Ear Your Monitor! Use the Bookmark Command

As the scatterbrained type, I often find myself working on several parts of a document at once. Maybe you do that, too. Or perhaps you're reading what you wrote and need to remember a specific spot to come back to. Whatever the reason, often it's necessary to, well, put a bookmark in your document. That's tough to do without bending the corner of your monitor, which I doubt would work anyway.

Welcome to Word's Bookmark command.

Setting a bookmark

To mark your place in your document, set a bookmark. Follow these steps:

1. **Put the toothpick cursor where you want to place a bookmark.**

2. **Choose the Insert⇨Bookmark command (or, if you have three hands, try Ctrl+Shift+F5).**

   The Bookmark dialog box opens, as shown in Figure 3-3.

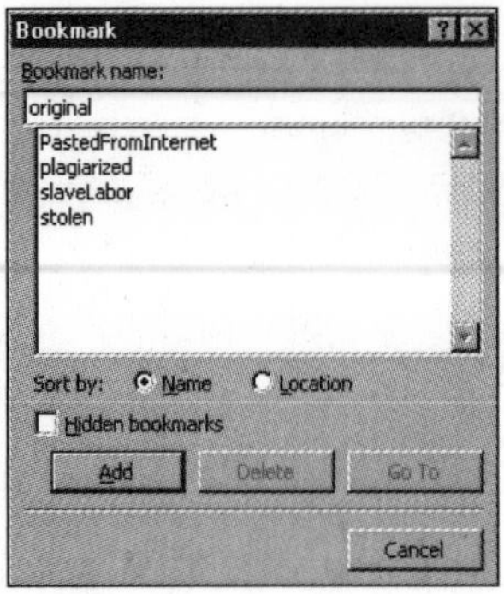

Figure 3-3:
The
Bookmark
dialog box.

3. **Type a name for the bookmark.**

Be clever! The name reminds you of where you are in your document. So if you're creating a term paper, memorable flags for various parts of your document (and their original sources) would be proper.

By the way, bookmark names cannot contain spaces. However, you can use unique capitalization if you like, as shown in Figure 3-3.

4. **Press Enter or click the Add button.**

Finding a bookmark and moving to that spot in your document

To return to a bookmark, use the Go To command, as covered in "Going Here or There with the Go To Command," earlier in this chapter. These steps keep you from turning the page and losing your train of thought:

1. **Press the F5 key.**

The Find and Replace dialog box splats across your screen.

2. **Highlight Bookmark on the Go To What list.**

Bookmark is the fourth item down.

The Enter Page Number box changes to read Enter Bookmark Name. Your most recent bookmark appears in that space.

If you don't see your bookmark, click the down-arrow and you see a long list of bookmarks in your document. Click the one you want.

3. **Click the Go To button.**

You're there!

4. **Click the Close button to get rid of the Find and Replace dialog box and return to editing your document.**

Using Secret Scroll Bar Buttons to Navigate

Lurking at the bottom of the vertical scroll bar are three buttons, as shown in the margin. These are the *browse* buttons, which allow you to scroll through your document in leaps and bounds of various sizes.

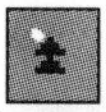

The top button is the *Browse Up* button.

The bottom button is the *Browse Down* button.

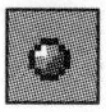

And the center button is the *What The Heck Am I Browsing For?* button.

When you click the center button, a pop-up palette of things to browse for appears, as shown in Figure 3-4. Pointing the mouse at any one of the items displays text that explains the item in the bottom part of the palette.

Figure 3-4:
Various
things to
browse for.

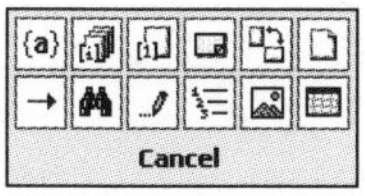

Normally, the page item is selected (see margin). That means clicking the Browse Up or Browse Down buttons jumps you back or ahead in your document one page at time.

These buttons are also related to the Search command (covered in Chapter 5). Clicking the Browse Up or Browse Down button locates the last item you've searched for. You can manually select that option by selecting the binoculars icon from the pop-up palette (refer to Figure 3-4), though whenever you use the Search command, the Browse buttons automatically take on the find-next or find-previous functions.

Other icons on the pop-up palette let you browse through your document by the items or edits they represent, though I've used only the Find and Page buttons myself.

Meanwhile, back in PgUp and PgDn keyboard land, you can now be fully informed of the functions of the Ctrl+PgUp and Ctrl+PgDn keys. Basically, they're shortcuts for the Browse Up and Browse Down buttons. If you haven't yet browsed for anything, Ctrl+PgUp and Ctrl+PgDn scroll through your document one screen at a time. Otherwise, those two key combinations take on the Browse button functions, letting you hop through your document by whichever item you've chosen from the pop-up palette. Nifty.

Chapter 4

Basic Editing

· ·

In This Chapter

▶ Using Insert and Overtype modes

▶ Deleting text with Backspace and Delete

▶ Deleting lines, sentences, and paragraphs

▶ Undoing your mistakes

▶ Using Redo (un-undo) command

· ·

*E*diting. It sounds so neat and tidy, doesn't it? It's a helping word. To edit is to help, "Here, let me edit this for you. I'm just going to touch it up a tad. Nip and tuck. Hone your points. Focus your thoughts." That's the way I'd like to think of editing. But the truth is far more ugly. Yes, editing is about destruction.

To edit is to cut. To whack. To destroy. To lay down swaths of burnt text, the stubble and stumps of excess words and mangled thoughts too gross and graceless for the printed page. That's the legacy of editing. And it's the subject of this chapter.

Word processing is more than just typing and moving the cursor around. It's playing with the text. Retyping. Deleting. Undoing. These are the basic editing tasks you find in the text that follows (which I typed, retyped, overtyped, deleted, and undid many times over).

To Insert or to Overtype: That Is the Question

Betcha didn't know that Word is usually in Insert mode. That means that any new text you type is inserted just before the blinking toothpick cursor. The new stuff pushes any existing text to the right and down as you type. This is Insert mode.

Insert mode's evil twin is Overtype mode. In Overtype mode, all the text you type overwrites the existing text onscreen, replacing it as you go.

To switch to Overtype mode, press the Insert key on your keyboard. Either the key labeled Insert or the Ins key on the numeric keypad (with Num Lock off) does the trick.

When you're in Overtype mode, the three letters OVR are highlighted on the status bar. In fact, you can double-click those letters to switch between Insert and Overtype modes.

Honestly, there is no reason to type in Overtype mode. Insert mode is fine by itself; you can use the various commands in this chapter to delete text at your whim.

> ✔ In Overtype mode, new text gobbles up text already on the screen. If you see this weirdness happen, double-click the OVR thing on the status bar to stop it, and then use the Ctrl+Z (Undo) keyboard shortcut to yank back any deleted text.

> ✔ So the answer to this section's title is that Insert mode is the answer.

Deleting Stuff

I knew a writer who was utterly afraid to delete *anything*. Rather than toss out the random paragraph or two, he'd merely copy the paragraphs as *blocks* and move them to the end of the document for "safekeeping." Yeah. And if he eventually becomes the next Bill Shakespeare, posterity will have all those discarded blocks of text to marvel over. Aren't we lucky?

Sad but true, deleting text is a part of the editing process, just like writing. Everyone edits and everyone deletes text. In fact, I'm fond of saying that you can probably delete the opening paragraph of any first draft you do. If that's your urge, or if even deleting small stuff is in order, this part of the book is the right place to come.

> ✔ It's said that Isaac Asimov never did second drafts of anything. That's not to say that he didn't go back and self edit — just that he was probably much better at writing than most folks I know.

> ✔ Moving blocks is covered in Chapter 6.

Your basic delete keys: Backspace and Delete

You can use two keys on the keyboard to delete single characters of text:

- ✔ **Backspace key:** Deletes the character to the left of the toothpick cursor.
- ✔ **Delete key:** Deletes the character to the right of the toothpick cursor.

```
Bread mold held special mean|ing for Brenda. Her refrigerator
            was full of samples.
```

In the preceding line, the toothpick cursor is "flashing" (okay, it *would* be flashing on a computer screen) between the *n* and the *i* in *meaning*. Pressing the Backspace key deletes the *n;* pressing the Delete key deletes the *i*.

- ✔ After deleting a character, any text to the right or below the character moves up to fill the void.
- ✔ If you're in Overtype mode, the Backspace key still pulls the rest of the text to the right.
- ✔ Backspace doesn't work like the Backspace key on a typewriter. The difference is that when you press Backspace in Word, the cursor backs up and *erases*. (The Word equivalent of the typewriter's Backspace key is the left-arrow key.)

- ✔ Special types of text in Word cannot easily be deleted using either the Backspace or Delete keys. An example is an updating text field, which is special text that always shows, say, today's date. Such text appears shaded in a light gray color when you try to delete it. That's Word reminding you of the text's specialness. You need to press the Delete or Backspace key once again to delete such text.
- ✔ You can press and hold Backspace or Delete to continuously "machine-gun-delete" characters. Release the key to halt such wanton destruction.

Deleting a word

Word has two commands that gobble up an entire word:

- ✔ Ctrl+Backspace deletes the word in front (to the left) of the cursor.
- ✔ Ctrl+Delete deletes the word behind (to the right) of the cursor.

To delete a word by using Ctrl+Backspace, position the cursor at the last letter of the word. Press Ctrl+Backspace, and the word is gone! The cursor then sits at the end of the preceding word or the beginning of the line (if you deleted the first word in a paragraph).

To delete a word by using Ctrl+Delete, position the cursor at the first letter of the word. Press Ctrl+Delete, and the word is gone. The cursor then sits at the beginning of the next word or the end of the line (if you deleted the last word in a paragraph).

Unfortunately, if you're in the middle of the word, you delete only from that middle point to the start or end of the word. Therefore, I bestow the following trick:

To delete a word, the whole word, and nothing but the word, point the mouse at the offending critter and double-click the mouse button. This action selects the entire word, highlighting it on the screen. Press the Delete key to zap the word away.

After deleting the text, Word neatly wraps up the remaining text, snuggling it together in a grammatically proper way.

No mere pencil eraser can match Ctrl+Delete or Ctrl+Backspace for sheer speed and terror!

Deleting lines, sentences, and paragraphs

In Word, there is a difference between a line of text, a sentence, and a paragraph. Heed these definitions:

- ✔ A *line of text* is merely a line across the page (not really a grammatical thing at all). The Ln indicator on the status bar tells you which *line* of text you're on, as measured from the top of the page. For example, right now Word tells me that I'm editing line 23. Whatever.

- ✔ A *sentence* is a sentence. You know: Start with a capital letter and end with a period, question mark, or exclamation point. You probably learned this concept in grammar school, which is why they call it *grammar* school anyway.

- ✔ A *paragraph* is a bunch of text ending with a press of the Enter key. So a paragraph can be one line of text, a sentence, or several sentences.

And just who cares? Well, all this stuff comes into play when you want to delete various bits of text. There are different ways to delete lines, sentences, and paragraphs.

Deleting a line of text

Word has no single command for deleting a line of text from the keyboard. But with the mouse, deleting a line is only a matter of a click and a key press. Follow these steps:

1. **Move the mouse into the left margin of your document.**

   The cursor changes into an arrow pointing northeast rather than northwest.

2. **Point the mouse pointer arrow at the line of text you want to obliterate.**

3. **Click the left mouse button.**

   The line of text is highlighted, or selected.

4. **Press the Delete key to send that line into the void.**

When the mouse cursor is pointing northeast, you can drag it down the left margin and select as many lines of text as you care to. All the lines can then be deleted with one stroke of the Delete key.

Also see Chapter 6, where I talk about marking text as a block and then blowing it to Kingdom Come.

Deleting a sentence

Making a sentence go bye-bye is cinchy. Well, you could just press the Delete key once for each character in the sentence. But, as with everything in a computer, there's always a better, easier way:

1. **Place the toothpick cursor firmly in the midst of the offending sentence.**

   Click.

2. **Press the F8 key thrice.**

   Pressing the F8 key once turns on *extended selection mode,* which is covered in Chapter 6. Pressing F8 twice selects a word, and pressing it thrice selects a sentence.

3. **Press the Delete key.**

   Oomph! It's gone.

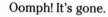

Pressing the F8 key three times highlights (selects) a sentence.

If you change your mind, press the Esc key. That cancels Extended Selection mode. Press any arrow key or click the mouse in your text to unhighlight.

Deleting a paragraph

There are two, nay, *three* ways to mark a paragraph for destruction:

✔ **The triple-click method.** Click the mouse three times on the paragraph. Click-click-click. Be quick about the triple click. That highlights the paragraph, and a deft press of the Delete key mooches it off the page.

> ✔ **The F8, F8, F8, F8 method.** You can also select and delete a paragraph by placing the toothpick cursor in the paragraph and pressing the F8 key fourice, er, four times. Press the Delete key and — presto! — vaporized text!
>
> ✔ **The northeast cursor/double-click method.** If you're fond of the north-east-pointing mouse, move the mouse pointer into the left column on the page (where it turns into the northeast pointer) and then double-click. The paragraph to the right of the mouse cursor is selected and primed for deletion with a quick tap of the Delete key.

Deleting odd shapes with blocks

Word can delete characters, words, and lines with nifty, specific commands. To delete anything else, you have to mark it as a block of text and then delete the block.

Refer to Chapter 6 for more information on marking a block of text. After any block is marked in your document, pressing the Delete key removes it. (If only getting rid of warts were so easy. . . .)

Erase Your Mistakes with Undo Haste

Now mark me how I will undo myself. — Richard II, William Shakespeare

There is no need to be afraid of doing anything in Word. Anything! That's because Word has a handy Undo command. The Undo command remembers the last several things you added or deleted and quite easily unravels any mistakes you made. Furthermore, there's a Redo command, which is essentially Undo-Undo, though that's a double negative, and it hurts my brain to think about it.

The blessed Undo command

To undelete any text you just accidentally zapped, do any of the following:

> ✔ Press Ctrl+Z.
>
> ✔ Choose Edit⇨Undo with the mouse.
>
> ✔ Click the Undo tool on the toolbar.

These are the three ways to use the Undo command. (I prefer the Ctrl+Z key combination myself).

✔ Unlike other programs, using the Undo command in Word twice doesn't undo your last undo. For example, pressing Ctrl+Z may replace text you just deleted. If you press Ctrl+Z again, it does not re-delete the text (undoing the undo).

✔ The Undo item on the Edit menu changes to pertain to whatever needs undoing: Undo Bold, Undo Typing, Undo Boo-boo, and so on.

✔ If you click the down arrow by the Undo button, you see a drop-down list of the last several things you've done in Word. You can select the whole group of them (by dragging the mouse through the list) to undo all your previous actions in one swift swath.

✔ To undo an Undo, choose Redo. See the section "Redo, or take two" a couple of sections from now.

Can't Undo? Here's why. . . .

Sometimes it eats you alive that Word can't undo an action. On the menu bar, you even see the message Can't Undo. What gives?

Essentially, whatever action you just did, Word can't undo it. This result can be true for a number of reasons: There is nothing to undo; not enough memory is available to undo; Word can't undo because what you did was too complex; Word just forgot; Word hates you; and so on.

I know that it's frustrating, but everyone has to live with it.

Redo, or take two

If you undo something and — whoops! — you didn't mean to, you must use the Redo command to set things back. To undelete any text you just accidentally zapped, do any of the following:

✔ Press Ctrl+Y.

✔ Choose Edit⇨Redo with the mouse.

✔ Click the Redo tool on the toolbar (if available).

How does this work? Well, pretend that after one particularly heavy lunch you return to the office for some vigorous typing. Alas, sleep eventually overcomes you, and your head slams into the keyboard for some random typing. After you snap awake — and check to ensure that no one witnessed such an embarrassing episode — you decide to undo the typing your forehead just did: Ctrl+Z, Ctrl+Z, Ctrl+Z.

But — whoops! — you pressed one Ctrl+Z too many times. In that case, use the Edit⇨Redo command (or Ctrl+Y) to yank back the stuff you just undid.

And what if there's nothing to redo? Then the Redo command becomes the Repeat command, which is covered in the section about taking advantage of the Repeat key, in Chapter 10.

✔ Honestly, no one uses the Redo command that much. If you do, you find that it can be very frustrating because it tends to redo things you really wanted undone in the first place. (You'll understand this if you ever use Redo several times in a row.)

✔ The Redo button on the toolbar may not be visible. I implore you to rearrange your toolbars, which I cover in Chapter 30.

✔ Like the Undo command, the Redo command has a button on the Standard toolbar. Next to the button is a down arrow, which you can click to review the last few things you just undid. Or redid. Or katydid. Oy.

Chapter 5

Search for This, Replace It with That

T he alchemists believed that you could turn lead into gold. Sure, you laugh at that now. "Ha, ha," you say — because you know that both gold and lead are basic elements and one cannot change into the other. At least that's what your high school chemistry teacher swore up and down about. But wouldn't it be swell if you could change lead into gold? Or water into gasoline? Or cardboard into pizza?

Well I'm here to tell you that the alchemists were right. It *is* possible to change lead into gold — as long as those are words in your document and you're using Word's nifty Find and Replace command. Yes, Word can deftly locate any occurrence of the word *lead* and swiftly substitute in the word *gold,* all neat and tidy. It may not be the lucrative retirement machine the alchemists dreamed of, but it's certainly possible. This chapter has all the details.

Text, O Text! Wherefore Art Thou?

Word can quickly locate any tidbit of text anywhere in your document, from a bombastic oratory to the tiniest iota of plot. The command used to find text is called, surprisingly enough, the Find command. It dwells on the Edit menu. Follow these steps to use the Find command and locate text lurking in your document:

1. **Think of some text you want to find.**

   For example, *lead*.

2. **Choose the Edit➪Find command.**

   You see the Find and Replace dialog box, as shown in Figure 5-1. Notice that this dialog box is also used for replacing text and using the Go To command, as indicated by the tabs. But you want to find text, so the Find tab is up front. Good.

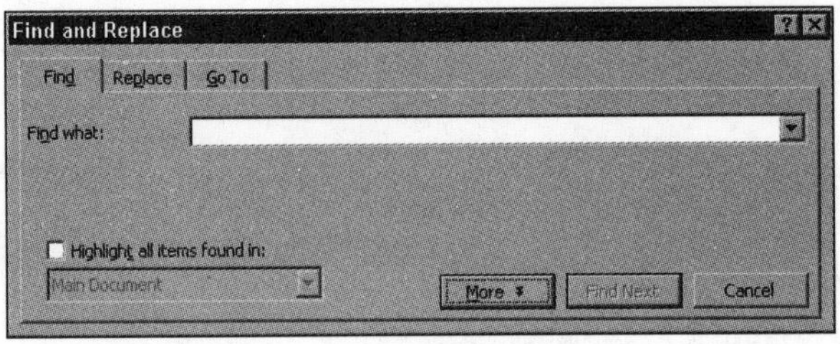

Figure 5-1:
The Find
and Replace
dialog box.

3. **Type the text you want to find.**

   Enter the text in the Find what box; for example, **lead**. Type it exactly as you want to find it.

   If you're not sure whether the text is typed in uppercase or lowercase letters, use lowercase.

4. **Click the Find Next button to start the search.**

   Or you can just press Enter.

If any text is found, it's highlighted onscreen. The Find and Replace dialog box does not go away until you click the Cancel button or press the Escape key. (The dialog box remains so that you can keep searching for more text, if you're so inclined.)

   ✔ The quick shortcut key for finding text is to press Ctrl+F (the F stands for Find in this case).

   ✔ Type exactly the text you want to find. It can be one word, multiple words, or a complete sentence you want to find. (Do not end the text with a period unless you want to find the period also.)

   ✔ If the text isn't found, the dog (or the Office Assistant of your choice) asks whether you want to search again from the beginning. Click Yes or No, accordingly. Or, if the text isn't found, the Office Assistant lets you know. (If you sent the dog outside, the message is displayed in a plain old dialog box.)

   ✔ If the text isn't found and you're *certain* that it's in there, try again. Check your typing first, though.

✔ If you're working on more than one document at a time, be aware that Word finds text only in the current document (the one you see on the screen). To find text in another document, click that document's button on the taskbar and try again.

✔ Refer to Chapter 28 for information on searching for text in multiple documents.

✔ To find an additional occurrence of the text, click the Find Next button.

✔ You can also use the Browse Up or Browse Down buttons to find the next occurrence of text — even if the Find and Replace dialog box is no longer visible on the screen. So, if you've already searched for and found *Denise,* clicking the Browse Down button finds her name again. (You can also use Ctrl+PgUp or Ctrl+PgDn to find the previous or next occurrence of the text.)

✔ Your Office Assistant may grow a light bulb over its head after you close the Find and Replace dialog box. Clicking the light bulb displays additional information about the Find command, most of which is summarized in the preceding bullets.

Re-searching

Word remembers the last bit of text you searched for. It appears selected (highlighted) the next time you summon the Find and Replace dialog box. That's handy if you want to find the same bit of text again — or you can edit that text, modifying it slightly, to find something else.

If you cast your eyes to the right side of the Find what text box, you see a drop-down arrow gizmo (refer to Figure 5-1). Clicking that gizmo displays a scrolling list of text you've previously searched for. To re-search for a bit of text you've already searched for, click the drop-down arrow and click on the text you want to find again. Click the Find Next button and you're off on your way.

Finding more stuff

The basic finders-keepers dialog box (refer to Figure 5-1) is okay for quickly finding tidbits of text. But sometimes you may want to find more detailed stuff, or stuff you can't readily type from the keyboard (like a new paragraph's Enter keystroke). Or, you may want to find text that specifically matches *Poobah* rather than plain old *poobah.* In those cases, you need to use the more robust Find and Replace dialog box.

To activate more options in the Find and Replace dialog box, press Ctrl+F. Click the More button. The Find and Replace dialog box gets taller, with a bunch of options and doodads at the bottom, as illustrated in Figure 5-2.

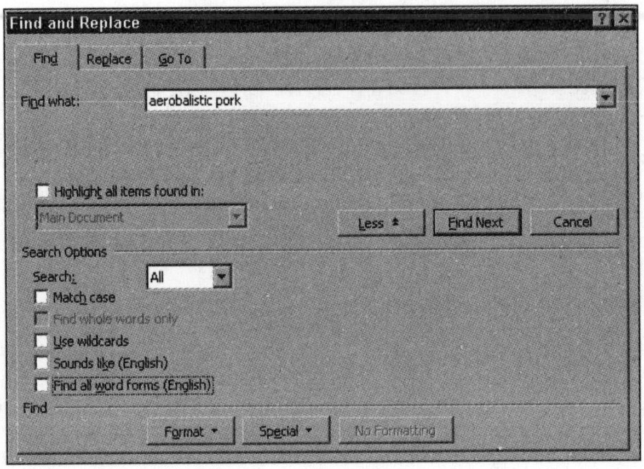

Find and Replace

Find what: aerobalistic pork

☐ Highlight all items found in:

Main Document

Less ≛ | Find Next | Cancel

Search Options

Search: All

☐ Match case
☐ Find whole words only
☐ Use wildcards
☐ Sounds like (English)
☐ Find all word forms (English)

Find

Format ▾ | Special ▾ | No Formatting

Figure 5-2:
The more detailed Find and Replace dialog box.

The following sections tell you why you may want to mess with some of those doodads.

Finding an exact bit of text

There is a difference between *Pat* and *pat*. One is a name and the other is to swat something gently. To use the Find command to find one and not the other, select the Match Case option under Search Options. That way, *Pat* matches only words that start with an uppercase *P* and have lowercase *at* in them.

Finding a whole word

The Find Whole Words Only option allows you to look for words such as *right* and *set* without finding words like *alright* and *upset*.

Finding text that you know only a small part of (using wildcards)

Here's a can-o-worms for you. It's possible to use wildcards to find words you know only a part of, or a group of words with similar letters. This trick is a highly technical thing, so I advise you not to drive or operate heavy machinery when reading the following.

The two basic wildcard characters are ? and *, where ? represents any single letter and * represents a group of letters. So, suppose that you type the following line in the Find what box:

```
?up
```

If you select the Use Wildcards option, Word searches for any 3-letter word that starts with any old letter but must end with *up: cup, pup,* and *sup,* for example.

The asterisk finds a group of characters, so the following wildcard locates any word starting with W and ending with S (there are lots of them):

```
w*s
```

You can use a bunch of other wildcard characters to find text in a number of interesting and strange ways. For example:

```
adverti[sz]e
```

This bracket-and-wildcard nonsense actually finds the word *advertise* or *advertize* depending on how you prefer to spell it.

Word has many more variations of wildcards available, although * and ? are the most popular and should get you by. To see the rest of the wildcards available, click the question mark button in the upper-right corner of the Find and Replace dialog box and then select the Use Wildcards option.

Finding text that sounds like something else

The Sounds Like option allows you to search for homonyms, or words that sound the same as the search word. You know: their and there, or deer and dear, or hear and here. How this is useful, I'll never know.

Oh! This is not a rhyming search command. If you try to use it to find everything that rhymes with *Doris,* for example, it doesn't find *Boris, chorus, pylorus,* or anything of the like.

Finding variations of a word

"No, no, no! Superman doesn't walk anywhere! He flies! Change this!" So off you go into Word, searching for every variation of the word *walk: walking, walked,* and so on. Word can do it. Just type **walk** into the Find what box and click the Find All Word Forms option.

Searching up, down, left, and right

Janus was the Roman god of beginnings and endings. He had two faces looking in two directions, ideal for watching a tennis match or for finding stuff you've lost. Alas, the Find command is not Janus. It looks only one way, usually toward the end of your document, when you go hunting for text.

As soon as you reach the end of your document, Word (or the Office Assistant) asks whether you want to search again from the beginning. You do, so you click Yes. Eventually, the Find command stops looking when it returns to where the toothpick cursor was when you first cast the Find command spell.

Of course, you don't have to look "down" all the time. You can tell the Find command to look from the toothpick cursor to the *start* of your document. That's looking "up." Or, you can look through the entire document. You do all this in the More part of the Find and Replace dialog box.

Locate the Search drop-down box (refer to Figure 5-2) and click the down-arrow. There you find three options:

- ✔ **Down:** Searches from the toothpick cursor to the end of the document.
- ✔ **Up:** Searches from the toothpick cursor to the beginning of the document.
- ✔ **All:** Fie on the toothpick cursor — Word searches the entire document.

I was just kidding about searching left and right in this section's title. Left is actually "up," or before the toothpick cursor; right is "down," or after the toothpick cursor. And starboard is right and port is left, if you happen to be using Word on a laptop somewhere in the ocean.

Finding stuff you just can't type in

No, this isn't a censorship issue. Some characters you just can't properly type in the Find and Replace dialog box — unprintable, unmentionable stuff. No, not Victoria's Secret types of things. I'm talking about characters you can't rightly type. For example, try finding a Tab character: You can't! Press the Tab key in the Find and Replace dialog box and — whoops! — nothing happens. That result is because Tab and a few other keys are special, and you must force-feed them to the Find and Replace dialog box.

To find a special, unprintable character, click the More button to see the expanded Find and Replace dialog box, and then click the Special button (refer to Figure 5-2). Up pops a list of various characters Word can search for but that you would have a dickens of a time typing (see Figure 5-3).

Choose one of the items from the list to search for that special character. When you do, a special, funky shorthand representation for that character (such as ^t for Tab) appears in the Find what box. Click the Find Next button to find that character.

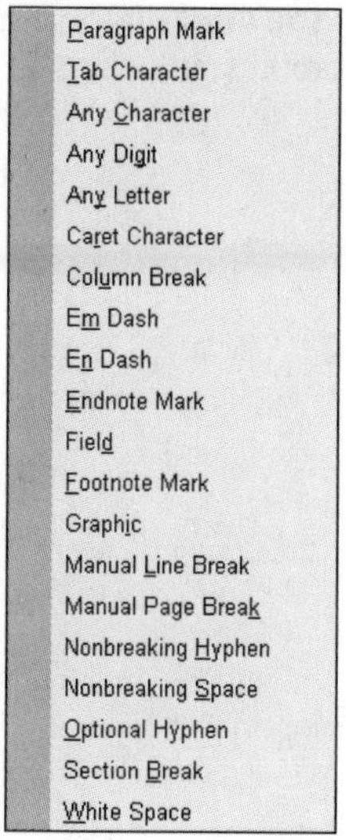

Paragraph Mark
Tab Character
Any Character
Any Digit
Any Letter
Caret Character
Column Break
Em Dash
En Dash
Endnote Mark
Field
Footnote Mark
Graphic
Manual Line Break
Manual Page Break
Nonbreaking Hyphen
Nonbreaking Space
Optional Hyphen
Section Break
White Space

Figure 5-3:
Items to
search for
that you
can't type.

Here are some of the most useful special characters available when you click
the Special button in the Find dialog box:

- **Any Character, Any Digit, and Any Letter** are special characters that
  represent, well, just about anything. These buttons are used as wildcards for matching lots of stuff.

- **Caret Character** allows you to search for a caret (^) symbol, which is a
  special character. If you just type the caret symbol itself (^), Word thinks
  that you're trying to type another special character.

- **Paragraph Mark** (¶) is a special character that's the same as the Enter
  character — what you press to end a paragraph.

- **Tab Character** is the character that moves the cursor to the next tab
  mark.

- **White Space** is any blank character: a space or a tab, for example.

Yes, you can mix and match the special characters with other text you want
to find. If you want to find a Tab character followed by *Hunter,* you use the
Special button to insert the tab character (^t on the screen), and then you
just type **Hunter** using your fingers. It looks like this:

```
^tHunter
```

You don't have to use the Special pop-up menu, as long as you can keep a list
of the special characters in your head. I do this all the time; because I know
that ^p is the shortcut for the Enter key, I can just type it in and not even

have to bother with clicking the More button in the Find dialog box. Here's a handy shortcut list of the common special characters, in case you want to memorize them:

Paragraph mark	^p
Tab character	^t
Any character	^?
Any digit	^#
Any letter	^$
Caret character	^^
Manual line break	^l
Manual page break	^m
White space	^w

Finding formatting

The final and most insane thing the Find command can do for you is to find formatting codes laced throughout your document. For example, if you want to find only those instances of the word *lie* in boldface type, you can do that.

Many formatting searches require that you know a bit about how Word formats text, characters, and documents, so I highly recommend that you familiarize yourself with the chapters in Part II of this book if you haven't yet done so.

To find formatting stuff in a document, use the More part of the Find and Replace dialog box (refer to Figure 5-2). Click the Format button to see a pop-up list of formatting options in Word, as shown in Figure 5-4.

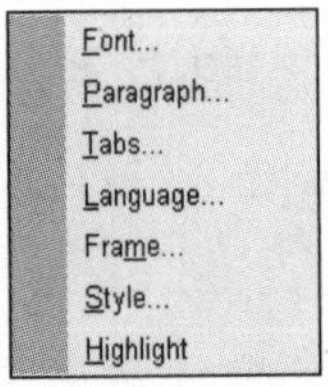

Figure 5-4:
Various
formatting
options to
search for.

> Font...
> Paragraph...
> Tabs...
> Language...
> Frame...
> Style...
> Highlight

Each one of the menu items displays one of Word's formatting dialog boxes. Within those dialog boxes, you can select the formatting attributes to search for. You use the Font dialog box to select specific font formats to search for and use the Style dialog box to search for text formatting using a specific style, for example. (Again, it helps if you know how Word uses these dialog boxes to format your text.)

Suppose that you want to find the bold-faced *lie* in your document. Follow these steps:

1. **Summon the Find and Replace dialog box.**

   Pressing Ctrl+F is the only sane way to do this step.

   Optionally, delete any previously searched for text in the Find what text box. (The last text you searched for always hangs around, just in case you forget what you last found.)

2. **Click the More button to display the bottom part of the Find and Replace dialog box.**

   This step isn't necessary if the bottom part is already showing. (And we all know how embarrassing that can be.)

3. **Click the Format button.**

   Up pops the Format list. Use the Font dialog box to apply bold to your text.

4. **Click the Font button.**

   The Font dialog box appears (which is covered in Chapter 11, in case you need to look). Because the text you're searching for is bold, you need to apply the Bold formatting option in the Font dialog box.

5. **Choose Bold from the Font style list.**

6. **Click OK.**

   The Font dialog box goes away and you return to the Find and Replace dialog box.

   Notice the text just beneath the Find what box? It says `Format: Font: Bold`. That's telling you that Word is now geared up to find only bold text.

   If you were to click the Find Next button now, Word would simply locate the next occurrence of bold text in your document. However, if you want to find a specific example of bold text, you need to fill in the Find what box.

7. **Type lie in the Find what box.**

8. **Click the Find Next button to find your formatted text.**

   Word locates the text you formatted — however you formatted it.

Word remembers your formatting options! When you go to search for non-formatted text, you need to click the No Formatting button. Doing so removes the formatting options and allows you to search for plain text again. After you forget this a few times, it really heats you up that Word cannot find your text. Do not forget to click the No Formatting button to return Word to normal text-finding mode!

✔ You can use this technique to look for specific occurrences of a font, such as Courier or Times New Roman, by selecting the font from the selection list. Scroll through the font menu to see what you can choose.

✔ You can look for a particular size of type (24 point, for example) by selecting it from the Size list. See Chapter 11 for information about character formatting.

✔ You can also search for paragraph formatting by choosing Paragraph rather than Font from the Format menu in the Find and Replace dialog box. See Chapter 12 for information about paragraph formatting.

✔ The remaining options on the Format pop-up list are fairly obscure, although if you become fluent with Word, know that you can search for text formatting with those, well, whatever-they-ares.

Finding and Replacing

By itself, the Find command is really handy. But its true power lies in its ability to not only find text but also replace that text with something else. It's one of the word-processor features that helped put various typewriter companies out of business.

If you've mastered the Find command, your black belt in the Replace command is only a paragraph away. In fact, the only trouble you'll have with the Replace command is its shortcut key.

No, it's not R — the Ctrl+R shortcut command is used to right-align text in a paragraph. (Nice try, though.) Apparently, Microsoft thought that more folks out there would be desperate to right-align paragraphs than who would desire to search and replace.

Okay, just give up now. Every other word you can think of for *replace* (oust, relieve, substitute, zap) has a shortcut key of its own. So the shortcut key for the Replace command is . . . Ctrl+H!

Enough dallying. Suppose that you want to replace the word *pig* with *pork*. Both mean the same thing, but you don't eat pig, you eat pork — well, unless your religion forbids such things, in which case you eat chicken or one of the many delightful vegetarian dishes. Enough!

1. **Choose Edit⇨Replace.**

   Or, if you can remember what the Heck H stands for, type Ctrl+H. Honestly.

   The Find and Replace dialog box, as shown in Figure 5-5, appears onscreen. This tab is actually another panel in the Find and Replace dialog box — which makes sense because finding is a big part of find and replace.

Figure 5-5:
The Replace
part of the
Find and
Replace
dialog box.

Find and Replace	? ×
Find	Replace	Go To
Find what:	pig
Replace with:	pork

More ≠   Replace   Replace All   Find Next   Cancel

The Find and Replace dialog box also has a More button. If you see the More options, click the Less button to make your screen look like Figure 5-5. (Refer to the section "Finding more stuff," earlier in this chapter, for information on what those options mean; they all apply to finding and replacing.)

2. **In the Find what box, type the text you want to find.**

   This is the text you want to replace with something else.

   Press the Tab key when you're done typing.

3. **In the Replace With box, type the text you want to use to replace the original text.**

4. **Ask yourself, "Do I want a chance to change my mind before replacing each bit of found text?"**

   If so, click the Find Next button (taking this action is usually a good idea). If not, you can click the Replace All button; text is found and replaced automatically, giving you no chance to change your mind.

5. **If you click Find Next, Word pauses at each occurrence of the text.**

   The found text is highlighted onscreen just like in the regular Find task. When this highlighting happens, you can click the Replace button to replace it or click Find Next to skip it and find the next matching bit of text. Click the Cancel button or press the Escape key when you tire of this process.

   Word may find your text, such as *use,* in the middle of another word, such as *causes.* Oops! Click that More button and select the Find Whole Words Only option to prevent that from happening.

If there's nothing more to replace, the dog says:

```
Word has completed its search of the document and has made 9
                        replacements.
```

Of course, the number of replacements depends on what you were searching for.

✔ If you don't type anything in the Replace with box . . . oops! Forgetting to type replacement text does not turn the Replace command into the Find command. No, Word just assumes that you want to find the text and replace it with *nothing*. Yup, that means deleting all the text that's found. This process can be a scary thing, so be sure to click <u>F</u>ind Next. Otherwise, you may zap parts of your document and, boy, would you be bummed (until you used the Undo command).

✔ My advice is to click Find Next most of the time. Only if you're absolutely certain (a rare occurrence, at least in my travels) should you click Replace All.

✔ The Undo command restores your document to its preceding condition if you foul up the Replace operation.

✔ Having Ctrl+H be the shortcut key for the Replace command makes no sense to me. But diligent reader Robin R. has pointed out that the H key is right there with the F and G keys on the keyboard. It just so happens that Ctrl+F for Find, Ctrl+G for Go To, and Ctrl+H for Replace are the three commands represented in the Find and Replace dialog box. Clever.

✔ You can also find and replace formatting — for example, to replace all the underline formatting in your document with italics. To do this, click the mouse in the Fi<u>n</u>d what text box, and then choose the formatting you want to find, as described earlier in this chapter. Next, click the mouse in the Replace w<u>i</u>th text box and then choose the formatting you want to replace with. Needless to say, this is a tricky — nay, an "advanced" — aspect of using Word, so save your document before you try any formatting search and replacements.

Chapter 6

Working with Blocks of Text

*W*hat would writing be without blocks? No, I'm not talking about writer's block. That's the brain lock some people claim to have when they can't find the right word or when the opening paragraph of a chapter seems to elude them. It's a myth, in my opinion; writer's block is a catchy phrase and easier to blame than the fact your fingers just aren't doing what your brain wants.

In Word, though, a *block* is a piece of text. Word lets you rope off a chunk of text — words, sentences, paragraphs, or the whole document — and then do fun and interesting things with that block of text. This chapter is all about those blocky things. Hey! It's time to play with blocks, boys and girls!

Marking Blocks of Text

A seasoned and famous writer once told me to triple-space everything, to type on thick, 20-pound paper, and to keep scissors and rubber cement handy to help me rearrange and edit. After all, he boasted, cutting and pasting your text beats typing it over and over again. His advice may have been true in 1978, but it's nuts today.

Word lets you do numerous things with blocks of text. And you don't have to worry about triple-spacing, typing on 20-pound paper, or even spending $1.29 for the industrial-size vat of rubber cement. Instead, you need to know how to mark the block. As usual, Word offers you several trillion ways to do this. I describe some of those methods here, each of which is well-suited for marking different-size chunks of text.

A Shifty way to mark tiny bits of text

To quickly mark a small chunk of text — a word, line, or paragraph — you can use the Shift key in combination with any of the arrow keys (also known as cursor-movement keys). This technique is best suited to marking a small slab of text onscreen. Let Table 6-1 be your guide.

Table 6-1	Shifty Selection Wizardry
To Do This	*Press This*
Select a character at a time to the right of the toothpick cursor	Shift+→
Select a character at a time to the left of the toothpick cursor	Shift+←
Select a block of text from the toothpick cursor to the end of the line	Shift+End
Select a block of text from the toothpick cursor to the beginning of the line	Shift+Home
Select a block of text from the toothpick cursor to a line above	Shift+↑
Select a block of text from the toothpick cursor to a line below	Shift+↓

Some thoughts on using the Shift key to select text:

✔ Either Shift key works.

✔ Using the Shift key is handy for marking small bits of text. There are better ways, however, of marking blocks larger than a line or two.

✔ Refer to Chapter 3 for more information about cursor-movement keys.

✔ I use the left Shift key and then work the arrow keys on the right side of the keyboard. If you can train yourself to work that way also, you find you can get quite deft at these Shift+arrow-key selection methods.

✔ If you use the Shift key to mark to the end of a paragraph, note that the Enter keypress (marking the end of the paragraph) is also selected. That means if you delete or reformat the block, it may also change the formatting of the next paragraph. To avoid that, press Shift+← to back up and not select the Enter keypress at the end of the paragraph.

Marking a block with your mouse

Mickey may have been born to rule a kingdom, but your computer's mouse was born to select text. Seriously! Outside of tweaking graphics, computer mice are the darlings of the text-selecting world.

It's a drag to select text

To best select a block of text with your mouse, follow these rodent-like steps:

1. **Position the mouse pointer where you want the block to start.**

2. **Hold down the left mouse button and drag the mouse over your text.**

   As you drag, the text becomes highlighted, or selected, as shown in Figure 6-1. Drag the mouse from the beginning to the end of the text you want to mark as a block.

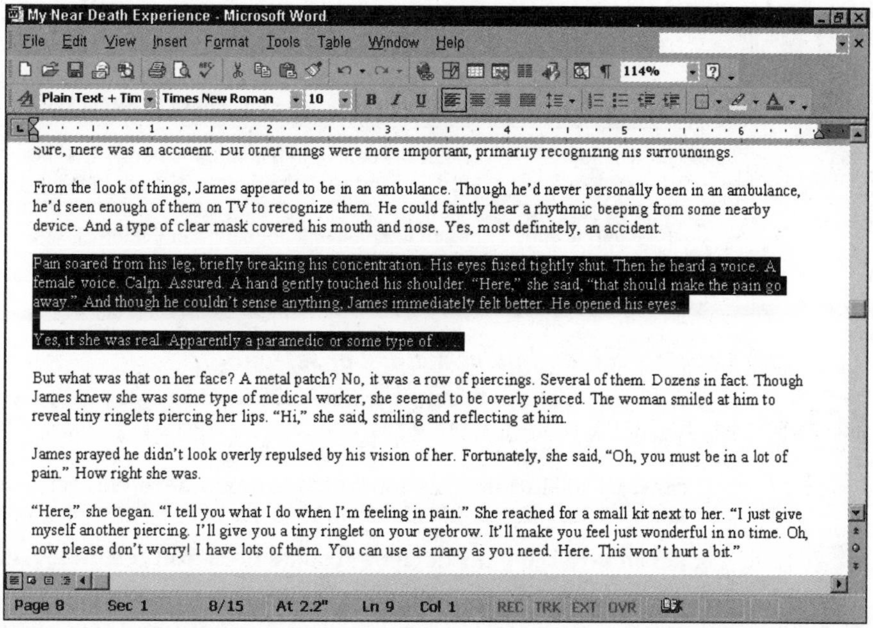

Figure 6-1:
A block of text is selected.

Notice how Word automatically selects whole words when you drag over them with your mouse. To tell Word not to select whole words, choose Tools⇨Options from the menu. On the Edit panel, deselect the check box labeled When selecting, automatically select entire word by clicking in the check box to remove the check. Click the OK button to save your change.

3. **Release the mouse — stop the dragging — to mark your block's end.**

You can select a chunk of text of any size with a mouse. However, my advice is to select only as much text as you can see on the screen at one time. If you try to select text beyond what you see on the screen, you have to select and scroll — which can be unwieldy; the mouse scrolls the text up and down quickly and, well, things get out of hand.

Quick-click mouse techniques to mark your text

Table 6-2 tells you how to put your roborodent to work selecting specific-size chunks of stuff.

Table 6-2	Mouse Selection Arcana
To Accomplish This	**Perform This Bit of Mouse Magic**
Select a word	Point at the word with your mouse and double-click.
Select a line	Move the mouse into the left margin beside the line you want to select. The mouse pointer changes to a northeasterly-pointing arrow. Click the mouse to select a line of text, or drag the mouse to select several lines.
Select a sentence	Point the mouse at the sentence and Ctrl+click; press the Ctrl key and click the mouse. The sentence is selected.
Select a paragraph	Point the mouse somewhere in the paragraph's midst and triple-click.

The old poke-and-point method of selecting

A final technique I use to select a block of text of any size with the mouse is what I call the poke-and-point technique:

1. **Start by positioning the toothpick cursor where you want the block to start — the anchor point.**

2. **Scroll through your document using the scroll bar.**

    You must use the scroll bar to scroll through your document. If you use the cursor-movement keys, you reposition the toothpick cursor, which isn't what you want.

3. **To mark the end of the block, press the Shift key and click the mouse where you want the block to end.**

   The text from the toothpick cursor to wherever you clicked the mouse is selected as a block.

This method works well for selecting a chunk of text of any size, especially when you need to scroll the document to mark the block's end.

Using the miraculous F8 key to mark a block

Who in their right mind would assign the F8 key to mean "select text?" Probably the same gang of microbrew-swilling, Volvo-driving, stock-option-obsessed people at Microsoft who brought you the F4 key. Remember F4? It's the Repeat key, so naturally the F8 key should mean select text. Drink some Talking Rain and you'll understand.

Never mind! If you can find room in your skull to remember the F8 key, you can put it to good use. F8 selects text in unique chunks, unavailable with other commands. What follows is a small sampling of what it does best.

Select a word. Pressing the F8 key twice selects a word. But, honestly, if you're going to point at the word to move the toothpick cursor there anyway, you may as well go ahead and double-click the word to select it.

Select a sentence. Position the toothpick cursor in a sentence and then press the F8 key three times to select the sentence.

Select a paragraph. Position the toothpick cursor in a paragraph and then press the F8 key four times to select the whole paragraph.

Select your document. Pressing the F8 key five times selects your entire document, but there's a better way to do that as well, which is covered in the section, "Marking the whole dang-doodle document," later in this document.

Oh! And pressing the F8 key only one time? Does that order you a new cup of coffee? Turn on WebTV? Activate Voice mode? Nope! Keep reading in the next section to learn the awful secret.

Dropping anchor with the F8 key

What the F8 key does is place Word into handy (but potentially annoying) Extended Selection mode. In this mode, the F8 key "drops anchor" on one end of a block. You can then use the cursor keys, the mouse, or even a letter key to continue marking the block. However — and this is most important — the entire time you're in Extended Selection mode, you cannot use Word for anything other than selecting a block.

Don't let this annoy you! Sure, it may confuse you at times, but using the F8 key in Extended Selection mode is the best way to select a chunk of text spanning more than one screen.

Heed these steps to use Extended Selection mode:

1. **Position the toothpick cursor at the start of the block of text you want to mark.**

2. **Press the F8 key.**

   The F8 key drops anchor, marking one end of the block.

   Notice the three letters EXT on the status bar? This is an important hint. You're now in Extended Selection mode, and the keys on your keyboard serve to select text, not to write anything. Beware!

3. **Select the block of text.**

   You can select the block of text by using the arrow keys or any of the cursor-navigation keys discussed in Chapter 3.

   You can also press a letter key to select text up to and including that letter. If you press N, you select all text up to and including the next N in your document. Nice. Nifty. Bitchen.

   Word highlights text from the point where you dropped anchor with F8 to wherever you move the toothpick cursor (refer to Figure 6-1). Text appears in white-on-black.

4. **After the block is marked, you're ready to do something with it.**

5. **Do something with the selected block of text.**

This is the annoying part. After you mark a block, you *must* perform some block command. See the status bar? The EXT is still highlighted. You're still marking a block! So unless you copy, cut, paste, spell check, or do something else, you're still in block-marking mode.

If you want to cancel the extended selection, press the Esc key. Or, you can double-click EXT on the status bar (which forces you to pay attention to EXT so that it doesn't frustrate you later).

> ✔ You can use the mouse and the F8 key to get really fancy. Position the cursor at either end of the block you want to mark and press the F8 key. Then position the mouse cursor at the other end of the block and press the left mouse button. Everything from there to there is marked.

✔ No matter how many times you press F8, be aware that it always drops anchor. If you press it twice or thrice (see the preceding section), F8 marks a chunk of text — but you're still in Extended Selection mode. Do something with the block or press Esc to cancel that mode.

✔ Get used to using the keyboard commands to block your text, and you will be much happier, believe me.

Selecting more than one chunk of text

It's possible, though not really practical, to select more than one bit of text as a block. For example, you can select a group of names from a document as a block, even though the names aren't all in the same place. Figure 6-2 shows this feature in action.

Figure 6-2:
Selecting
multiple
blocks.

```
Tuesday

    Slept in. Damn alarm clock didn't go off. Was late for my 9:30
with Charlie T. Funny, but Fat Tony also showed up. That saved me
from having to make my 11:30, so I phoned Vinny and Tito for lunch
at Rosetti's. Met Don V. at 3:00. Whacked Fat Tony out at the
junkyard. Early dinner with Maria. Then home to Sadie and the kids
for dinner at 7:00.
```

To select multiple chunks of text in a single document, you need two tools: the mouse and the Ctrl key on your keyboard. Follow these steps:

1. **Initially select a block of text.**

   You can use any of the block-marking techniques covered earlier in this chapter.

2. **Press and hold the Ctrl key.**

   You can use either Ctrl key on your keyboard.

3. **Drag the mouse to select an additional block of text.**

   Keep repeating this step to select additional blocks of text.

Note that each block of text is separate. Only the text highlighted on the screen is contained in the block. The text between, which is unselected, is not part of the block. The secret is pressing and holding the Ctrl key while you drag with the mouse.

The text you select this way is still considered by Word as a single block; it's just that the text is culled from several locations in your document. If you cut the text, it all disappears from the various places you've selected. Pasting the text back into the document pastes each separate chunk as a paragraph of text.

Marking the whole dang-doodle document

To mark everything in your document as a block, choose Edit➪Select All. The Windows key equivalent for the Select All command is Ctrl+A.

In Word, you can also use the obscure Ctrl+5 (the 5 on the numeric keypad) key combo or whack the F8 key five times.

Naaaa: Just press Ctrl+A to mark the whole thing.

Deselecting a Block

Now that you have a block marked, uh, what were you going to do with it? And how do you go back to Normal mode, getting rid of the highlighted block so that you can actually type something? Frustrated? Be no more!

Here are some handy ways to deselect that pesky block of highlighted text:

✔ **Press the ← key.** This action unhighlights the block and returns the toothpick cursor to the point where the block started, or to the top of your document if you selected the whole document. This technique works for stuff you've selected with the mouse or with the Shift key.

✔ **Click the mouse.** This method deselects the block and puts the toothpick cursor wherever you click. This method works for selections made with the mouse or with the Shift key.

✔ **Press the Esc key and then the ← key.** This method works when you're using the Extended Selection command (the F8 key or the EXT button on the status bar — remember?).

✔ **Don't forget the Shift+F5 command!** Pressing this key combo not only deselects the block (whether you selected it with the mouse, the Shift key, or the F8 key) but also returns you to the text you were editing before making the selection. Nifty!

Copying a Block

After a block is marked, you can copy it into another part of your document. The original block remains untouched by this operation. Follow these steps to copy a block of text from one place to another:

1. **Mark the block.**

   Detailed instructions about doing this task are offered in the first part of this chapter.

2. Choose Edit⇨Copy.

Word places a copy of the marked block in the Clipboard — a storage area for text or graphics that you cut or copy. To complete the copy operation, all you have to do is paste the block, which is covered in the section "Pasting a Block," later in this chapter.

✔ The shortcut key for copying in Word (and Windows) is Ctrl+C.

✔ You can also click on the Copy tool on the toolbar to copy a selected block of text.

✔ If you accidentally press Ctrl+C twice to copy a block, you display the Clipboard view pane. More information on this topic is in the section "Copying Multiple Blocks (Collect and Paste)," later in this chapter.

✔ Also refer to the section "Copying Multiple Blocks (Collect and Paste)" for more information about the Clipboard.

Moving a Block

To move a block of text, you cut and paste it. This is Microsoft terminology, not mine. Traditionally, word processors move blocks of text. Cutting and pasting is what kids do in school. But I digress.

Moving a block of text works like copying a block except that you use the Ctrl+X (or Edit⇨Cut) command rather than Ctrl+C. The selected block of text disappears. Well, actually, it goes into the Clipboard. But from there, you can paste it anywhere else in your document.

Don't be alarmed when the block disappears. Remember, this is a move operation; the original block will be put somewhere else (as covered in the next section).

✔ You can use the Cut tool on the toolbar to move a block of text.

✔ Additional information about marking a block is in the first two sections of this chapter.

✔ The Ctrl+Z Undo shortcut undoes a block move.

✔ After you cut and move a block, you can paste it into your document a second time. This subject is covered in the next section, "Pasting a Block."

Pasting a Block

After you've copied or cut a block of text, the next step is to paste that chunk of text. It doesn't matter whether the block was copied or cut; pasting works the same for both. Follow these steps:

1. **Move the cursor to the position where you want the block.**

   Don't worry if there isn't any room there! Word inserts the block into your text just as though you had typed it yourself.

2. **Choose Edit⇨Paste.**

   You now have two copies of the block in your document.

When you paste text in Word, the Paste Options icon appears near the end of the pasted text, as shown in the margin. Do not be alarmed. That button allows you to select formatting for the pasted block because occasionally the block may contain formatting that, well, looks very ugly after you paste in the text.

Using the Paste Options icon is utterly optional. In fact, you can continue typing or working in Word and the icon instantly disappears. But if you want to adjust the pasted text's formatting, follow these steps:

1. **Point the mouse at the Paste Options icon.**

   The icon turns into a "button," with a downward-pointing triangle on one end. If you've been using Windows for any length of time, you'll recognize this as a drop-down menu gizmo.

2. **Click the downward-pointing triangle.**

   A menu appears, from which you can select various formatting options (see Figure 6-3).

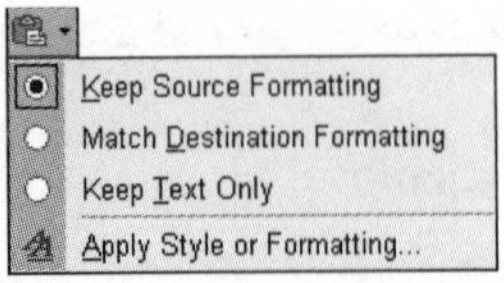

Figure 6-3:
Various
Paste
command
formatting
options.

Keep Source Formatting
Match Destination Formatting
Keep Text Only
Apply Style or Formatting...

More than pasting, it's special pasting!

When Word pastes text into your document, it does so by pasting it in fully formatted and with all the bells and whistles. You can override this setting by choosing one of the options from the Paste Options icon. Or, you can just tell Word *how* to paste your text before you paste it, by using the Edit⇨Paste Special command.

The Paste Special command may not be readily visible on the Edit menu. To see it, click the down arrow at the bottom of the Edit menu. This action displays the full menu, complete with lots of options you'll probably never use. Among them, you'll find Paste Special.

Choosing the Paste Special command displays the Paste Special dialog box, which lists several options for pasting in the text: Document Object, Formatting Text, Unformatting text, Picture, and so on. Each of these items tells Word how to paste in the information. To discover what each option does, select it from the list and read the description in the Result area of the dialog box.

For example, when I want to paste in text from a Web page but don't want all that HTML-blah-blah formatting, I use the Paste Special command and choose the Unformatted Text option. I click OK and the text is pasted into Word as plain text and not as some Web object.

By the way, this dialog box is how Word pastes in links to other Office applications, such as an Excel spreadsheet or information from Access. To link the pasted object, you choose the Object item from the list.

Here's a quick summary of the options available:

Keep Source Formatting	The formatting is fine; don't do a thing.
Match Destination Formatting	Reformat the pasted block so that it looks like the text it's been pasted into.
Keep Text Only	Just paste in the text. No formatting.
Apply Style or Formatting	Display the view pane with various text and styles and other stuff to junk up the screen.

Choose an option to match the formatting you want. I can recommend either the first or second choices. The last one is definitely opening the door to the land of the strange and ugly.

- ✔ You can also use Ctrl+V shortcut key to paste a block of text.

- ✔ Oh, and you can click on the Paste tool to paste a copied or cut block of text. Decisions, decisions. . . .

- ✔ The Paste Options icon generally doesn't go away until you start typing new text or use some other text-editing command.

- ✔ If you tire of the Paste Options button, you can turn off that feature: Choose Tools⇨Options and select the Edit tab. Remove the check mark next to the Show Paste Options buttons item. Click OK.

✔ After you copy a block, you can paste it into your document a second time. That's because whenever a block of text is cut or copied, Word remembers it. You can yank that block into your document again at any time — sort of like pasting text again after it's already been pasted in. You use Ctrl+V, the Paste shortcut. Pasting text again simply pastes down a second copy of the block, spit-spot (as Mary Poppins would say).

✔ You can even paste the block into another document you're working on, or into another application. (This is a Windows trick, which most good books on Windows discuss.)

Copying or Moving a Block with the Mouse

If you have to move a block only a short distance, you can use the mouse to drag-move or drag-copy the block. This feature is handy, but usually works best if you're moving or copying between two locations you can see right on the screen. Otherwise, you're scrolling your document with the mouse, which is like trying to grab an angry snake.

 To move any selected block of text with the mouse, just point and drag the block: Point the mouse cursor anywhere in the blocked text, and then drag the block to its new location. Notice how the mouse pointer changes, as shown in the margin. That means you're dragging and copying text.

Copying a block with the mouse works just like moving the block, though you press the Ctrl key as you drag. When you do that, a plus sign appears in the mouse pointer (see the margin). That's your sign that the block is being copied and not just moved.

✔ The Paste Options icon appears after you've "dropped" the chunk of text. Refer to the preceding section for more information on the Paste Options icon.

✔ When you drag a block of text with the mouse, you're not copying it to the Clipboard. You cannot use the Paste (Ctrl+V) command to paste in the block again.

✔ A *linked copy* is created by dragging a selected block of text with the mouse and holding down *both* the Shift and Ctrl keys. When you release the mouse button, the copied block plops down into your document looking very ugly:

```
{LINK Word.Document.1 "Document2" "OLE_LINK2" \a \r}
```

Gadzooks! This advanced feature of Word (hence that techy guy in the margin) links the copied block to the original so that a change to one affects both. They made it ugly so that, like Medusa, you would avoid it and not want to look at it. Better save this trick for the advanced Word book I haven't written yet.

Copying Multiple Blocks (Collect and Paste)

One of Word's nifty features, one that other Windows programs lack, is the ability to store more than one cut or copied block of text in the Clipboard at a time. So you can cut, cut, cut or copy, copy, copy and then pick and choose which of those blocks you want pasted back into your document. They call it "collect and paste," and I firmly believe that this is a handy and welcome feature — but one that also takes a bit of explaining.

The Clipboard can hold blocks of text large and small. But, normally, the Clipboard holds only one item at a time.

Looking at the Clipboard

You can view items copied or cut by peering into Word's special Clipboard. Here's how:

1. **Summon the task pane.**

   If the task pane isn't already visible (on the right side of the document area, as shown over in Figure 1-3), choose <u>V</u>iew⇨Tas<u>k</u> Pane.

2. **View the Clipboard task pane.**

   Click on the downward-pointing triangle in the task pane. Choose Clipboard from the menu. The Clipboard task pane appears, as shown in Figure 6-4.

The scrolling list contains the last several items you've copied, not only from Word but from other programs as well.

Pasting items from the Clipboard is covered in the next section.

   ✔ The Clipboard can hold only 24 items. If any more than that are copied or cut, the older items in the list are "pushed off" to make room for the new ones. The current number of items is shown at the top of the task pane.

Point the mouse here
to see an item's menu.

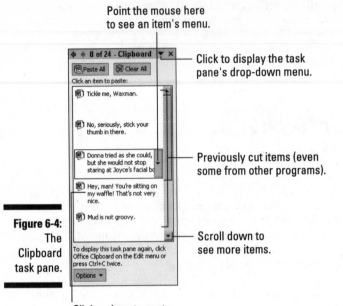

Click to display the task
pane's drop-down menu.

Previously cut items (even
some from other programs).

Scroll down to
see more items.

Figure 6-4:
The
Clipboard
task pane.

Click an item to paste
into your document.

✔ Other programs in Microsoft Office (Excel and PowerPoint, for example), also share this collect-and-paste feature.

✔ You can close the task pane when you're done with collect and paste: Click on the X in the upper-right corner of the task pane window.

Pasting from the Clipboard

To paste any collected text in the Clipboard, click on that chunk of text with the mouse. The text is copied from the Clipboard to the toothpick cursor's location in your document.

To paste in everything in the Clipboard — all that stuff — click the Paste All button. Thwap! Everything is pasted into your document at once.

It's possible to pick and choose what you paste. For example, position the toothpick cursor and choose a specific item to paste. Then move the toothpick cursor and paste in something else. You can paste like this all day as long as the Clipboard task pane is visible.

After pasting, the Paste Options icon appears next to the pasted text. Refer to the section "Pasting a Block," earlier in this chapter, for what do to with that thing.

Cleansing the Clipboard

You're free to clean up Word's Clipboard whenever the Clipboard task pane is visible. To remove a single item, point the mouse at that item and click on the downward-pointing triangle (see Figure 6-4). Choose <u>D</u>elete from the shortcut menu, and that one item is zapped from the Clipboard.

To whack all the items on the Clipboard, click the Clear All button at the top of the Clipboard task pane. I do this if I plan on collecting several items to be pasted at once elsewhere. For example, I click Clear All and then go out and copy, copy, copy. Then I move the toothpick cursor to where I want everything pasted and click the Paste All button, and I'm done.

Note that you cannot undo any clearing or deleting done in the Clipboard task pane. Be careful!

Other Things to Do with Your Blocks

There are hat blocks, engine blocks, building blocks, mental blocks, nerve blocks, down-blocks, and finally blocks of text. I don't know about the other things, but when you have a block of text, you can do any of a number of things to it. The command you use affects only the text within that block.

Aside from using the Copy, Cut, and Paste commands, you can do the following with a block of text in Word:

- ✔ Format the block (see Part II).
- ✔ Use the Replace command to find and replace only in the block of text (refer to Chapter 5).
- ✔ Print the block (see Chapter 9).
- ✔ Delete the block with the Delete or Backspace keys.

Chapter 7

Minding Your Ps and Qs

The ability to spell correctly is a talent, not an acquirement. — Mark Twain

What's wrong with English spelling? Vowels, that's what. Add to that an ugly assortment of rules and exceptions that make no sense to anyone. Putty things over with a little Latin grammar to keep the academics pleased. And, finally, toss in an influx of words from other languages, accepted into the English gene pool with no phonetic modification. There. No wonder spelling and grammar in English are so utterly insane.

Admit it, English teachers of the world: There are no real rules. (Twain called them "arbitrary.") So that leaves you with three choices: 1) Forget it all and re-adopt Latin as the language of the world (*lingua mundum*, which sounds good, but is most likely incorrect) 2) speak English but never write it down or 3) use Word's spelling- and grammar-checking abilities to ensure that your written English is perfect, pluperfect, past perfect, but never imperfect. Or something like that.

Ewe Spell Grate

It's widely known that word processors come with the ability to flag incorrectly spelled or otherwise suspect words. Heck, even your e-mail program does that (and if not, you haven't upgraded to the latest version).

Today's computers are so fast that they can catch a misspelled word or awkward grammar the instant you type it. In some cases, the boo-boo is corrected automatically. Ta-da. In other cases, it's underlined with Word's wiggly pen — red ink for bad spelling or green ink for ugly grammar. Don't let this intrusion of linguistic propriety vex you! Instead, peruse the next few sections to learn the ways of Word's spell checker in depth.

Word's spell checker instantly tells you whether it recognizes a word. It does not, however, tell you whether the word is properly used. Just because a document contains no misspelled words doesn't mean that the document is perfect.

Let's turn this on (or off)

To ensure that Word automatically checks your typing, choose Tools⇨ Options from the menu. Click the Spelling & Grammar tab, which is shown in Figure 7-1.

Look up top for the Check spelling as you type option. A check mark by that option means that Word's automatic spell checking has been activated.

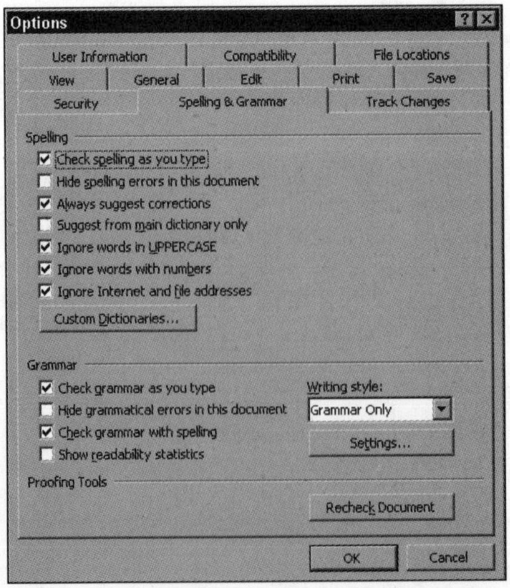

Figure 7-1:
Various
spelling and
grammar
options.

TECHNICAL STUFF

Automatic spell-checking doesn't work!

In a few instances, automatic spell-checking doesn't seem to work. If that happens to you, try these things:

First, check to ensure that on-the-fly spell checking is activated. See the nearby section "Let's turn this on (or off)."

Second, go visit the Options dialog box: Choose Tools⇔Options. Click the Spelling & Grammar tab. If a check mark is by the Hide spelling errors in this document item, click to remove it. Click OK.

Third, your document may be formatted with "no proofing" language. To solve that problem, select your entire document by pressing Ctrl+A. Then choose Tools⇔Language⇔Set Language. (You may have to click the down arrows at the bottom of the Tools menu to see the Language item.) In the Language dialog box, choose English (US) (for the United States), and click OK. This should reactivate the on-the-fly spell-checking.

If you detest automatic spell checking, you can click in the box to remove the check mark. Word no longer annoys you with red wiggly-underline text, though you can still use the Tools⇔Spelling and Grammar command to check your document at any time.

Click OK to dismiss the Options dialog box.

The automatic spelling checker in action

Word automatically checks everything you type as you type it. Make a boo-boo, and Word lets you know. The second you press the Spacebar or type some punctuation character, Word examines what you typed and immediately flags it as wrong, wrong, wrong. It does this by underlining the word using a red zigzag pattern. See Figure 7-2 for a sampling.

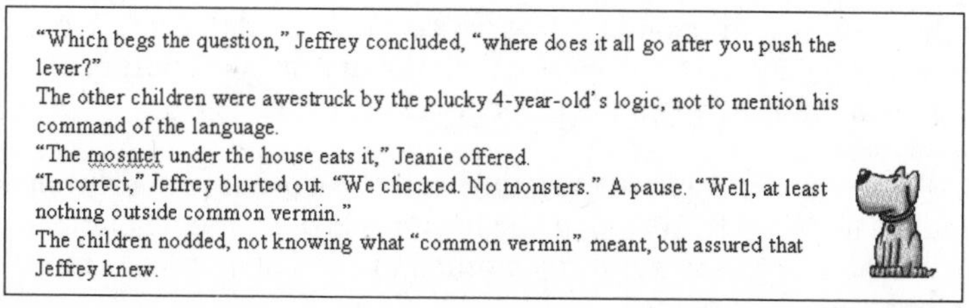

Figure 7-2: The word *mosnter* is flagged as misspelled.

"Which begs the question," Jeffrey concluded, "where does it all go after you push the lever?"

The other children were awestruck by the plucky 4-year-old's logic, not to mention his command of the language.

"The mosnter under the house eats it," Jeanie offered.

"Incorrect," Jeffrey blurted out. "We checked. No monsters." A pause. "Well, at least nothing outside common vermin."

The children nodded, not knowing what "common vermin" meant, but assured that Jeffrey knew.

My advice: Keep typing. Don't let the "red zigzag of a failed elementary education" tweak you. It's more important to get your thoughts up on the screen than to stop and fuss over inevitable typos. (Besides, I show you a trick in the next section to automatically correct your more common mistakes.)

When you're ready, go back and fix your spelling errors. I do this every two or three paragraphs:

1. **Find the misspelled word.**

   Look for the red underline.

2. **Right-click on the misspelled word.**

   This step pops up a shortcut menu, similar to the one shown in Figure 7-3.

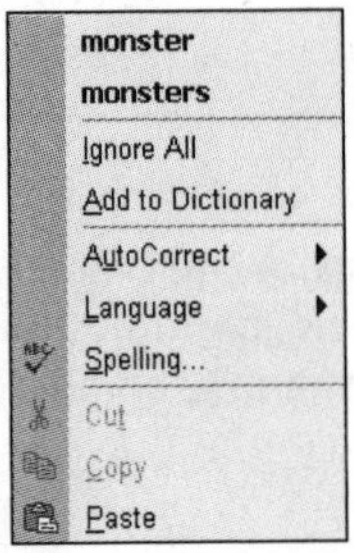

Figure 7-3: Choose the properly spelled word from the list.

```
monster
monsters
Ignore All
Add to Dictionary
AutoCorrect        ▶
Language           ▶
Spelling...
Cut
Copy
Paste
```

3. **Choose from the list the word you intended to type.**

   In Figure 7-3, the word *monster* fits the bill. Click that word, and it's automatically inserted into your document, replacing the bogus word.

4. **Continue with the next misspelled word.**

   You can scan the page for the next word, but it's better to double-click the spelling thing on the status bar (see the margin). Double-clicking that, uh, "book" takes you instantly to the next misspelled word (or grammatical error).

If the word you intended to type isn't on the list, don't fret. Word isn't *that* smart. You may have to use a real dictionary or take another stab at spelling the word phonetically and correct it again.

Select the Ignore All item from the list if the word is properly spelled and you don't want Word to keep flagging it as misspelled. For example, if I really want little Jeanie in the story to say *mosnter* instead of *monster,* I could tell Word to ignore it just this once.

Un-adding words to the dictionary

Over time, you find yourself adding lots of words to the dictionary — words that you know are spelled correctly but that the dictionary doesn't recognize. You know: street names, cities, relatives, alien names, and stuff like that. Word stores those added words in what's called the Custom dictionary.

The Custom dictionary is not something you normally mess with, which is why I'm talking about it here, in a techy sidebar. But I do occasionally get e-mail from readers who desperately need to delete a word they accidentally added to the Custom dictionary. Oops. When that happens, you need to access the Custom dictionary to remove the improperly added word. Here's how:

1. Choose Tools⇨Options from the menu.

2. In the Options dialog box, click the Spelling & Grammar tab.

3. Click the Custom Dictionaries button.

This step displays a list of all custom dictionaries you may have. Most likely, only one is on the list, CUSTOM.DIC.

4. Select the CUSTOM.DIC dictionary file and click the Modify button.

You see a scrolling list of words you've previously added to the Custom dictionary. You can delete any of those words by selecting the word and then clicking the Delete button.

(You can also add words here by typing the word into the Word text box and then clicking the Add button.)

When you're done, keep clicking the various OK buttons until all the dialog boxes have gone away and you're back to using Word.

The Add to Dictionary item is used to add commonly used words to Word's dictionary. For example, my last name is Gookin, which Word thinks is a misspelling of the word *Goofing*. No, no, no. So I click the Add to Dictionary menu item to insert the word *Gookin* into Word's internal dictionary.

✔ The Ignore All command ignores spelling mistakes for a certain word only in the document you're editing. If you want to ignore the word forevermore, choose the Add to Dictionary command to add the word to Word's this-is-spelled-okay list.

✔ If the word looks right but is red-wiggly-underlined anyway, it may be a repeated word. Those are flagged as misspelled by Word, so you can either choose to delete the repeated word or just ignore it.

The Joys of AutoCorrect

The truth is that you cannot misspell the word *mosnter* as *monster* in Word. Try it! Word auto-corrects the misspelling the second you press the Spacebar or type a punctuation symbol. That's because *mosnter* is on Word's internal

AutoCorrect list. Word assumes that whenever you type *mosnter,* you really mean *monster.* Ditto for other common misspellings: *acheive* for *achieve* and *teh* for *the,* for example. That's one of the joys of AutoCorrect: It's hard to misspell commonly misspelled words as you type.

Another joy of AutoCorrect is that you can add your own list of commonly mistyped words to the AutoCorrect repertoire. For example, if you often type *ecxuse* rather than *excuse,* you can tell — nay, *order* — Word to always AutoCorrect it for you. The following sections tell you how.

Using AutoCorrect

There's nothing to using AutoCorrect; it happens automatically. The only trick is how to add your own slate of words to AutoCorrect's list. That's easy.

To throw any misspelled word into the AutoCorrect bin, right-click on the word. Rather than choose the proper spelling from the menu, choose the AutoCorrect item. Up pops a submenu containing various corrections, as shown in Figure 7-4. Choose the properly spelled word from the submenu that appears. That word is then added to AutoCorrect's list and, as a special favor, Word corrects the word in your text as well.

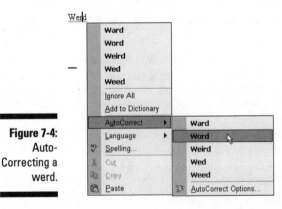

Figure 7-4:
Auto-
Correcting a
werd.

If possible, try to add only lowercase words with AutoCorrect. For example, Figure 7-4 shows the word *Werd* being added; *Werd* will be corrected to *Word.* It would be better, however, to add the word *werd*, with no capital letters. That way, AutoCorrect fixes all variations of *werd,* upper- or lowercase.

Undoing AutoCorrect's correction

If AutoCorrect makes a change you don't like, you can undo it. Usually, pressing the Ctrl+Z shortcut for the Undo command right after you see the automatically corrected text does the trick. Sometimes, pressing the Backspace key also works.

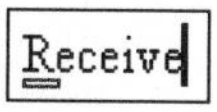

Receive

When you correct an AutoCorrected word, a small, blue rectangle appears under the word. Point the mouse at that rectangle to see the AutoCorrect Options icon. Clicking the downward-pointing arrow on the icon displays some choices (see Figure 7-5) because Word is concerned about why you undid the AutoCorrection.

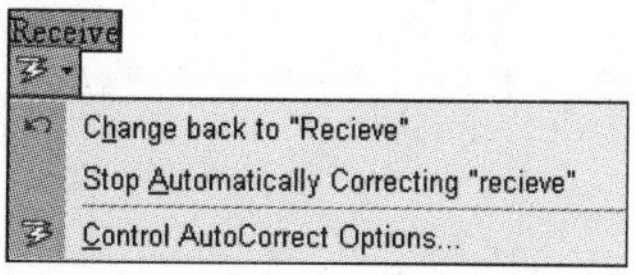

Figure 7-5:
Adjusting an
Auto-
Correction.

You can undo your undo by selecting the first menu item, Change back to [whatever].

Choosing the second item removes the word from AutoCorrect's repertoire.

The final option displays the AutoCorrect dialog box, which is covered later in this chapter.

Click anywhere else in your document or press the Esc key to hide the pop-up AutoCorrect Options menu.

Other AutoCorrect tricks

Try typing the following line in Word:

```
Copyright (C) 2001 Blorfomatic Inc.
```

When you type the (C), Word automatically converts it into the copyright symbol. That's also a function of AutoCorrect in action.

Try this one too:

```
Look at the ugly picture of Doris-->
```

The - -> turns into a right-pointing arrow.

And then there's the ever-popular:

```
I'm sorry about the cat.  :-)
```

See how the :-) turns into a ☺. It really lightens the tone of the message, don't you think?

How about some AutoText tricks?

Another Word trick that works like AutoCorrect is AutoText. Unlike AutoCorrect, which rewrites text you may misspell, AutoText *finishes* writing words you start to spell.

As an example, try to type the following line in Word:

```
Ladies and Gentlemen:
```

When you get to about the *i* in *Ladies,* a box of text appears above the tooth-pick cursor. It says "Ladies and Gentlemen: (Press ENTER to Insert)." That's AutoText in action. Press the Enter key to have Word complete the tidbit of text for you.

Reviewing your AutoCorrect and AutoText settings

You can check out the AutoCorrect and AutoText vocabularies, because either you're curious or you want to remove or add words or phrases. To do this, you must summon the AutoCorrect dialog box.

From the menu, choose Tools⇨AutoCorrect Options. (You may have to click the down arrows on the menu to find the AutoCorrect menu item.) Make sure that the AutoCorrect tab is selected, as shown in Figure 7-6.

You can have AutoCorrect fix several common boo-boos for you by using the options at the top of the dialog box: Two capital letters at the start of a sentence (for you fast typists); the first letter of a sentence; names of days, and a fix for those times when you accidentally have the Caps Lock key on.

The last item is the Replace text as you type check box, which turns on AutoCorrect. Make sure that this box is selected.

The following sections assume that the AutoCorrect dialog box is open and ready for business.

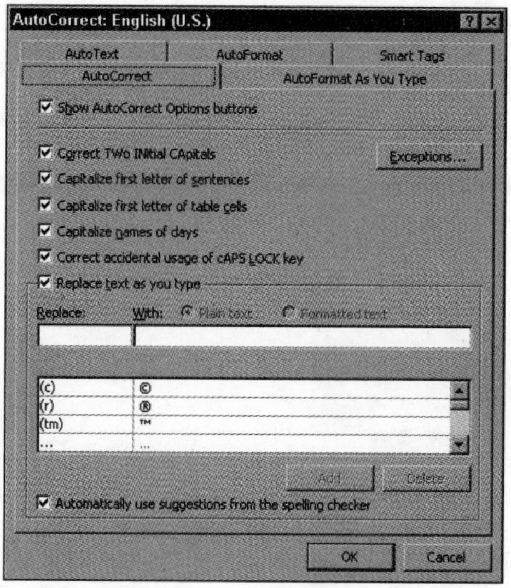

Figure 7-6:
The
AutoCorrect
dialog box.

Manually adding an AutoCorrect entry

On the AutoCorrect tab in the AutoCorrect dialog box, you can manually create your own entries by using the Replace and With boxes:

✔ Typos and misspellings go in the Replace box.

✔ The correct word goes into the With box. (Choose "Plain text" to ensure that your formatting stays okay.)

✔ Click the Add button to add an entry.

✔ Click OK to close the AutoCorrect dialog box when you're done.

Being cruel with AutoCorrect is entirely possible. For example, inserting a meanie like *thier* for *their* would drive some people nuts. Remember, AutoCorrect is subtle. If you type looking at the keyboard rather than the screen, you never know what it's up to.

Removing unwanted AutoCorrect entries

To remove an item from AutoCorrect, locate it on the list. For example, AutoCorrect lists *hda* as a correction for *had*, but you're working on a project named HDA and you don't want it corrected to *had* every time you type it.

When you find the offending spelling on the list, position the mouse pointer over it and click to select it and then click the Delete button. The offender is gone.

Click OK to close the AutoCorrect dialog box when your destructive urges have been quenched.

Adding a new AutoText entry

To add a new AutoText entry (remember, that's where Word finishes the typing for you), click the AutoText tab in the AutoCorrect dialog box. This action displays information about AutoText, as shown in Figure 7-7.

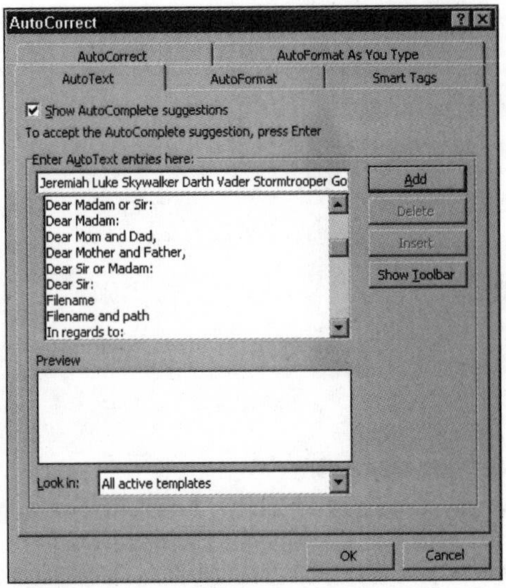

Figure 7-7:
The
AutoText
dialog box.

AutoText has no Replace/With type of setup. Just type the word or phrase you want Word to finish typing for you, such as your address or name, into the Enter AutoText Entries Here box:

```
Sir Jeremiah Robert Eddington III, Esquire, Ret.
```

Clicking the Add button places that item in AutoText's bin. Now, whenever you type **Sir** in a document, AutoText takes over and displays the rest of the name. Press Enter to insert it.

Click the OK button to close the AutoCorrect dialog box.

Any selected text in your document automatically appears in the AutoCorrect/AutoText dialog box. That's a nifty way to put long, detailed information into the dialog box without having to retype it: Just select the text you want to add to AutoText, summon the AutoCorrect or AutoText dialog box, and click Add; the selected text is added.

Removing an AutoText entry

You don't need a midget clairvoyant to rid your AutoText house of unwanted spirits. Instead, just choose the item you don't want, highlighting it on the list, and click the Delete button.

Click OK to close the AutoCorrect dialog box when you're done cleaning house.

Grammar Be Good

If spelling is arbitrary, grammar is a myth. Oh, I could rant on this for hours. Suffice it to say, no matter what the grammarians think, English is not Latin. It can't be. Latin usually has one, very proper way to say something. English has many ways and many words with which to express the same thought. That's why English is so poetic.

Regardless of what I think, Word does come with a grammar checker, and it does, at times, underline suspicious words or phrases in an angry green zigzag. That's your clue that you've somehow offended Word's sense of grammatical justice. Figure 7-8 shows an example. Right-clicking on the green-underlined text displays a pop-up menu, similar to the spell-checker's menu.

Figure 7-8:
An evil preposition lurks at the end of this sentence!

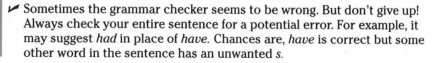

That's the broom I rode to the castle on

| I rode to the castle on that broom |
| Ignore Once |
| Grammar... |
| About This Sentence |
| Cut |
| Copy |
| Paste |

The pop-up menu either lists some alternatives, such as the one offered in Figure 7-8, or simply tells you that the sentence is too long or a fragment and offers no suggestions or poor grades for your efforts. Just choose a correct sentence and Word replaces the foul sentence in your document, or try again until you please the Grammar Gods.

- ✔ If you select About This Sentence from the pop-up menu, the Office Assistant dog explains which part of the English Language Book of Rules you offended. (Well, more or less. Sometimes the dog is way off in his explanation.)

- ✔ Sometimes the grammar checker seems to be wrong. But don't give up! Always check your entire sentence for a potential error. For example, it may suggest *had* in place of *have*. Chances are, *have* is correct but some other word in the sentence has an unwanted *s*.

✔ If you detest on-the-fly grammar checking, you can turn it off. Choose Tools➪Options from the menu. Click the Spelling & Grammar tab. Near the bottom of the dialog box, in the Grammar area is the Check grammar as you type check box. Click in the check box to deselect the option and click OK. Grammar is off.

✔ You can also use the Spelling & Grammar tab in the Options dialog box to customize what types of offending grammar you want Word to flag for you. Click the Settings button and you can pick and choose from various subtle or overtly offensive types of English grammar to have Word sniff for.

Thesaurus, Find Me a Better Word

If you want to add more punch to your prose, consider the thesaurus as your punching bag. Traditionally, a bound thesaurus was second only to the dictionary as the ultimate writer's tool. The thesaurus allowed you to look up a common, dull word, like *big,* and replace it with something that means the same thing but would be a better choice, such as *large* or *immense* or even *humongous.* Well, just like Word's spelling and grammar checking, a thesaurus is available to help you find just the right word.

The quickie thesaurus

A *thesaurus* is a book of synonyms. A *synonym* is one word that carries the same or similar meaning to another, like *giant* and *big* or *wee* and *small.* English is full of these, and so is Word. Synonyms are as close as a right-click of the mouse: To find the synonym of any word, right-click that word in your document. From the pop-up menu, choose the Synonyms submenu to see a list of words with a similar meaning (see Figure 7-9).

The Synonyms submenu displays a list of a dozen or so synonyms for *big,* plus one antonym (a word with the opposite meaning), as shown in Figure 7-9. To replace the word in the document with a synonym, just choose it from the submenu.

Not all words have synonyms. If so, the Synonyms submenu displays (No Suggestions). Oh, well.

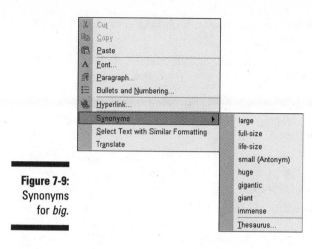

Figure 7-9:
Synonyms
for *big*.

The official thesaurus

A more traditional way to use Word's thesaurus is the Thesaurus dialog box. Unlike the Synonyms submenu (refer to the preceding section), the Thesaurus dialog box is more of a place to explore words than to look up simple synonyms. Here how to get there:

1. **Place the toothpick cursor within a simple word, such as *big*.**

    Adjectives are best for the thesaurus, although the Word Statistical Department tells me that the thesaurus contains more than 120,000 words.

2. **Do the Thesaurus command.**

    Choose <u>T</u>ools⇨<u>L</u>anguage⇨<u>T</u>hesaurus or press the Thesaurus shortcut, Shift+F7. Instantly, the Thesaurus dialog box opens (see Figure 7-10). Word displays several alternatives for the word. They're grouped into categories by meanings on the left and synonyms on the right.

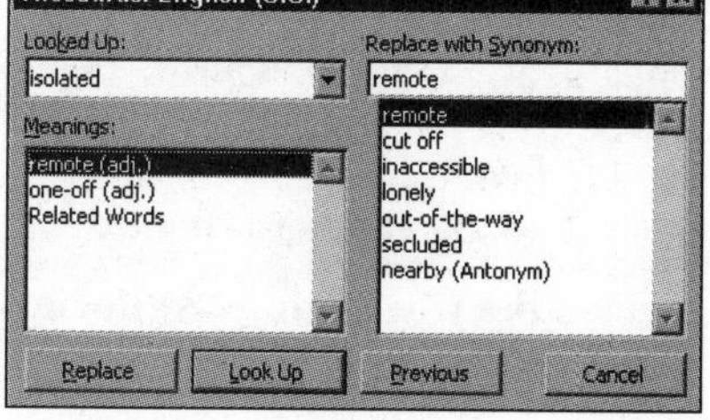

Figure 7-10:
The
Thesaurus
dialog box.

3. **To replace the word in your document, highlight your choice and click the Replace button.**

   After selecting a word, you return to your document. If you don't find a word, click the Cancel button to return to your document.

   ✔ If one of the words in the left column is close but not exactly what you want, select it and click the Look Up button. The new word's synonyms appear in the right column.

   ✔ If the word you select has no synonym, the thesaurus displays an alphabetical list of words. Type a new, similar word or click the Cancel button to get back to your document.

   ✔ After inserting a new word, you may have to do a bit of editing: Add *ed* or *ing* to the word or maybe replace *a* with *an* in front of it. A bit of editing is usually required whenever you replace one word with another.

   ✔ You can also access the Thesaurus dialog box by choosing Synonyms⇨Thesaurus from the pop-up menu you see whenever you right-click a word.

Say that in French

Another Thesaurus-like feature in Word is its ability to translate words into another language. Word does this best one word at a time, which is always good because computers still haven't quite mastered the ability to accurately translate complete sentences. Yet, for adding a wee little — nay, *petit* — French to your document, the Translate command works swell. Or *gonfler*, perhaps.

To translate a word from English into French, follow these steps:

1. **Right-click the word to translate.**

   The word must be spelled correctly and free of grammatical errors. If not, fix the word and try right-clicking again.

2. **Choose Translate from the pop-up menu.**

   The Translate view pane appears, as shown in Figure 7-11. Translations appear in the Results part of the view pane; if not, click the Go button. Note that you may be required to install this feature, which means that you need the original Word or Microsoft Office CD handy.

3. **Click the Replace button to stick the word into your document.**

   Comment facile!

Figure 7-11:
The
Translate
view pane.

- ✔ This feature works best one word at a time. Though it looks like you can select a whole sentence, that's just too much for Word to deal with.

- ✔ My copy of Word came with only French and Spanish translations. Hopefully, more will be available in the future, including the important Latin translator and the often-ridiculed but equally necessary Klingon translator.

- ✔ I would avoid visiting the Internet for a translation, at least not in the way Word attempts to do things.

- ✔ On the other hand, my favorite web page for translating from English or into English is `http://babelfish.altavista.com/`. You can copy and paste text from there into Word, no problem.

Making Every Word Count

Writers get paid by the word. If you're lucky enough to be paid for your writing, you know the "word count" quite well. Magazine editors demand articles based on word length. "I need 350 words on how utterly funny it is to buy a computer for the first time," an editor once told me. And novel writers typically boast of how many words are in their latest effort. "My next book is 350,000 words," they say in a stuffy voice. How do they know how many words there are? Why, they use Word's handy Word Count feature!

To see how many words are in your document, choose Tools⇨Word Count. You see a summary of your document's statistics, as shown in Figure 7-12. Many other things are summarized, too: pages, characters, paragraphs, lines, and other stuff.

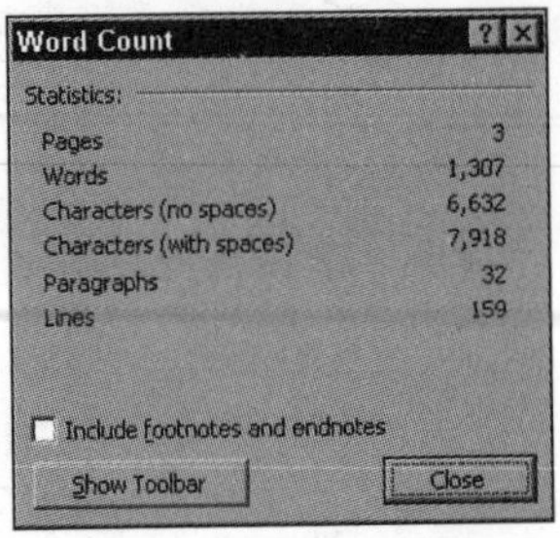

Figure 7-12:
Pulling a
word count.

The Word Count dialog box is okay, but Word has a more interactive way to tell you how many words you have to go — or how many words too many you may have. It's the Word Count toolbar: Click the Show Toolbar button in the Word Count dialog box (see Figure 7-12) or choose View➪Toolbars➪Word Count from the menu. This action displays the Word Count floating palette, as shown in Figure 7-13.

Figure 7-13:
Word
counting
on-the-fly.

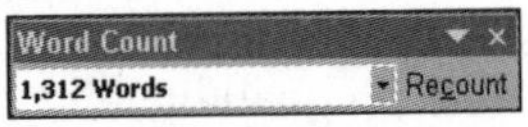

The Word Count floating palette hovers over your document as you type. To see the current word count, click the Recount button. You can also choose some other item to count from the drop-down list, such as paragraphs, characters, pages, and lines.

Click the X button in the Word Count floating palette window to make it disappear.

Chapter 8

Basic Document Tricks

· ·

· ·

*R*ight after you type the smallest modicum of text, you should save your document. There, on the disk, your document becomes a *file,* a permanent record you can open again for editing or printing or review. As long as you save your work to disk — even the most seemingly insignificant stuff — you have it forever. And don't worry about it taking up too much space. Word processing documents are space-savers on disk. Keep the lot of 'em!

This chapter shows you how to save a document to disk and how to open a document you created that's already been saved to disk. And just because it's a sunny day outside, I also tell you how to open one document *inside* another. Yes, the secrets can now be told.

✔ What you save to disk is a *document* — all the text and stuff you've created in Word. Some people refer to a document saved on disk as a *file.* Same thing.

✔ Relatively speaking, a word processing document takes up little space on a hard drive. Each chapter in this book is 5 to 10 pages long, and the document files on disk for each chapter average about 42K in size, compared with 100K or more for a simple picture file.

Saving a Document to Disk (The First Time)

Don't think that you have to wait until you finish a document to save it to disk. In fact, saving should be done almost immediately — as soon as you have a few sentences or paragraphs. Save! Save! Save!

To save a document that hasn't already been saved to disk, follow these steps:

1. Summon the Save command.

Just click the Save button on the toolbar. The Save As dialog box enlightens you with its presence, as shown in Figure 8-1.

Figure 8-1: The Save As dialog box.

If you don't see the Save As dialog box, it means that you already saved your document once. This time, you're merely saving it again. That's fine.

2. Type a name for your document.

Word automatically selects the first line or first several words of your document as a filename and puts it in the Save dialog box. If that's okay, you can move on to Step 3.

If you want to give your document a name other than the one listed in the Save As dialog box, type the new name. You can use letters, numbers, spaces, and a smattering of symbols. Though the filename can be tediously long, my advice is to keep it short, simple, and descriptive (which prevents most lawyers from effectively naming files).

3. Click the Save button.

If everything goes right, your disk drive churns for a few seconds and the file is saved.

Your clue that the file has been successfully saved is that the filename now appears on the document's title bar, near the top of the screen.

If a problem arises, you likely see one of two error messages:

```
The file [whatever] already exists
```

You have three choices. Select the middle one, Save change with a different name. Then type a different name into the Save As dialog box. (If you choose either of the other options, you risk destroying a file on disk in a manner that cannot be undone.)

The second problem message reads something like this:

```
The file name, location, or format '[whatever]' is not valid.
        Type the filename and location in the correct
            format, such as c:\location\filename.
```

Whatever. Basically you used a boo-boo character to name the file. To be safe, stick to letters, numbers, and spaces. Going beyond that means that you may offend Word's sense of what a filename is or isn't. Check the nearby side-bar, "Complicated — but important — information about filenames." Then click OK and try again.

✔ In addition to using the Save button on the toolbar, you can save a file by using the File➪Save menu command, the Ctrl+S keyboard shortcut, or the very bizarre Shift+F12 keyboard shortcut.

✔ Always save your document, even after you've typed only a few lines of text.

✔ You should also organize your files by storing them in their own special folders on your disk.

✔ If you want to save the document as a Web page, choose File➪Save as Web Page from the menu. This is also known as saving in HTML format, which is a common file format for sharing documents and stuff like that.

✔ Although Word can handle large documents (the absolute size is unlimited), smaller documents are easier to deal with in the long run. If you're writing a book or anything with multiple parts, save each part as its own document.

TECHNICAL STUFF

Complicated — but important — information about filenames

You must name your file according to the loving, yet firm, Windows filenaming rules. This task isn't as tough as memorizing stuff for a DMV test, and it's not as horrid as things were in the ancient days of DOS — but it's darn close:

- ✔ A filename can be up to 245 characters long; even so, try to keep your filenames short and descriptive.

- ✔ A filename can include letters, numbers, and spaces and can start with a letter or a number.

- ✔ A filename can contain periods, commas, and hyphens.

- ✔ A filename cannot contain any of these characters: \ / : * ? " < > |

- ✔ Don't bother typing a three-letter extension (.DOC) on the end of any of your Word files. (This is for anyone who used an older version of Word where the .DOC at the end of the name was required. It's not anymore.)

Saving a document (after it's already been saved once)

Just because you save your document to disk once doesn't mean that you're all done. Every so often, you should save your document again. That way, any changes you've made since the last time you saved are remembered. This doesn't mean that you have to be obsessive about saving. For example, I save once every few pages of text I write, or whenever the phone rings or I need to get up and stretch my legs, get coffee, or go potty.

 To save a document after saving it the first time (described in the preceding section), press Ctrl+S or click the Save button on the toolbar. You see the status bar change oh-so-quickly as the document is saved. The Office Assistant may even animate in a manner showing that you've saved your document — a graphical reward for being a good Word citizen.

Saving a document to disk with a new name

With a word processor, there is no such thing as a "draft." You know: rough draft, first draft, third draft, and so on. Well, in a way, whenever you print the document, you're printing a draft. But the draft concept isn't necessary because you just keep saving the same document to disk after you fix it up.

If you do want to save drafts, or you want to save any document to disk with a new name, choose File⇨Save As. This action displays the Save As dialog box (refer to Figure 8-1), in which you can type a new name for the file, such as **Invasion Plans, 2nd Draft**.

You must choose File⇨Save As to save a file under a new name. If you use one of the regular Save commands (File⇨Save, the Save button on the toolbar, or Ctrl+S, for example), you're merely resaving your document to disk, not making a second file.

Automatic recovery (in case you forget to save)

Save your document. Save it often. I use Ctrl+S or click the Save button on the toolbar all the time. The justification here is fear: You're afraid that something nasty will happen to the computer and you'll lose everything you typed. (That's happened to me enough, let me tell you.)

To be even safer, and therefore ensure that you always have a saved copy of your stuff, Word sports an AutoRecover feature.

What AutoRecover does is to secretly save information about your document every few minutes or so. That way, if a power outage or other mishap occurs and you forgot to press Ctrl+S, you can get some of your document back. This is a handy feature everyone should use.

To turn on AutoRecover, follow these steps:

1. **Choose Tools⇨Options.**

   You may have to click the down arrows at the bottom of the menu to find the Options menu item.

2. **Click the Save tab.**

   The Options dialog box has lots of tabs. Locate the Save tab and click it to display information about saving your document.

3. **Ensure that the Save AutoRecover check box is selected.**

   The check box is named Save AutoRecover info every. It's in the middle of the dialog box.

4. **Enter the backup interval in the minutes text box.**

   For example, the number **10** directs Word to back up your documents every ten minutes. If the power is unstable at your home or office, enter **5, 3, 2,** or even **1** minute as the backup interval. (The smaller the interval, the more often Word may interrupt your work to do the backup.)

5. Press Enter to return to your document.

Even though Word has the AutoRecover option, don't get sloppy! It's still best to save with Ctrl+S or the Save button on the toolbar as often as you can.

AutoRecover works all the time without your thinking about it. But suppose something does happen — say, a rabid moose knocks over a telephone pole in your neighborhood. The power goes out, but you didn't have time to save your documents. Uh-oh. Better hope AutoRecover saved most of it for you.

Eventually, they fix things (including the moose) and the power comes back on. When you run Word again, you see the Document Recovery panel, as shown in Figure 8-2. It lists any files that were automatically saved by Word. For example, the Fourmyle [Original] document, shown in Figure 8-2, was saved to disk, but the AutoRecover copy was saved at a later time, making it more up-to-date.

Select the document you want to recover; just click on it on the list. The document is opened and displayed. You should immediately scour it for whatever text may be missing. There's no way to recover that text, but, hopefully, it's fresh enough in your mind that you can sort of reconstruct it.

Click the Close button to dispense with the Document Recovery window.

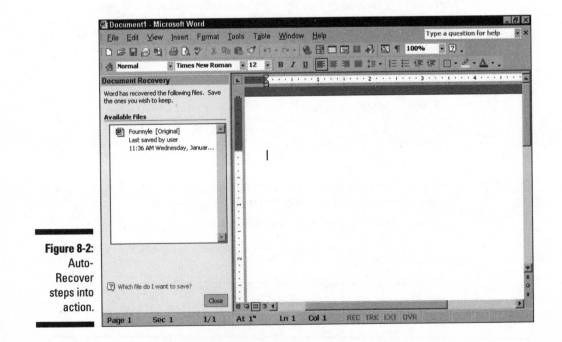

Figure 8-2:
Auto-
Recover
steps into
action.

WARNING!

Other options in the Options/Save dialog box

You may have noticed quite a few interesting settings on the Save panel in the Options dialog box. Avoid temptation here. Ignore such seductive choices as Allow fast saves. That one in particular can cause problems because it saves only a document's changes and not the entire document at once. Sure, it works. But you may have problems down the road, especially if the document grows very big.

The Always create backup copy item is interesting. What it does is to create two copies of the document you're saving: the current copy and a backup of the old copy. That's okay, but

it's really a holdover from older versions of Word that lacked its current, powerful Undo command. Also, all those backups consume disk space.

Other options in the Options/Save dialog box should be set only if you need that feature or are being directed to use the option for some specific purpose. Generally speaking, the options are all okay as Word is installed. The only one you may want to mess with is the time interval for AutoRecover, as covered in the nearby section "Automatic recovery (in case you forget to save)."

Saving when you're done

You're done. Your fingers are sore. Your eyes are crusted over. Images flicker when you close your eyelids. Yup. It's time to call it a Word day. Get up and stretch. But before you move off into the real world, you have two choices:

- **Choose File⇨Close.** This method closes the document you're working on without actually quitting Word. That allows you to stick around, start a new document, open an old document, or just play with the Office Assistant.

- **Choose File⇨Exit.** This method closes Word and lets you return to Windows for fun and folly.

Either way, when you close the document you're working on, Word may ask whether you need to save. Click Yes. The document is saved to disk one final time.

If the document you're working on has yet to be saved, you see the Save As dialog box (refer to Figure 8-1), in which case you need to give the file a name and save it that way.

The point is that Word doesn't let you quit or close any document that isn't saved to disk.

If you choose File⇨Close or File⇨Exit and if Word doesn't ask you to save, the document has already been saved to disk. No need to fret. Everything is okay.

- ✔ The shortcut key for the File⇨Close command is Ctrl+W.

- ✔ The shortcut key to close Word is — are you ready? — Alt+F4.

- ✔ There is no reason to quit Word and start it again to begin working with a blank slate.

- ✔ Always quit Word properly. Never turn off your PC or reset when Word or Windows is still onscreen. Turn off your PC only when Windows tells you that it's safe to do so. If you don't, your computer starts running slower and Windows may crash (more frequently).

Opening a Document on Disk

To fetch a document from disk, you use the Open command. This command retrieves a document you saved to disk, opening it in a window where you can read, edit, print, or do whatever to it all over again.

To grab a file from disk — to open it — follow these steps:

1. **Summon the Open command.**

   Choose File⇨Open to display the Open dialog box, as shown in Figure 8-3.

Open				? X
Look in:	My Documents		← · 🗀 🔍 X 🗁 ⬛ · Tools ·	
	Name ▲	Size	Type	Mo ▲
History	🗀 Audio		File Folder	12/
	🗀 Downloads		File Folder	11/
	🗀 Galleries		File Folder	11/
	🗀 My Music		File Folder	11/
My Documents	🗀 My Pictures		File Folder	11/
	🗀 Original Desktop Items		File Folder	11/
	🗀 random		File Folder	12/
Desktop	🗀 theater		File Folder	11/
	📄 86 the fish	39 KB	Microsoft Word Document	7/1
	📄 Airline food	39 KB	Microsoft Word Document	7/1
	📄 Dawn is ugly	39 KB	Microsoft Word Document	7/1
Favorites	📄 Evil Poetry	39 KB	Microsoft Word Document	7/1
	📄 Letter to the Editor	39 KB	Microsoft Word Document	7/1
	📄 Lies and Omissions	39 KB	Microsoft Word Document	7/1 ▼
My Network Places	File name:			Ope
	Files of type:	All Files		Canc

Figure 8-3: The Open dialog box.

The shortcut key for the Open command is Ctrl+O, and there's also a quick shortcut button on the toolbar, as shown in the margin.

2. **Click the document's name.**

   The Open dialog box — vast and wild as it is — contains a list of documents previously saved to disk, as you can see in Figure 8-3. Your job is to find the one you want to open.

Sometimes, you may have to open a folder icon to locate your document. For example, the theater folder, as shown in Figure 8-3, contains stuff I've written for the stage (my other life).

When you find the file, click once on its name. This highlights the file.

3. Click the Open button.

Word opens the file, carefully lifting it from your disk drive and slapping it down on the screen, where you can edit it, print it, read it, or just look at it in glowing admiration.

✔ Opening a document does not erase it from your disk drive.

✔ Opening a document is one of the first things you can do when you start your Word day.

✔ Word may complain that it can't open a document because a certain conversion feature is unavailable. If so, click Yes to load that feature. (You may need to obtain the Word or Office CD to complete the operation.)

✔ If you can't find your document, see Chapter 28.

A handy way to open a recent file

Word remembers the last several files you've been working on. It keeps them in a list on the File menu. Chances are good that you probably need to open one of them, so choosing one from the File menu is a handy way to open that document quickly.

The number of files Word remembers on the File menu is adjustable. To set the value, choose Tools⇨Options. In the Options dialog box, click on the General tab. Look for the Recently used file list item. Next to it is a spinner gizmo, normally with the number 4 in it. You can adjust that value up or down to have Word remember more or fewer files, which it keeps track of on the File menu. Click OK when you're done modifying this value.

Using the Files of type drop-down list

The Open dialog box displays two things: folders and files. The types of files that appear are set by the Files of type drop-down list. In Figure 8-3, it says All Files, which means that the Open dialog box displays all the files in the My Documents folder.

To see only files of a specific type, choose that file type from the drop-down list. For example, to see only Word documents, choose Word Documents from the list.

If you want to see only WordPerfect documents, choose one of the WordPerfect file types from the drop-down list.

Bottom line: if you don't see the file you know is there, check the Files of type drop-down list to ensure that the Open dialog box is showing you the files you're expecting. (Also refer to Chapter 28 for more information on working with other file types in Word.)

Opening one document inside another

Word places all documents it opens into their own windows. Each window even has a button on the taskbar, so you can click those buttons to switch between the various Word documents you may have open. What isn't so obvious, however, is how Word can open one document inside another.

Suppose that you're editing some general report and you need to combine several smaller documents created by other people into a single, larger document. Or maybe you have a common bit of text you've saved to disk, which needs to be inserted into other documents. You could open those other documents and then copy and paste their contents. But Word has a better way.

To insert the contents of one document into another, follow these steps:

1. **Position the toothpick cursor right where you want to insert the document.**

   This step works just like copying or moving a block; the new text appears right where the toothpick cursor is blinking.

2. **Choose Insert⇨File.**

   If you don't see the File command, click the "show more" arrows at the bottom of the menu.

3. **Use the Insert File dialog box to hunt down your file.**

   The Insert File dialog box works exactly like the Open dialog box.

4. **Click the Insert button to open the document and insert it into your text.**

   And there it is.

Unlike pasting a block, no Paste Options button is available, so you're pretty much stuck with whatever formatting was in the original document. Refer to Part II of this book for information on reformatting the inserted file, if you need to do so.

If you don't like the document you inserted, the Undo command can get rid of it for you; choose Edit⇨Undo or press the handy Ctrl+Z key command.

Chapter 9

Getting It Down on Paper

· ·

In This Chapter

▶ Getting the printer ready to print

▶ Previewing your document before printing

▶ Printing specific parts of a document

▶ Printing several documents

▶ Printing multiple copies of a document

▶ Canceling the Print command

· ·

This chapter is about the final step you take after creating your masterpiece. No, no, no! Forget publishing for now. Sure, you can send off your efforts to That Big Publishing House In New York, sign a massive advance, and sell millions of books. But what are you going to send? Hmmm?

A-ha! It's printing. Getting it down on paper. Printing sounds easy: Coax your document out of the computer and into the printer, where it prints and looks just like you want it to look. Of course, some problems and issues may occur, which this chapter addresses. After all, no single device in your entire computer system deserves a good flogging like the printer.

Preparing the Printer (Do This First!)

Before printing, you must make sure that your printer is ready to print. Check these few items:

1. **Make sure that your printer is plugged in and properly connected to your computer.**

   A cable connects the computer and your printer. The cable should be firmly plugged in at both ends. (This cable needs to be checked only if you're having printer problems.)

Never plug a printer cable into a printer or computer that is on and running. Always turn your printer and computer off whenever you plug anything into them. If you don't, you may damage the internal electronic components.

2. **Make sure that your printer has enough toner and ink or a decent ribbon.**

   Laser printers should have a good toner cartridge installed. If the laser printer's "toner low" indicator is on, replace the toner at once.

   Most ink printers let you know when they're out of ink, or you notice that the image appears streaked or faded or is missing information. Replace the ink cartridge at once.

   Frayed ribbons in older printers produce faint text and are bad for the printing mechanism.

3. **Check the printer for paper.**

   The paper can feed from the back, come from a paper tray, or be manually fed one sheet at a time. However your printer eats paper, make sure that you have it set up properly before you print.

4. **Your printer must be *online* or *selected* before you can print anything.**

   This is weird: Some printers can be on but not ready to print. The power is on, but unless the printer is online or selected, it ignores the computer. To force the printer to listen to the computer, you must press the Online, Select, or similar button.

   - If you're printing to a network printer — and the thought makes me shudder — someone else is in charge of the printer. The network printer should be set up and ready to print. If not, someone to whom you can complain is usually handy.

   - The printer you use affects the way Word displays and prints your document, so before you do lots of formatting, check to be sure that you selected the correct printer.

Preview before You Print

Word shows you exactly what your document looks like, right there on the screen. Especially if you choose Print Layout view (View⇨Print Layout), you see the page just as it prints — headers, footers, graphics, page breaks, and all. Even so, sometimes that's just not good enough. Certain people go ahead and print a sample anyway, just to see whether they like things — totally unaware that what they're doing is needlessly destroying trees and consuming so much paper that all the forests will disappear and Mr. Bunny will have nowhere to live.

Save Mr. Bunny!

 To sneak a preview of how your printed document will look, choose File➪Print Preview or click the handy Print Preview button on the Standard toolbar. Doing so displays your document in a rather standoffish view, as shown in Figure 9-1.

Figure 9-1:
A document
is being
previewed
before
printing,
which saves
a few trees
here and
there.

Take note of how your text looks on the page. Look at the margins. If you're using footnotes, headers, or footers, look at how they lay out. The idea here is to spot something dreadfully wrong *before* you print.

When you're done gawking, click the Close button to return to your document.

Or, if everything looks hunky and dory, click the little Print button and your document prints instantly.

✔ Use the scroll bars to see more of your document.

✔ If you have a wheel mouse, like the Microsoft Intellimouse, you can roll the wheel up or down to scroll one page up or down in your document.

✔ If your mouse is wheel-less, you can use the Page Up and Page Down buttons to peruse various pages of your document.

✔ Click the mouse on your document to zoom in and get a closer look. Click the mouse again to zoom back out. If this doesn't work, click the Magnifier button and try again.

✔ I don't really use Print Preview mode much. However, if I'm really formatting something heavily — with footnotes, strange columns, and stuff like that — Print Preview can be a godsend.

Printing a Whole Document

All ancient cave paintings were rough drafts. You, living in the 21st century, have the luxury of editing, formatting, and rewriting, all on the screen. But when you're ready to write it to the wall (or paper, in this case), follow these steps:

1. **Make sure that the printer is online and ready to print.**

   See the first section in this chapter, "Preparing the Printer (Do This First!)"

2. **Save your document.**

   Ha! Surprised you. Saving before you print is always a good idea. Click the little Save tool for a quickie save, and if you need any extra help, refer to Chapter 8 on saving your stuff to disk.

3. **Print your document.**

   The quickest way to do this is to click the Print tool. Click it and your document starts to print. Quick. Easy. But you can't change any settings; it just prints!

   If you choose File⇨Print or press Ctrl+P rather than use the Print tool on the toolbar, the Print dialog box appears (see Figure 9-2). You need to then click OK or press the Enter key to print your document.

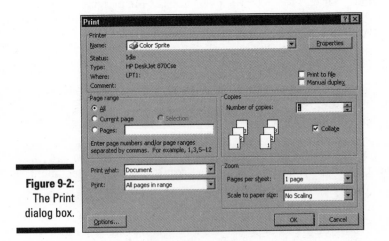

Figure 9-2:
The Print
dialog box.

Printing may take some time — really. A long time. Fortunately, Word lets you continue working while it prints in the *background*. To ensure that Word works this way, refer to the "Printing and getting on with your life," techie sidebar later in this chapter.

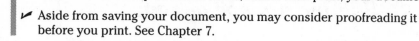

✔ If nothing prints, don't hit the Print command again! There's probably nothing awry; the computer is still thinking or sending (downloading) text to the printer. If you don't get an error message, everything will probably print, eventually.

✔ The computer prints one copy of your document for every Print command you incant. If the printer is just being slow and you impatiently click the Print button ten times, you get ten copies of your document. (See the section "Canceling a Print Job (Omigosh!)," later in this chapter.)

✔ If you have a manual-feed printer, the printer itself begs for paper. Your printer says, "Beep, feed me!" You must stand by, line up paper, and then shove it into the printer's gaping maw until your document is done printing. See Chapter 30 to figure this one out.

✔ If your computer has more than one printer attached, or can access other printers through the network, you can choose which printer to use by selecting it from the Name drop-down list in the Print dialog box. This is also how many fax programs work: You select the Fax modem from the Name drop-down list to fax, rather than print, your document.

✔ Aside from saving your document, you may consider proofreading it before you print. See Chapter 7.

Printing Bits and Pieces

You don't have to print your entire document every time you want some hard copy. No, Word lets you print a single page, a range of pages, or a selected block of text. This is all done in the Page range area of the Print dialog box (in the middle, on the left).

The following sections assume that your printer is on and ready to print.

Printing a specific page

Follow these steps to print only one page of your document:

1. **Move the toothpick cursor so that it's sitting somewhere in the page you want to print.**

   Check the Page counter in the lower-left corner of the screen (on the status bar) to ensure that you're on the right page.

   You can use the Go To command (the F5 key) to go to any specific page in your document. See Chapter 3.

2. **Choose File➪Print or press Ctrl+P.**

3. Select the Current Page option on the Print Range panel.

4. Click OK.

The dialog box closes and that one page prints. (It may take some time to print as Word organizes its thoughts.)

The single page prints with all the formatting you applied even though it's only a single page that prints. For example, if you have a document with headers, footers, and a page number, all that information is included on the one page you print — just as though you had printed the complete document.

Printing a single page in this manner is great for when you (or the printer) goof up one page in a document and you need to reprint only that page. This saves trees over reprinting the whole document just to fix one boo-boo. And it keeps Mr. Bunny happy.

Printing a range of pages

Word enables you to print a single page, a range of pages, or even some hodgepodge combination of random pages from within your document. To print a range or group of pages, follow these steps:

1. Conjure up the File⇨Print command.

2. Click the Pages button in the Page Range area of the Print dialog box.

3. Type the page numbers and range of page numbers.

To print pages 3 through 5, type **3-5**.

To print pages 1 through 7, type **1-7**.

To print pages 2 and 6, type **2,6**.

4. Click OK.

The pages you specify — and only those pages — print.

You can get very specific with the page ranges. For example, to print page 3, pages 5 through 9, pages 15 through 17, and page 19 (boy, that coffee went everywhere, didn't it?), you type **3, 5-9, 15-17, 19**.

TECHNICAL STUFF

Printing and getting on with your life

Word has the capability to print while you do something else. If this background printing capability isn't coddled to life, you may wait a dreadfully long time while your documents print. To ensure that the background printing option is on, click the Options button in the Print dialog box (press Ctrl+P and then Alt+O to get at the Options button). A special dialog box appears.

In the upper part of the dialog box, you find the Printing Options corral. The top item in the right column is the Background Printing check box, which should have a check mark in it. If not, click in the check box or press Alt+B to put one there. Click the OK button to close that dialog box, and then click the Close button to banish the Print dialog box. Now you're all set with background printing.

Printing a block

After you mark a block of text onscreen, you can beg the Print command to print only that block. Here's how:

1. **Mark the block of text you want to print.**

   See Chapter 6 for all the block-marking instructions in the world.

2. **Choose File⇨Print.**

3. **Tickle the button by the word Selection.**

   The Selection item in the Print dialog box is available only when a block is selected. Press the Alt+S key or click the button by the word Selection. (Selection is located in the Page range area of the Print dialog box.) This step tells Word that you want to print only your highlighted block.

4. **Click the OK button.**

   In a few moments, you see the hard copy sputtering out of your printer. The page selection prints in the same position and with the same headers and footers (if any) as it would if you had printed the entire document.

Printing Several Documents

You may think that the best way to print several documents at a time is to open each one and print them one at a time. Oh, but you couldn't be more wrong! A better way exists, and it's hidden in the Open dialog box, the same one you use to open any old document on disk.

To print several files at a time, follow these steps:

1. **Make sure that the printer is on, selected, and rarin' to print.**

2. **Choose File⇨Open.**

   Or, use one of the many other ways to summon the Open dialog box.

3. **Select the documents you want to print.**

   To select a document, Ctrl+click it with the mouse: Press and hold the Ctrl key and click the file. This step highlights that document.

   Keep Ctrl+clicking documents until you highlight all those you want to print.

4. **Click the Tools button at the top of the Open dialog box.**

   A list of commands appears on a pop-up menu (see Figure 9-3). The one you want is the Print command.

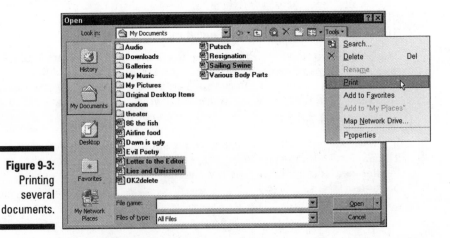

Figure 9-3:
Printing
several
documents.

5. **Choose the Print command.**

   Word happily prints all the documents you selected.

When you print a gang of documents, they just all print. No Print dialog box or no warning asks you whether the printer has enough paper or whether you're really spiritually prepared to print all those documents at once.

Printing More Than One Copy of Something

Every year, I concoct a family Christmas letter and bring joy to the hearts of dozens of friends and relatives by sending them a copy. Rather than drive off to Kinko's and pay the exorbitant fee of six cents per copy, I instead opt to do my own printing and direct Word to have the printer spew out the several dozen copies I need. This approach is easy for anyone to try, as long as you have enough paper and you know which part of the Print dialog box to tweak.

To print several copies of a document, heed these steps:

1. **Prepare everything.**

   Ensure that the document is up to snuff (use Print Preview for that task, as discussed earlier in this chapter) and make sure that the computer is stocked with the proper festive paper.

2. **Choose File⇨Print.**

   Or, press Ctrl+P. As with other printing variations, you cannot use the Print button on the toolbar to print multiple copies (unless you just want to click it twice to get two quick copies.)

3. **Enter the number of copies in the Number of copies box.**

   The Copies area is in the middle on the right side of the Print dialog box (refer to Figure 9-2). In the box, type the number of copies you want Word to spew out. For three copies of a memo, type **3**.

4. **Click OK to print your copies.**

Under normal circumstances, Word prints each copy of the document one after the other. This process is known as *collating*. However, if you're printing seven copies of something and you want Word to print seven page 1s and then seven page 2s (and so on), click in the Collate check box to *remove* the check mark. (Normally, you leave the check mark there.)

Canceling a Print Job (Omigosh!)

Since you probably need to quickly cancel your printing, here goes:

 1. **Double-click the li'l printer dude by the current time on the taskbar.**

   This step opens up your printer's window (see Figure 9-4) and displays a list of documents waiting to be printed.

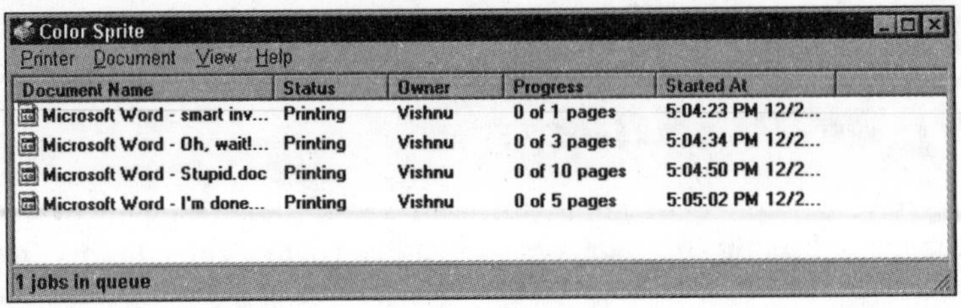

Figure 9-4:
Documents
waiting in
your
printer's
queue.

Color Sprite					
Printer Document View Help					
Document Name	Status	Owner	Progress	Started At	
Microsoft Word - smart inv...	Printing	Vishnu	0 of 1 pages	5:04:23 PM 12/2...	
Microsoft Word - Oh, wait!...	Printing	Vishnu	0 of 3 pages	5:04:34 PM 12/2...	
Microsoft Word - Stupid.doc	Printing	Vishnu	0 of 10 pages	5:04:50 PM 12/2...	
Microsoft Word - I'm done...	Printing	Vishnu	0 of 5 pages	5:05:02 PM 12/2...	
1 jobs in queue					

2. **Click the name of your Word document "job" on the list.**

3. **Choose Document⇨Cancel Printing.**

4. **Click OK to terminate the job.**

   If you're using a network printer, you may not be able to cancel the document. Oh, well.

   Note that it may take a while for the printer to actually stop printing. That's because the printer has its own memory (RAM), and a few pages of the document may be stored there *and* continue to print even after you've told the printer to stop. (Stupid printer, stupid.)

5. **Cancel more print jobs if you're in an especially vicious mood.**

   Repeat Steps 2–4 for each job you want to sack.

6. **Close your printer's window after you're done.**

   Choose Printer⇨Close to make the window run away from the desktop. You're zapped back to Word, ready for more editing action.

Obviously, canceling a print job is the act of a desperate person. In its efforts to make life easy for computer users, Windows tries hard to help us change our minds. Canceling something that's printing may or may not work as planned. My advice is just to be careful with the Print command in the first place.

Chapter 10

Tips from a Word Guru

*F*or the past 10 years or so, I've been using Microsoft Word as my main word processor. That may or may not make me an expert, but at least I'm enough of an experienced user that I have oodles and oodles of tips stored away. Because I'm a nice guy, I want to pass those tips on to you.

In this chapter are suggestions and random thoughts that relate to other topics in this part of the book, but I've put them all here for easy reference. These tips and tricks are ones I wish that *I* had known about when I first started using Word — some of these tips surprise even longtime Word users.

The Office Assistant Has Thought of Something!

Here's one reason to turn the Office Assistant on: The light bulb! After you do certain common tasks in Word, the Office Assistant grows a halo of sorts, shaped like the light bulb pictured in the margin. That means the Office Assistant has a suggestion that may make your task easier.

To see the suggestion, click the light bulb. A cartoon bubble with helpful or insightful information is displayed, as shown in Figure 10-1. Click OK when you're done reading.

Figure 10-1:
The Office
Assistant
says
profound
things.

To see the Office Assistant, choose Help⇨Show the Office Assistant from the menu.

Finding Your Place Quickly

At the start of the day, you open your document and then what? You scroll down, reading and editing until you think that you get to where you were last editing yesterday. Needless to say, this can be a tedious waste of time.

Alas, the Shift+F5 shortcut (Go Back) doesn't remember where you were when you open a document (unless you never quit Word). A trick I use is to insert two ampersands (&&) into the document where I was last editing. For example:

```
Our Beauty Through Power Tools Salon is unique in the
          industry. I mean, let's be honest, creams and gels
          can do only so much. To get to the meat of the
          problem, so to speak, you need a good belt sander,
          jig saw or &&
```

In this example, the two ampersands mark the spot where I was writing last. To find that spot after opening a document, I press Ctrl+F to display the Find and Replace dialog box and then search for &&. I close the Find and Replace dialog box and then get on with my work.

You don't have to use the && symbols (which is Shift+7 twice, if you've been mentally geared by Word to think that way). You can use any symbols to mark your place. Just remember what they are.

Taking Advantage of the Repeat Key

When the Redo command, Ctrl+Y, has nothing left to redo, it can be used as the Repeat command. This command can be a real time-saver. If you press a Word command, cursor key, or character and then press the Repeat key, that command, cursor key, or character is repeated.

For example, type the following lines in Word:

```
Knock, knock.
Who's there?
Knock.
Knock who?
```

Now press Ctrl+Y. Word repeats the last few things you typed. (If you had to press the Backspace key to back up and erase, Ctrl+Y repeats only from that point on.)

You can also use the Edit⇨Repeat command, or, if you can remember it, press the F4 key to do the same thing as pressing Ctrl+Y.

Another handy Repeat deal: Type a bunch of underlines onscreen, like blank lines on a form. Then press Enter. Press Ctrl+Y a few times, and the page is soon filled with blank lines. Hey! Create your own ruled paper!

Previewing Documents Before You Open Them

You can name a file with the most descriptive and useful name you can think of and then ten days later forget what's in it. Or, maybe you're working on a book and need to double-check the real name you gave Chapter 8. Naturally, you say (because you're with-it), "I can just open that document for a sneak peek."

Oh! But there's a better way. You can use the Open dialog box to preview any document *before* you open it, saving valuable time and effort. Here's how:

1. **Choose File⇨Open.**

   Or click the Open button on the toolbar or use Ctrl+O. Whatever. The Open dialog box appears.

2. **Click the down-arrow by the Views button.**

   The Views button is located in the upper-left part of the dialog box. (It's similar to the Views button in Windows 98.) Clicking the down arrow by that button drops down a menu.

3. Choose Preview from the menu.

The look of the Open dialog box changes to reveal Preview mode. Any file you choose on the left side of the Open dialog box is previewed on the right side, as shown in Figure 10-2.

Figure 10-2:
Previewing
a document
before you
open it.

You can scroll the Word document down to read more of it, if you like.

Choose another file to preview by clicking its name.

4. To open the file, just click the Open button. Or, if you're done looking, click Cancel.

The Open dialog box stays in Preview mode until you choose another mode from the Views button drop-down list. (Normally, Word uses Details view.)

  ✔ If you choose All files from the Files of type list, you can use the Open dialog box's preview window to preview other types of files: graphics files, text documents, and even Excel documents.

  ✔ Previewing some types of documents may prompt Word to display a File Conversion dialog box. Click OK if you want to open the file; otherwise — if you're just poking around — click Cancel.

  ✔ If you attempt to preview a Web page document you saved to disk, Windows may attempt to connect to the Internet to update the information on the document. (Just a warning in case something like that tends to bug you.)

  ✔ If the file is of a mysterious type that Word cannot display, you get the message Preview not available. Oh, well.

> ✔ Personally, I prefer List view.
>
> ✔ See Chapter 8 for more general information on opening documents.
>
> ✔ See Chapter 28 for information on other things you can do with files in the Open dialog box.

Counting Individual Words with Find and Replace

A nifty thing about the Replace command is that it tells you, when it's done, how many words it found and replaced. You can take advantage of that in a sneaky way to see how many times you use a certain word in your document.

Suppose that you know that you use the word *actually* way too much. One or two *actually*s are okay, but more than that and you're being obsessive.

To discover how many *actually* words (or any words) are in your document, summon the Find and Replace command (Ctrl+H) and enter the word in *both* the Find what and Replace with boxes. The same word. Two times. Click Replace <u>A</u>ll and Word dutifully counts the instances of that word in your document.

Nothing is replaced with this trick because you're searching for a word and replacing it with the same word. (Believe it or not, this does not confuse the Office Assistant.)

Multiple Document Mania

Word lets you work on up to a zillion documents at once. Well, actually, you can work on several documents at once. Whenever you open a new document or choose <u>F</u>ile➪New to start a new document from scratch, Word opens another document window.

All the document windows appear as buttons on the taskbar. To switch from one document to another, click its button on the taskbar.

> ✔ Yes, in a way, having all those buttons means that you do have more than one copy of the Word program running at a time. There isn't anything wrong with that. In fact, I encourage you to open as many document windows as you need.
>
> ✔ A quick way to switch from one document window to another is to press the Alt+Tab key combination.

✔ Another way to switch documents is to use the Window menu. Alas, the Window menu displays only the first nine documents you have open (which is a bunch). For any more than nine windows, you see a More Windows menu item that displays the entire list of all the documents and windows you're working on in Word.

✔ The goings-on in one document are independent of any other: Printing, spell checking, and formatting affect only the document you can see onscreen.

✔ You can copy a block from one document to the other. Just mark the block in the first document, copy it (press Ctrl+C), open the second document, and paste it in (Ctrl+V). Refer to Chapter 6 for detailed block action.

Closing your documents

When you're working with several open documents or windows at a time, you can close the documents by clicking the X (Close) button in the window's upper-right corner. However, when you get to the last open document, do not click the X button unless you want to quit Word as well as close the document.

Seeing more than one document

You can arrange all your documents onscreen by choosing <u>W</u>indow⇨Arrange All. (You may need to click the "show more" arrows at the bottom of the menu to see this command displayed.) The Arrange All command arranges each document window in a tiled pattern on the screen, allowing you to view more than one document at a time.

Of course, choosing <u>W</u>indow⇨Arrange All works best with two documents. Three or more documents arranged on the screen looks more like modern art than anything designed to help you get work done more efficiently.

✔ Although you can see more than one document at a time, you can *work* on only one at a time. The document with the highlighted title bar is the one "on top."

✔ After the windows are arranged, you can manipulate their size and change their positions with the mouse.

 ✔ Clicking a window's Maximize button restores the document to its normal, full-screen view.

Working on one document in two windows

It's possible in Word to show one document in two windows. You can view two or more different parts of the same document in a large window.

To set up a second window for your document, choose the Window➪New Window command. (You may need to click the "show more" arrows at the bottom of the menu to see the New Window command.) The second window opens, as does a second button for that window on the taskbar.

Even though two windows are open, you're still working on only one document. The changes you make in one of the copies are immediately included in the other. (If you want to make a copy of the document, use Windows to copy the document file.)

When you're done with the second window, click the X button to close it. This action closes the window without closing your document; the first window stays open.

✔ This feature is useful for cutting and pasting text or graphics between sections of the same document, especially when you have a very long document.

✔ The title bar tells you which copy of your document you're looking at by displaying a colon and a number after the filename: for example, `Boring Stuff:1` in one window and `Boring Stuff:2` in the second window.

✔ Another way to view two parts of the same document is by using the old split-screen trick. This feature is discussed . . . why, it's right here.

Using the old split-screen trick

Splitting the screen allows you to view two parts of your document in one window. No need to bother with extra windows here. In fact, I prefer to use Word with as little junk onscreen as possible. When I need to view two parts of the same document, I just split the screen — Moses-like — and then undo the rift when I'm done. You can accomplish the same splitting-screen feat by following these steps:

1. **Place the mouse cursor on the little gray thing located just above the up-arrow button on the vertical scroll bar (on the upper-right side of your document).**

   Oh, brother. Just refer to Figure 10-3 to see what I'm talking about.

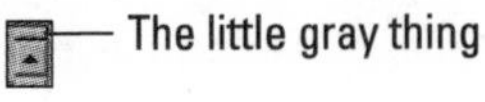

Figure 10-3:
The little
gray thing
you use to
split a
window.

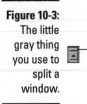 — The little gray thing

When you find the sweet spot, the mouse pointer changes shape and looks like a pair of horizontal lines with arrows pointing down and up.

2. Hold down the left mouse button and drag the pointer down.

As you drag, a line drags with you and slices the document window in half. That marks the spot where the screen splits.

3. Release the mouse button.

Your screen looks something like Figure 10-4.

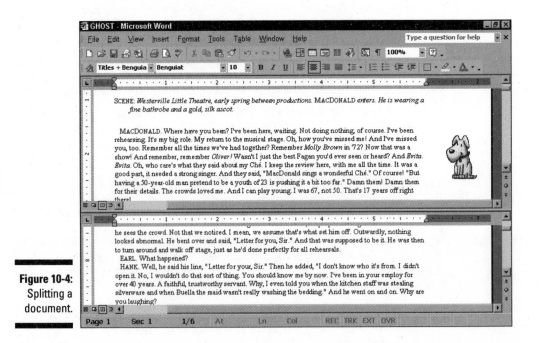

Figure 10-4:
Splitting a
document.

- ✔ Each section of the document can be manipulated separately and scrolled up or down. Even so, you're still viewing only one document; changes you make in one of the copies are immediately included in the others.

- ✔ This feature is useful for cutting and pasting text or graphics between parts of the same document.

- ✔ The fastest way to split a window is to point the mouse at the little gray area and double-click. It's also the fastest way to undo a split screen: Put the mouse pointer on the little gray area and double-click.

- ✔ You can also choose Window⇨Split to split your screen and Window⇨ Remove Split to undo it. (The Remove Split command can be seen if you click the "show more" arrows at the bottom of the Window menu.)

Part II

Letting Word Do the Formatting Work

In this part . . .

Formatting is the art of making your document look less ugly. It's the second part of word processing, coming right after the writing part, yet often consuming far more time. After all, text is text. You have a gift for it or you don't. If you don't, Word is capable of taking plain, boring text and making it look pretty. (It may still read bad, but it *looks* pretty.) Ah, let me tell you, nothing makes you swell with pride like a well-formatted document.

This part of the book tells you how to format your document. You can format text, characters, paragraphs, sentences, and entire documents. I also tell you about styles and templates plus automatic-formatting tips and tricks to sate the desires of documents most demanding.

Chapter 11

Formatting Characters, Fonts, and Text

*T*he most basic thing you can format in a document is a character. Characters include letters, symbols, and Uncle Cedric, who trims his ear hairs by using a lit match.

You can format characters to be bold, underlined, italicized, little, big, in different fonts or colors — or even animated if you're building a Web page. Word gives you a magnificent amount of control over the appearance of your text. This chapter contains all the details.

How to Format Your Text

You can change your text formatting in two ways:

✔ Choose a text formatting command, and then type the text. All the text you type has the format you chose.

✔ Type the text, and then select the text as a block and apply the formatting. This technique works best when you're busy with a thought and need to return and format the text later.

You use both methods as you compose text in your document. Sometimes, it's easier to use a formatting command and type the text in that format. At other times, you review your document and select text to apply formatting to that block. Either way works.

See Chapter 6 for more information on marking blocks of text.

Changing the Font

One of the fun things about Word is its capability to use lots of different fonts. Sure, you can make text bold, italic, underlined, big, little, and on and on, but adjusting the font to match your mood takes expression to an entirely new level.

To switch to a different font, follow these steps:

1. Drop down the Fonts list.

Click the down arrow by the Font dialog box to display a drop-down list of fonts, similar to the one shown in Figure 11-1.

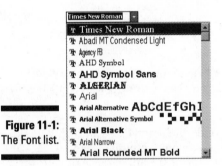

Figure 11-1:
The Font list.

2. Scroll to the font you want.

The fonts are listed by name in alphabetical order, and the font style is displayed on the menu (see Figure 11-1).

3. Click to select a font.

Everything you type after choosing a new font appears onscreen in that font. The text should print and look the same as well. If you select a block of text, all the text in that block switches over to the new font.

Quickly reusing fonts

The Fonts list can get long, as long as the number of fonts you have installed in Windows. Fortunately, Word remembers the last several fonts you've recently chosen from the Fonts list. Those fonts appear at the top of the list, as shown nearby. If you want to reuse any font for a document, just scroll to the top of the list and pluck out the font.

For example, the following image shows the fonts Poor Richard (which I didn't make up), Broadway, Arial, and Times New Roman as being recently selected. Because they now appear at the top of the list, choosing them again is simple.

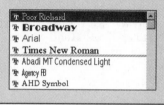

✔ The Fonts text box displays whichever font you're using. Normally, that's the Times New Roman font. When you switch to another font, its name appears in the text box.

✔ If you know the name of the font you want, you can save time by typing it in the box on the toolbar. In some cases, all you need to do is type the first few letters of the font's name and Word automatically completes the rest, such as typing **CO** to select the Courier font.

✔ Oddball shortcut key for this one? Try Ctrl+Shift+F. Then press the ↓ key to scroll through the font list and press Enter to choose your font. (Tiring, isn't it?)

✔ Fonts are the responsibility of Windows, not Word. New fonts are installed in the Control Panel's Fonts folder (the procedure is really no big deal). Thousands of fonts are available for Windows, and they work in all Windows applications.

✔ The Fonts list appears on the Formatting toolbar. To see more about that toolbar, see Chapter 29. (Also look there if you can't find the Fonts list.)

Basic Character Formatting

After you pick out a font, the most basic way to format your text is to make it **bold,** *italic,* or <u>underlined</u>. Easy-to-use keyboard shortcuts and buttons on the formatting toolbar make these the handiest text-formatting tools.

To make text bold, press Ctrl+B or use the Bold button on the toolbar.

Use **bold** to make text stand out on a page — for titles and captions, for example — or to emphasize text that carries a great deal of weight, speaks its mind at public meetings, or wears a cowboy hat; you know the type.

To make text italic, press Ctrl+I or use the Italic tool on the toolbar.

Italics are replacing underlining as the preferred text-emphasis format; it looks so much better than shabby underlined text. Italics are light and wispy, poetic, and free. Underlining is what the Department of Motor Vehicles does when it feels creative.

Underline text by pressing Ctrl+U or use the Underline tool on the toolbar.

Underlined text is really a holdover from the typewriter days. In most cases, where underlined text is required (and who are those people, anyway?), you can get away with italics instead. So, no matter what that stodgy professor may think, *Crime and Punishment* just looks better than boring old <u>Crime and Punishment</u>.

- Basic character formatting affects only selected text or any new text you type.

- To turn off a text attribute, use the command again. For example, press Ctrl+I to type something in *italics*. Then press Ctrl+I again to return to normal text.

- You can mix and match character formats; text can be bold and underlined or bold and italicized. Yes, you may have to type several Word character-formatting commands before typing your text: Ctrl+B, Ctrl+I, and Ctrl+U for bold, italicized, and underlined text all at once, for example. Then you have to type each of those commands again to switch the text back to normal.

- To apply text formatting to a single word, put the toothpick cursor in that word and give the formatting command. For example, putting the toothpick cursor in the word *incredulous* and pressing Ctrl+I (or choosing the Italic button from the toolbar) makes the word italicized.

- The Bold, Italic, and Underline tools on the toolbar can show you which formatting attributes are applied to your text. For example, when the toothpick cursor is in a bold word, the B on the toolbar appears depressed. (Don't try to cheer it up, it's just doing its job.)

An example: Making italic text

To italicize your text, follow these steps:

The boring difference between a bold font and bold text

In Windows, you can have bold fonts and bold text. Weird, huh? For example, there's the regular Arial Rounded MT font, which you can make bold with Ctrl+B, and then there's the Arial Rounded MT Bold font, which sounds like it's already bold. So what's the difference?

The difference between a bold font and the Bold command is that a bold font is designed to be bold. It looks better on the screen and when it's printed. Making text bold with the Bold command merely tells Windows to redraw the current font, making it look fatter. Although this approach works, the Bold command doesn't display or print the font as nicely as a font that's born to be bold.

Obviously, using the Bold command is easier than switching to a bold font in the middle of a paragraph. But if you can, consider using a bold font for long expanses of text, titles, headings, or captions wherever possible. The Bold command is okay for making text bold in the middle of a sentence. But bold fonts always look better.

1. **Press the Ctrl+I key combination.**

   I   Italics mode is on! (You can also click the Italic button.)

2. **Type away to your heart's content!**

   Watch your delightfully right-leaning text march across the screen.

3. **Press Ctrl+I after you're done.**

   Italic formatting is turned off. (Or, you can click the Italic tool again.)

   ✔ You can use any text formatting command (or toolbar button) rather than italics in this step: Ctrl+B for bold or Ctrl+U for underline.

   ✔ If the text you want to italicize is already onscreen, you must mark the text as a block and then change the character format to italics. Mark the text as a block, following the instructions detailed in Chapter 6, and then press the Ctrl+I key combination or use the leaning *I* Italic tool.

Text-attribute effects roundup

Bold, italics, and underlining are the most common ways to dress up a character. Beyond that, Word has a whole bucketful of character attributes you can apply to your text. Table 11-1 shows the lot of them, including the basic bold, italics, and underline commands.

Table 11-1	Text-Format Samples and Commands	
Key Combination	*Toolbar Button*	*Applies This Format*
Ctrl+Shift+A		ALL CAPS
Ctrl+B		**Bold**
Ctrl+Shift+D		Double underline
Ctrl+Shift+H		Hidden text (it doesn't print — shhh!)
Ctrl+I		*Italics*
Ctrl+Shift+K		SMALL CAPS
Ctrl+U		Continuous underline
Ctrl+Shift+W		Word underline
Ctrl+=		subscript
Ctrl+Shift + =		superscript

Applying one of the weird text formats shown in Table 11-1 is cinchy. Just follow the instructions in the preceding section, "An example: Making italic text," and substitute the proper shortcut from Table 11-1.

✔ Some of the toolbar buttons you see listed in Table 11-1 are not on the toolbar. You can add them, if you like (if you plan on using that text attribute quite a bit). *Everything* in Word 2002 is customizable. See Chapter 29 for the details.

✔ Pay special attention to word underline and continuous underline. Some people like one and despise the other. If you prefer to underline only words, remember to use Ctrl+Shift+W and not Ctrl+U.

✔ Hidden text — what good is that? It's good for you, the writer, to put down some thoughts and then hide them when the document prints. Of course, you don't see the text onscreen either. To find hidden text, you must use the Find command (covered in Chapter 5) to locate the special hidden-text attribute. You have to click the Format button, choose Font, and then click the Hidden box. (This information really should have been hidden to begin with.)

Big Text, Little Text: Text Size Effects

Attributes — bold, italics, underline, and so on — are only half the available character formats. The other half deals with the text size. By using these text-formatting commands, you can make your text teensy or humongous.

Before getting into this subject, you must become one with the official type-setting term for text size: It's *point.* That's what Word uses: point rather than text size. It's not point, as in "point your finger" or the "point on top of your head." It's point, which is a measurement of size. One point is equal to ¹⁄₇₂ inch. Typesetters. . . .

- ✔ The bigger the point size, the larger the text.
- ✔ Most text is either 10 or 12 points in size.
- ✔ Headings are typically 14 to 24 points in size.
- ✔ Most fonts can be sized from 1 point to 1,638 points. Point sizes smaller than 6 are generally too small for the average person to read.
- ✔ Seventy-two points is equal to one-inch-high letters.
- ✔ The author is 5,112 points tall.

Setting your text size

Text size is set in the Font Size box on the toolbar (it's just to the right of the Font box). Clicking the down arrow displays a list of font sizes for your text, as shown in Figure 11-2.

Figure 11-2: Choose a font size from this list.

The new text size affects any marked block on the screen. If a block of text isn't marked, any new text you type appears in the new size.

Here are some things to remember about setting the font size:

- ✔ The weirdo keyboard shortcut for getting to the Font size box is Ctrl+Shift+P. (Sounds like a disposable undergarment to me.)
- ✔ You can type a specific text size in the box (though I rarely do).
- ✔ Bigger numbers mean bigger text; smaller numbers mean smaller text.

Making text bigger or smaller

You can use a couple of quickie shortcut keys to instantly shrink or grow text in a marked block. The two most popular ones are

Ctrl+Shift+>	Makes the font larger in the next "look good" size
Ctrl+Shift+<	Makes the font smaller in the next "look good" size

These are easy to remember because > is the greater-than symbol and < is the less-than symbol. Just think, "I'm making my text *greater than* its current size" when you press Ctrl+Shift+> or "I'm making my text *less than* its current size" when you press Ctrl+Shift+<.

If you want to increase or decrease the font size by smaller increments, use the following shortcut keys:

Ctrl+]	Makes text one point size larger
Ctrl+[	Makes text one point size smaller

These commands (all four of them) affect a selected block of text on the screen. Otherwise, the command affects only the word the toothpick cursor is in.

Hey! I did this whole section without a Viagra joke!

Making superscript or subscript text

Superscript text is above the line (for example, the 10 in 2^{10}). *Subscript* text is below the line (for example, the 2 in H_2O). Here are the two shortcut keys you need to use:

Ctrl+Shift+Equal turns on superscripted text.

Ctrl+Equal turns on subscripted text.

"Equal" means the = (equal sign) key on your keyboard. (It looks gross for me to put "Ctrl+Shift+=" here.)

Now you can use these commands as you type to create superscript or sub-script text. However, I recommend that you type your text, go back and select the superscript or subscript text as a block, and *then* use these commands. The reason is that the text you modify tends to be rather teensy and hard to edit. Better to write it first and then format.

Undoing All This Text-Formatting Nonsense

It's quite possible to junk up your text with so many formatting commands that undoing them all would be a frustrating exercise. Rather than delete the text and start over, you can use a simple and universal undo-formatting command — Word's equivalent of a text-formatting eraser. The command is Reset Character, and its shortcut key is Ctrl+Spacebar.

So if you encounter an expanse of ugly and overly formatted text, select it as a block and press Ctrl+Spacebar. This key combination strips the formatting from the text like a powerful and environmentally unsafe industrial-size can of paint remover. Thwoop! It's gone.

✔ Another key combination for Ctrl+Spacebar is Ctrl+Shift+Z. Remember that Ctrl+Z is the Undo command. To undo formatting, all you do is add the Shift key, which may make sense — well, heck, if any of this makes sense.

✔ Technically, the Ctrl+Spacebar command restores characters to the for-matting defined by the style you're using. So, if the Normal style is 12-point Times New Roman, pressing Ctrl+Spacebar restores that font and size. Don't let this information upset or confuse you! Instead, turn to Chapter 16 for more information on Word's styles.

Doing the Font Dialog Box

There is a place in Word where all your Font formatting delights are kept in a neatly organized fashion. It's the Font dialog box, as shown in Figure 11-3.

To summon the Font dialog box, choose Format➪Font from the menu. The handy keyboard shortcut is Ctrl+D.

This dialog box is definitely not for the timid — just like *Fantasy Island*. All sorts of exciting and exotic things happen here, most of which this chapter shows you how to do in other ways. But when you want it all done at once, this is the spot. You can change the font, size, text attributes — everything.

Changing the default font

I hate the word *default,* but the computer industry doesn't listen to me. So I live with it. What *default* means is the option selected for you when you haven't yet selected an option. In the case of Word, default text means the font, size, and settings of the characters that appear whenever you start a new document. Normally, that's 12-point Times New Roman, but you can change that.

Nestled in the lower-left corner of the Font dialog box (refer to Figure 11-3) is the Default button. Don't click it yet! Instead, make choices

in the Font dialog box for the font you want Word to use whenever you start a new document. If you want 14-point Arial, Italic, and Double-underline, select those options. When you have the font just the way you like, click the Default button. You're asked whether you really, really want to change the default font. Click Yes to do so or No to chicken out. Click Cancel when you're done with the Font dialog box.

Your newly chosen default font appears the next time you start a new document in Word.

Ah, please note the lovely Preview window at the bottom of the Font dialog box. This window allows you to preview changes to your text. One of my pastimes is to continuously select fonts in the Font dialog box to see what they look like in the Preview window.

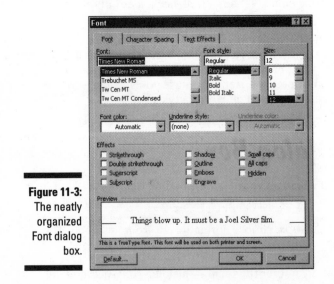

Figure 11-3: The neatly organized Font dialog box.

Changes you make in the Font dialog box affect any marked block on the screen or any new text you type after you click OK.

Click OK when you're done setting the font information. Or, click Cancel if you're just visiting.

- ✔ The best benefit of the Font dialog box is the Preview window at the bottom. That window shows you exactly how your choices affect text in your document.

- ✔ Note that the Underline attribute is selected from the Underline style drop-down list. Word can do several different types of underlining.

- ✔ Check out Emboss and Engrave! But please, on behalf of everyone who plans to read your stuff — don't do a whole document that way. Save the festive fonts for titles and headings.

- ✔ The Character Spacing tab displays advanced options for changing the size and position of text on a line. This tab is okay for messing with special text, such as a title, but don't make it a regular stop.

- ✔ The Text Effects panel is kind of fun to play in, though most of the effects shown there appear only on Web page documents you create (unless you plan on training actual ants to march around on your paper).

Changing the CASE of Your Text

Upper- and lowercase effects aren't considered part of a font, character attribute, or format. But still, the Word geniuses at Microsoft found room in their bustling bag o' tricks for a two-fingered command that lets you mix around the case of your text.

Press Shift+F3 to change the case of your text.

The Shift+F3 command works on a block of selected text or on any single word the toothpick cursor is in (or next to).

Press Shift+F3 once to change a lowercase word to an initial cap (or all words to initial cap). Press the key combination again to change the words to ALL CAPS. Press Shift+F3 again to change the text to lowercase. Press Shift+F3 again to start the process all over again.

Although I prefer using the Shift+F3 command, there is also the Format⇨ Change Case command. That command summons the Change Case dialog box, as shown in Figure 11-4, which lets you choose specific mangulations of upper- and lowercase letters for your text, as shown in the figure.

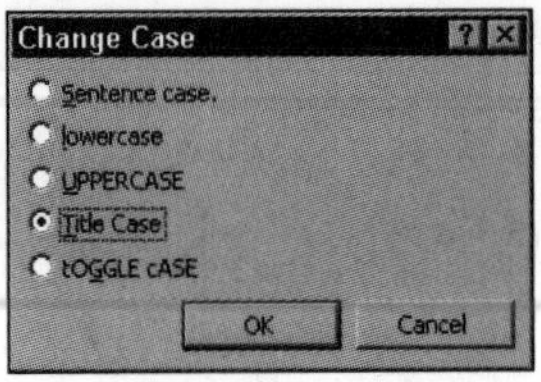

Figure 11-4:
The Change
Case dialog
box.

Text changes in the Change Case dialog box apply to the word the toothpick cursor is blinking in, or to a selected block of text.

Chapter 12

Formatting Paragraphs

· ·

· ·

Want to be really cool? Then call a paragraph a *graph*. That's what all the high-end typesetters call it. Apparently, they're all just too busy to say the "para" part. Think of all the time they save. Must be a few minutes total by the end of the day. Dern efficient, those folks.

Formatting characters is a bit more involved than formatting complete paragraphs — I mean graphs. There's just not that much you can do with a paragraph of text. You can slam it right or left, center it, and then adjust the spacing and indents. That's about it. Word tries its best to help you work with paragraphs in as easy a way as possible. This chapter shows you all the tricks.

Paragraph-Formatting Techniques

There are several ways to format a paragraph in Word:

✔ Use a paragraph formatting command, and then type a new paragraph in that format.

✔ Use the formatting command in a single paragraph to format that paragraph. (Place the toothpick cursor in that paragraph, and then use the formatting command.)

✔ Use the formatting command on a block of selected paragraphs to format them all together.

No matter which method you choose, keep in mind that the paragraph formatting commands work only on paragraphs, not on sentences or words. Of course, if your paragraph is only a single word or sentence, that's okay.

- ✔ Refer to Chapter 6 for specific and entertaining block-marking instructions.

- ✔ To make a single word a paragraph, just type the word followed by a press of the Enter key.

- ✔ Remember, a paragraph is a chunk of text that ends when you press the Enter key.

- ✔ If you want to format individual characters or the text inside a paragraph, refer to Chapter 11.

- ✔ You can format all the paragraphs in a document if you first select the entire document. Use Edit⇨Select All or press the Ctrl+A key combination.

- ✔ If you want to see the Enter key symbol (¶) at the end of each paragraph, choose Tools⇨Options. Click the View panel. In the second area down (Formatting Marks), select the Paragraph marks option. Click OK. Now, every time you press the Enter key, a ¶ symbol marks the end of the paragraph. (Many Word users prefer this mode of operation.)

Aligning Paragraphs

Paragraph alignment has nothing to do with politics. Instead, it refers to how the edges of the paragraph look on a page. There are four options:

Left

Center

Right

Fully Justified

Much to the pleasure of southpaws the world over, left-aligning a paragraph is considered normal. That's the way the old typewriter used to do things: The left side of the paragraph is all even and tidy. The right side is jagged, not lined up.

To left-align a paragraph, press Ctrl+L or choose the Align Left button on the toolbar.

Centered text appears centered on the page.

If you type more than one line in a centered paragraph, each line of the paragraph is centered on the page, one on top the other. I suppose artists and poets may like this. It's also good for headlines and titles. But this type of paragraph formatting isn't very easy to read in a long paragraph.

To center a paragraph, press Ctrl+E or use the Center tool on the toolbar.

A paragraph that is aligned to the right has its right margin nice and even. The left margin, however, is jagged. This style is also known as flush right because the right side is flush with the margin. When do you use this type of formatting? I have no idea, but it sure is funky to type a paragraph that's right aligned.

To flush your text along the right side of the page, press Ctrl+R or click the Align Right tool on the toolbar.

Finally, there's full justification, which is where both the left and right sides of the paragraph are lined up neat and tidy, flush with the margins. This is the style of paragraph formatting often used in newspapers and magazines, which makes the thin columns of text easier to read. Word makes each side of the paragraph line up by inserting extra space between the words in the paragraph.

To give your paragraph full justification, press Ctrl+J or click the Justify button on the toolbar.

- ✔ The left and right text alignments have other names: Left-aligned text is considered to be *left justified*. Right-aligned text is *right justified*. Typographers may refer to left-aligned text as *ragged right* and to right-aligned text as *ragged left*. Rush Limbaugh refers to left-aligned text as *liberal pinko commie text* and right-aligned text as *the light of truth*.

- ✔ There is no option for "no alignment." To unalign a paragraph, you simply choose Left alignment. Remember, left is normal.

- ✔ You can also use the Paragraph dialog box to change the paragraph(s) justification. Choose Format⇨Paragraph from the menu. The Alignment drop-down list in the top area contains Word's four paragraph-alignment options.

- ✔ You can best see the Align Right and Justify buttons if you arrange the Formatting and Standard toolbars on top of one another. Otherwise, you have to click the down arrow at the end of the Formatting toolbar to see those buttons. Refer to Chapter 29 for more information on moving around the toolbars.

- ✔ You can also center or left-justify a single word on a line by itself by using the center tab. This subject is covered in Chapter 13.

- ✔ When you type a new flush-right paragraph, the characters push to the right, always staying flush with the right side of the document. It's like writing in Hebrew!

- ✔ If you do manage to center your soul on the cosmic plane, you'll probably receive lots of respect and fame. If so, remember never to let your acolytes see you eat at Sizzler.

Adding Vertical Air to Your Paragraphs

You can space out your text in an up-and-down fashion in two ways. The first, traditional method is to change the line spacing, and the second is to add space before or after your paragraphs.

Changing the line spacing merely inserts extra space between *all* lines of text in a paragraph (or all paragraphs in a block). I cover this subject in the next section.

Adding space between paragraphs is roughly equivalent to pressing the Enter key twice after a paragraph — but with Word, the computer can do that work for you. See the section "Adding Elbow Room between Paragraphs," a little later in this chapter.

As with all paragraph formatting, changing the line spacing works on the current paragraph (the one the toothpick cursor is blinking in) or on all the paragraphs selected in a block.

Changing line spacing

There are three handy keyboard shortcuts for three common types of line spacing: single-spacing, 1½-line spacing, and double spacing.

> To single-space a paragraph (or all paragraphs in a block), press Ctrl+1.

> To double-space a paragraph (or paragraphs), press Ctrl+2.

> To use 1½-spaced lines, press Ctrl+5.

Line spacing is usually done to accommodate notes or rude comments to be penciled in later. For example, many fussy editors request that drafts be printed out in double — or even triple — spacing. The fussier the editor, the more spacing you should choose.

- ✔ Ctrl+5 means 1½-line spacing, not 5-line spacing.
- ✔ For your Ctrl+5 keypress, don't use the 5 key on the numeric keypad; that's the command to select all the text in your document. Instead, use the 5 key hovering over the R and T keys on your keyboard.

Quickly changing line spacing

A special button on the Formatting toolbar is geared specifically for changing the line spacing. Clicking the Line Spacing button displays a drop-down list of line-spacing options, as shown in Figure 12-1. To set the line spacing, choose a value from the list.

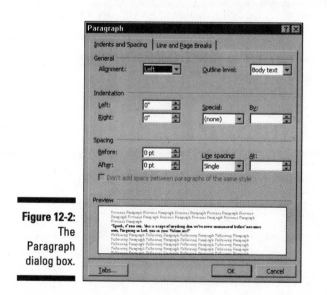

Figure 12-1:
Choose line
spacing
from this
menu.

✓	1.0
	1.5
	2.0
	2.5
	3.0
	More...

Changing line spacing to something specific

Plucky reader Robert J., a printer in Indianapolis, points out that Word is capable of line spacing at intervals other than 1, 1.5, 2, and so on. So, if you want to tighten up text on a page, you can select all the paragraphs and choose .9 for the line spacing. Or, choose 1.2 to get a little more air in there, but not as much as 1.5 spacing gives you. You do this by summoning the Paragraph dialog box:

1. **Choose Format⇨Paragraph from the menu.**

   This step summons the Paragraph dialog box, as shown in Figure 12-2.

2. **Choose Multiple from the Line spacing drop-down list.**

Figure 12-2:
The
Paragraph
dialog box.

3. **Enter the line spacing you want.**

   For example, **2** is double spacing, but **2.5** puts two-and-a-half spaces between a line. You can enter any value from **.1** on up to, well, whatever. Values such as **.9** or **.8** can really help to tighten up a paragraph.

4. **Click OK.**

The new line spacing affects the current paragraph, or all paragraphs in a selected block.

The Paragraph dialog box is a busy place. The next few sections discuss other things you can do there in addition to changing the line spacing.

Adding Elbow Room between Paragraphs

Some people, myself included, are in the double-Enter habit. That is, you press Enter-Enter to end a paragraph, when all Word really needs is a single Enter. It's a similar disorder to pressing Spacebar-Spacebar after a period — an utterly useless affliction in the age of modern word processing, an unnecessary legacy of the typewriter age. In Word, committing such a sin is like writing down your stutter.

If you want your paragraphs to automatically have some padding around them — like the cushions of air in Dr. Scholl's insoles — you need only to tell Word to stick some padding down there. Here's how:

1. **Position the toothpick cursor in the paragraph you want more air around or mark a block of paragraphs to affect them all.**

   The air can be either above or below the paragraph.

2. **Choose Format⇨Paragraph.**

   The Paragraph dialog box appears (refer to Figure 12-2).

   Make sure that the Indents and Spacing panel is forward, as shown in the figure. (Click that panel's tab or press Alt+I, if it isn't forward already.)

   You want to concentrate on the area that says Spacing.

3a. **To add space before a paragraph, enter a value in the Before box.**

3b. To add space after a paragraph, enter a value in the After box.

For example, to add space after every paragraph — just like pressing the Enter key twice — click twice on the up arrow by that box. The value 12 pt means that there will be just about one blank line after the paragraph.

Even though you're adding space *below* a paragraph, you need to click the up arrow to increase the value in the After box. This is weird, and you'll do it wrong occasionally because it's a bad mental model. (I've been reading Norman.)

Generally speaking, "6 pt" (points) is about half a line of text. A value of 12 pts means one extra line. The "pt" thing is an abbreviation for the point measurement, as explained in the nearby sidebar, "What's the pt?"

Use the Preview window at the bottom of the Paragraph dialog box to see how the spacing before or after your paragraph affects things.

4. Click OK.

The paragraph (or paragraphs) now has extra spacing.

✔ So which do you use, Before or After spacing? My advice is always to add the padding at the end of the paragraph, in the After box. I use the Before spacing only if I *really* want to separate something from the preceding paragraph (which is rare).

✔ To make a blank line between your paragraphs, follow these steps and select 12 pt in the After box.

✔ Adding space before or after a paragraph isn't the same as double spacing the text inside the paragraph. In fact, adding space around a paragraph doesn't change the paragraph's line spacing at all.

What's the pt?

The amount of space Word sticks between paragraphs is measured in points — which is a typesetter's measurement. If you've ever messed with the size of a font (see Chapter 11), you've already worked in points, though the Font size menu doesn't use the pt abbreviation.

There are 72 points to an inch. If you use a 12-point font, which is common, a space of 12 points between paragraphs adds an extra line. Six points (6 pt) is half a line of text.

The boxes where you enter point values in the Paragraph dialog box use spinner gizmos. If you click the up or down arrows on the *spinner,* you increase or decrease the spacing between lines in 6-point increments. If you need more specific values, you can type them in directly (though I've used only 6, 12, and maybe 18 in my short life).

Changing a Paragraph's Indentation

Word can indent your paragraphs for you just as easily as a wandering shopping cart can indent your car door.

Right now, I'll bet that you're indenting each of your new paragraphs by pressing the Tab key. Although I won't sneer at that, there is a better way: Let Word do the indenting for you. Automatically!

The following sections discuss several indenting options.

Word has two methods of separating one paragraph from another. The first is to use spacing after the paragraph, as covered in the preceding section. The second method is to add no extra spacing between paragraphs and instead indent each paragraph's first line.

Automatically indenting the first line of a paragraph

There's no need to press Tab at the start of a new paragraph. No, Word can do that for you automatically:

1. **Choose the Format⇨Paragraph command.**

   The Paragraph dialog box appears. Make sure that the Indents and Spacing panel is up front (as shown in Figure 12-2).

2. **Locate the Special drop-down list.**

   You find this list off to the right in the Indentation area of the dialog box.

3. **Select First Line from the list.**

4. **Enter the amount of indenting in the By box.**

   Unless you've messed with things, the box should automatically say 0.5", meaning that Word automatically indents the first line of every paragraph a half-inch. Type another value if you want your indents to be more or less outrageous. (Things are measured here in inches, not points.)

5. **Click OK.**

   The selected block, or the current paragraph (and the remaining paragraphs you type), all automatically have an indented first line.

To remove the first-line indent from a paragraph, repeat the steps and select (none) from the drop-down list in Step 3. Then click the OK button.

Making a hanging indent

A *hanging indent* has committed no felonious crime. Instead, it's a paragraph in which the first line sticks out to the left and the rest of the paragraph is indented — like this:

Electrified toilet seat. Developed in Sweden, where it was originally a useful warming tool. Visitors from the United Kingdom discovered a humorous side effect when the voltage was increased 120 times. Works on a delay timer for the perfect gag. Limit 2 per customer. Cannot be shipped to Mississippi. Item #100.

To create such a beast for whatever fabulous reasons, follow these steps:

1. **Move the toothpick cursor to the paragraph you want to hang and indent.**

   Or, you can position the cursor to where you want to type a new, hanging-indent paragraph. Or, you can select a block — yadda, yadda, you know the drill by now.

2. **Press Ctrl+T, the Hanging Indent shortcut.**

   The Ctrl+T in Word moves the paragraph over to the first tab stop but keeps the first line in place.

You can also accomplish this task in the Paragraph dialog box. Choose `Hanging` from the Special drop-down list and enter the indent (usually half an inch) in the By box. Click OK!

- The hanging indent is really an indent-everything-but-the-first-line-of-the-paragraph type of indent.

- If you want to indent the paragraph even more, press the Ctrl+T key more than once.

- It's stupid that they have a shortcut key for a hanging indent but not for indenting the first line of a paragraph, which I feel more people do more often than this hanging nonsense.

- To undo a hanging indent, press Ctrl+Shift+T. That's the unhang key combination, and your paragraph's neck will be put back in shape.

Indenting the whole paragraph

Indenting a paragraph means that you indent, or *nest*, the entire paragraph by aligning its left edge against a tab stop. Here's how you do it:

1. **Move the toothpick cursor anywhere in the paragraph.**

   The paragraph can be already onscreen, or you can be poised to type a new paragraph. Or, you can try this command on a selected block of text.

2. **Press Ctrl+M, the indent shortcut.**

   Ummm — indent! Ummm — indent! Say it over and over. It kinda works. (You can also click the Increase Indent button on the Formatting toolbar.)

3. **Type your paragraph if you haven't already.**

   If you selected the paragraph as a block, it's indented to the next tab stop.

   ✔ To indent the paragraph to the next tab stop, press Ctrl+M again.

   ✔ To return the original margin, press Ctrl+Shift+M. You can also click the Decrease Indent tool.

   ✔ You can also indent or unindent a paragraph by using the Paragraph dialog box (refer to Figure 12-2). In the Indentation section, the Left item is used to move the left side of a paragraph over by a given amount.

   ✔ See Chapter 29 for information on tweaking the toolbars until you can see the Indent and Unindent buttons.

   ✔ Although the Ctrl+M and Ctrl+Shift+M shortcuts aren't mnemonic, their only difference is a Shift key. So, after you get used to using them (hopefully before the afterlife), they're easy to remember.

Double-indenting a paragraph

Sometimes an indent on the left just isn't enough. There are those days when you need to suck a paragraph in twice: once on the left and once on the right (for example, when you lift a quote from another author but don't want to be accused of plagiarism). I had someone quote an entire book I wrote (twice, actually), simply by double-indenting their paragraphs. No one went to jail, either!

1. **Pick your paragraph.**

   If the paragraph hasn't been written yet, move the cursor to where you want to write the new text. Or, put the toothpick cursor in the paragraph or just select multiple paragraphs as a block.

2. **Choose the Format⇨Paragraph command.**

   The Paragraph dialog box appears (refer to Figure 12-2). Locate the Indentation area.

3. **Enter the amount of <u>L</u>eft indentation.**

   For example, type **.5** to indent half an inch, or you can use the up or down arrows to increase or decrease the left indentation.

4. **Enter the amount of <u>R</u>ight indentation.**

   Type the same value as you did in the <u>L</u>eft box.

   Check the Preview part of the Paragraph dialog box to ensure that your paragraph is indented as you prefer.

5. **Click OK.**

To unindent the paragraph, you need to repeat these steps and enter **0** in both the <u>L</u>eft and <u>R</u>ight boxes.

Watch out when you try to mix left and right indenting with a first line indent or hanging indent. It could drive you insane, and Microsoft lawyers have proven that they cannot be held responsible for your mental health in such instances.

Who Died and Made This Thing Ruler?

Word's main throwback to the typewriter era is the ruler, which is the final strip/bar information on Word's screen (refer to Figure 1-3). The ruler can be used for on-the-fly indention changes in a paragraph as well as for setting tabs. (Tabs are covered in Chapter 13.)

If you don't see the ruler onscreen, choose the <u>V</u>iew⇨Ruler command. (You may have to click the "show more" arrows at the bottom of the View menu to see that command.)

Tab gizmo

First line indent   Right indent

Figure 12-3:
The ruler.

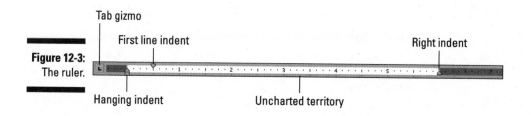

Hanging indent   Uncharted territory

Figure 12-3 shows the typical Word ruler. Note the three parts of the ruler that deal with indenting a paragraph (or a group of selected paragraphs).

The following actions affect the paragraph the toothpick cursor is in or a group of paragraphs selected as a block:

To adjust the indent for the right side of a paragraph, grab the Right Indent guy on the ruler and drag him right or left.

To adjust the indent for the left side of a paragraph, grab the Left Indent box. Note that moving this box moves both the First Line Indent and Hanging Indent triangles.

To adjust the left indent without moving the first line indent, grab the Hanging Indent thing and drag it left or right.

To adjust the first-line indent, grab the First Line Indent doojobbie with the mouse and drag it up or down, er, left or right.

✔ The ruler is a mouse gizmo; you use the mouse to make changes on it. Even so, just about everything you can do to a paragraph with the ruler can also be done in the Format Paragraph dialog box.

✔ You can select different types of tabs with the Tab gizmo. See Chapter 13.

✔ The ruler is fine for visually setting indents, but if you need to be precise, you must use the Paragraph dialog box. Only there can you enter exact amounts for indents. Refer to the previous several sections in this chapter for detailed information on setting various paragraph indents.

✔ Setting the indents for a paragraph is not the same thing as setting margins. Margins are set at the page-formatting level. See Chapter 14 for more information on setting margins.

Paragraph-formatting survival guide

This table contains all the paragraph-formatting commands you can summon by holding down the Ctrl key and pressing a letter or number. By no means should you memorize this list.

Key Combo	Does This	Key Combo	Does This
Ctrl+E	Centers paragraphs	Ctrl+T	Makes a hanging indent
Ctrl+J	Fully justifies paragraphs	Ctrl+Shift+T	Unhangs the indent
Ctrl+L	Left aligns (flush left)	Ctrl+1	Single-spaces lines
Ctrl+R	Right aligns (flush right)	Ctrl+2	Double-spaces lines
Ctrl+M	Indents text	Ctrl+5	Makes 1½-space lines
Ctrl+Shift+M	Unindents text		

Chapter 13

Formatting Tabs

• •

In This Chapter

▶ Finding tabs on the ruler

▶ Setting tab stops

▶ Using right, center, and decimal tabs

▶ Using the Tabs dialog box

▶ Removing tab stops

▶ Setting a leader tab

• •

Word's tabs are strange. Not *Twilight Zone* strange: The tab stops harbor no third eye or hideous intelligence, nor are they out to eat the human race. No, it's more of a new-food strangeness. You know, like sushi looks like raw fish until you taste it and discover that it's rather yummy. Then it's not so strange to *you* any more, but if you tell someone that you're craving monkfish liver pâté, well, then, *that's* strange.

Tabs in Word are confusing because the tab stops you set are more than just tab stops. They can be used to line up or arrange text in useful ways. In fact, knowing the proper tab to set can save you oodles of time. The problem is that tabs in Word are just not logical. That's why I wrote this chapter.

The Story of Tab

Once upon a time, a giant cola company searched for a diet beverage.

Whoops! Wrong Tab story.

A tab is like a big space. When you press the Tab key, Word zooms the toothpick cursor over to the next *tab stop*. You can use tabs to line up columns of information or to indent paragraphs or lines of text. They're handy. This you should know. This chapter tries dutifully to explain the rest of the tab mystery.

✔ Pressing the Tab key inserts a tab "character" in your document. That character moves the toothpick cursor, and any text you type, over to the next tab stop.

✔ Pressing the Tab key does not insert spaces. When you use Backspace or Delete to remove a tab, you delete one character — the tab character.

✔ Word can display the tab character for you if you like. It looks like a tiny arrow pointing to the right. To display this character, choose Tools⇨Options. Click the View tab. Choose Tab characters from the Formatting marks area. Click OK.

✔ Tab stops are set at ½-inch intervals on each line of text — unless you specify otherwise.

✔ It helps if you have the ruler visible when you work with tabs. Choose View⇨Ruler from the menu if the ruler isn't visible. You may have to click the down arrows on the menu to see the Ruler command. (Refer to Figure 1-3 for the location of the ruler on Word's screen.)

✔ Tab is short for *tab*ulator. It comes from the Latin root for *table,* which is handy because that's what tabs help you do: line things up into tables. Even so, Word does have a Table command. See Chapter 20.

The Tab Stops Here

Just to confuse you, there are two places in Word where you can set tab stops. The first is the ruler, as shown in Figure 13-1. The second is in the Tabs dialog box. Most folks use the ruler, but for some Tab options you must go to the Tabs dialog box.

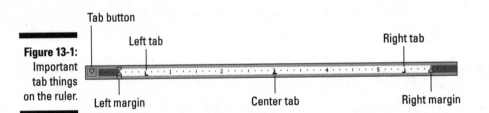

Figure 13-1:
Important
tab things
on the ruler.

Tab button

Left tab

Right tab

Left margin

Center tab

Right margin

The ruler is the first choice for setting tabs because of the Tab button on the left side (refer to Figure 13-1). The Tab button sports one of Word's five different types of tab stops. Here's the brief rundown (which you don't have to memorize):

The most common tab is the left tab, the plump L. This tab works like the Tab key on a typewriter: Press the Tab key, and the new text appears at the next tab stop. No mental hang-ups here.

The center tab stop centers text on the tab stop. This is strange, which is why it's covered later in this chapter in glorious detail. See the later section "The center of Tab."

The right tab causes text to line up right justified at that tab stop. This tab gives you leeway to do some fancy paragraph justification on a single line, some of which is demonstrated in the section "Right on, Tab," later in this chapter.

The decimal tab aligns numbers by their decimals. This proves to be a great boon to anyone printing a list of prices. See the section "The amazing decimal tab," later in this chapter.

The ugly stepsister of the Tab family is the bar tab. I'm sure that there were a few hoots in the Word programming lab the day they named this one. See the section "Paying the bar tab," somewhere a few pages to the right of here.

Clicking the Tab button displays one of the tab stops I just mentioned. Click the button a few times to watch it change from one type of tab stop to the other.

Also included on the Tab button, though they're not really tab stops, are the Left Indent and Hanging Indent items. Why they put them there, I'll never know. Chapter 12 shows you better ways to indent a paragraph, anyway.

The following sections describe the various tab stops and how they can be used in your documents.

Setting a Tab Stop

To set a tab stop, you generally follow these steps:

1. **Click the Tab button until you find the type of tab you want.**

   For example, click the Tab button until the standard left tab — looks like a Big L — appears (see the margin).

2. **Click on the ruler were you want the tab stop placed.**

   This is the tricky part. You must click right on the middle of the ruler. For example, to put a tab stop at 1⅛ inches, you position the mouse pointer as shown in Figure 13-2.

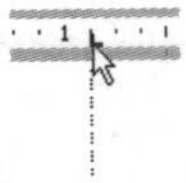

Figure 13-2:
Setting a
left tab.

You can drag the tab stop left or right. As you drag, notice a line that extends down into your document's text (refer to Figure 13-2). That line tells you *exactly* where text lines up for that tab stop.

Release the mouse button to set the tab.

3. To set another tab stop, repeat Step 2.

You set a new tab stop every time you click on the ruler. The type of tab displayed on the Tab button determines which kind of tab you set.

4. When you're done, just click in your document to set the toothpick cursor and type away.

Pressing the Tab key zooms the toothpick cursor over to the tab stop — at 1.125 inches, as shown in Figure 13-2. (That's 1⅛ inches, for those of you who don't follow the stock market.)

- ✔ The best thing about setting tabs and using the Tab key is that they line up text *exactly* with the tab stop. Pressing the Spacebar a zillion times just doesn't do that.

- ✔ Setting the tab affects only the paragraph the toothpick cursor is in. If you want to set the tabs for multiple paragraphs or an entire document, you must select a block and then set the tabs.

- ✔ Removing a tab stop is as easy as dragging the tab (the Fat L or other tab character) from the ruler. That's right, you can drag a tab stop down from the ruler into your text to remove it.

- ✔ The phantom tab stop you may see when you select a block appears when a tab is set in one of the paragraphs but not in all of them. You can remove the phantom tab stop by dragging it off the ruler, or click the tab stop with the mouse to set it for all the selected paragraphs.

Setting your standard left tabs

Left tabs are the standard, typical, boring types of tabs most everyone uses. But why are they left? Left over? Left out? Leftist?

Left tabs are called such because text typed after you press the tab aligns its left side to the tab stop. Figure 13-3 illustrates this concept. See how each bit of text lines up its left edge with the tab stop in the figure? Pressing the Spacebar doesn't do this. You must use a tab stop!

Figure 13-3:
Lining up
text on a tab
stop.

Name:	Olopee	Dandruh	Dirk Bunster
Position:	King of Mars	Asteroid Princess	Teenage Geek
Favorite food:	Naugahyde	Ice mints	Pizza
Favorite weapon:	Tweezers	Her bod	Leatherman

To make a new left tab stop for your current paragraph, follow these steps:

1. **Type the paragraph you want to stick the tabs in.**

   I'm a fan of typing the text *first*. That's because one tab stop does the trick. Just type your text, pressing the Tab key once — no matter how far you eventually want the text to go over. Too many people press the Tab key three or four times. That's okay, but it's inefficient. Word is smarter than that. Use the Tab key only once, and then use the ruler to set the tab stop. Trust me — this is the best way to work things.

2. **Make sure that the toothpick cursor is in the paragraph you want to change.**

3. **Choose the left tab stop from the Tab button.**

   Keep clicking the Tab button until the Left tab appears, as shown in the margin.

4. **Click the mouse in the ruler where you want a new tab stop.**

   For example, in Figure 13-3, the first tab stop is set at 1.25 inches, the second at 2.5 inches, and the third at 4 inches.

The center of Tab

The center tab is a unique character. It's normally used with only a single word or just a few words. What it does is allow you to center that word (or those words) on a line of text without centering the entire paragraph. Here's a demo:

1. **Start a new paragraph, one containing text you want to center.**

   You probably won't type a whole paragraph for a center tab. In fact, that would be very unusual. Instead, the best example for this situation is typing a header or footer — a single line of text. (See Chapter 15 for more information on headers and footers.)

2. **Press the Tab key.**

   Believe it or not, you need only one tab.

3. **Type the text to center.**

   A chapter title, your name, or whatever text you type is centered on that line when you set a center tab stop.

4. **Press Enter.**

   This step ends the line. Now you're ready to set the center tab.

5. **Click the mouse to put the toothpick cursor on the line you just typed.**

6. **Click the Tab button until the center tab appears.**

   The center tab is shown in the margin. It looks like an upside-down T.

7. **Click the mouse on the middle of the ruler to set the center tab.**

   Your text should line up as shown in Figure 13-4. See how the text "Plans for Invading Earth" appears centered on the center tab? The paragraph is still aligned to the left, but that tiny bit of text is centered.

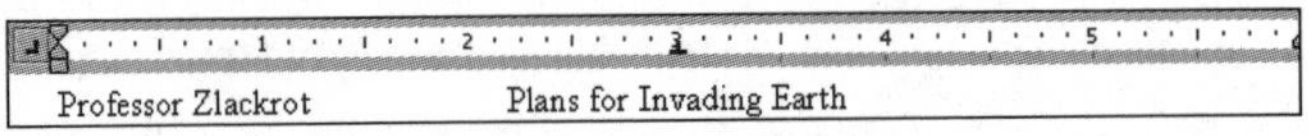

Figure 13-4:
A bit of text
is centered
with the
center tab.

Professor Zlackrot   Plans for Invading Earth

✔ Center tabs are best used on a single line of text, usually by themselves. There's no restriction on this; you can use as many center tabs on a line as you like. I just haven't seen it done that way.

✔ Most often, you use center tabs in headers and footers. See Chapter 15.

✔ Obviously, centering a paragraph beats the pants off using a center tab stop in most cases. In fact, the only time I use center tab stops is when I create headers or footers.

Right on, Tab

The right tab is a creature that aligns text to the right of the tab stop, not to the left. Figure 13-5 shows how a right tab stop lines up text using an example from the preceding section.

Figure 13-5:
A right tab
stop.

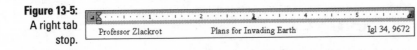

Professor Zlackrot   Plans for Invading Earth   Igl 34, 9672

- ✔ To set a right tab stop, choose the right tab from the Tab button on the ruler. Then click on the ruler where you want the right tab to be set.

- ✔ Figure 13-5 shows the right tab on the right side of a heading. After setting the right tab, I pressed the Tab key and then typed the date.

- ✔ Typing text at a right tab stop pushes the text to the left (the opposite of normal), which keeps the text aligned with the right stop.

- ✔ As with a center tab stop, the right tab stop is best used on a line by itself, usually in a header, footer, or some type of document title, as shown in Figure 13-5.

The amazing decimal tab

I love decimal tabs. Without them, columns of numbers would never match up. This feature is a serious boon to anyone who writes a financial summary report, as shown in Figure 13-6.

Figure 13-6:
Lining up
numbers
with the
decimal tab.

Present	From whom	Estimated cost
Tie	Aunt Debra	$15.00
Sweater	Mom	$30.00
Socks	Jonah	$6.50
Chain Saw	Virgil	$230.00
Massage	Renee	Priceless

You work with a decimal tab just like any other tab. The difference is that the text to the left of the decimal comes before the tab stop and text after the decimal goes to the right (as shown in Figure 13-6).

For example, in Figure 13-6, on the third line I typed *Sweater,* pressed Tab, *Mom,* Tab, and then *$30.00.* Pressing the first tab, a left tab, lined up *Mom* on the left with other text in the column. Pressing Tab again moved the text over to the decimal tab stop at 3" (see the ruler). I typed *$30* and it moved to the left. But when I typed the decimal, that determined the tab "stop," and the rest of the number moved to the right. (You really have to try this yourself to see how it works.)

If you need to rearrange things (perhaps the columns are too close together), select all the lines with numbers as a block. Use your mouse to slide the decimal tab left or right on the ruler. You can then realign the numbers in the selected block all at once.

By the way, the "Priceless" item in the figure doesn't line up because it lacks a decimal. A good way to fix it would be to replace the decimal tab with a regular right tab for that line — more work for later!

Paying the bar tab

Enough with the puns! Setting a bar tab puts a vertical line in your document wherever the bar tab is set, as shown in Figure 13-7.

Figure 13-7:
The mystery
of the
bar tab.

The bar tab doesn't actually set a tab stop. This is important to remember. A bar tab is basically a text decoration, like a vertical line, but one you can position like a tab stop. And as you can see in Figure 13-7, you can type text right through the bar tabs, which makes me wonder what their true purpose in life really is. Whatever.

Using the Tabs Dialog Box

Setting tabs in the ruler is fine for most folks. I like it because you can actu-ally see the effect the tab has on your text and can drag the tab stop to make adjustments. For purists, however, there is the Tabs dialog box.

Call forth the Tabs dialog box by choosing Format⇨Tabs from the menu. The Tabs dialog box appears in all its glory, as shown in Figure 13-8.

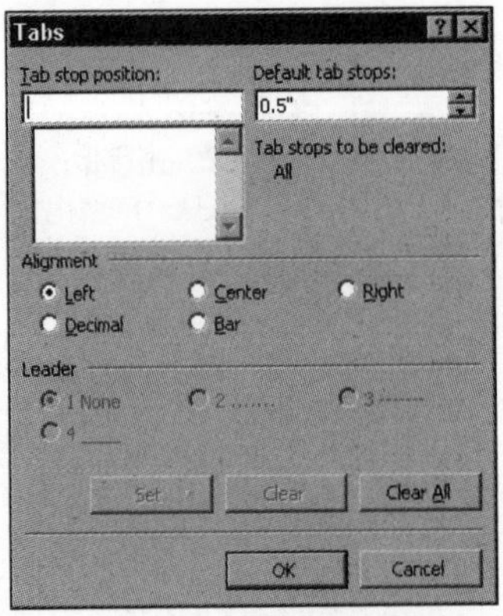

Figure 13-8:
The Tabs
dialog box.

Working with this dialog box is an awkward thing, most likely because the ruler just makes so much more sense for setting tabs. But suppose that you have some really uptight editor who wants you to set your tab stops at 1.1875 and 3.49 inches. If so, the Tabs dialog box is the only place to do it.

Setting a tab in the Tabs dialog box

To set a tab in the Tabs dialog box, follow these steps:

1. **Summon the Tabs dialog box.**

   Choose Format⇨Tabs from the menu.

2. **Enter the exact tab stop position in the Tab stop position box.**

   For example, type **1.1875** to set a tab at exactly that spot.

3. **Choose the type of tab stop from the Alignment area.**

   The standard tab stop is Left. Other tab stops are covered elsewhere in this chapter.

4. **Click the Set button.**

   The Set button — not the OK button — is what creates the tab stop. After clicking Set, your tab stop is placed on the list below the Tab stop position dialog box. (You may notice that numbers are rounded to the nearest tenth; Word interprets 1.1875 as 1.9.)

5. **Continue setting tabs.**

   Repeat Steps 1–4 for as many tabs as you need to set.

6. **Click OK.**

   You're returned to your document with the new tab stops visible on the ruler.

  ✔ If you need to set a row of tabs, with each one three-quarters of an inch apart, for example, type **0.75"** in the Default tab stops box and then click the OK button. Word automatically figures the tab stops and sets them for you. You can see these default tab stops, which appear as dark brown ticks on the gray line below the ruler (they're very hard to see).

  ✔ For setting precise tab stops, type in the Tab stop position box some measurements for each tab stop. For example, type **1** and click the Set button; type **1.67** and click Set; type **2.25** and click Set, and so on. Each tab stop is added to the list of tab stops in the Tabs dialog box. Click OK to set the tab stops for your paragraph.

  ✔ You must click the Set button to set a tab. I don't know how many times I click OK, thinking that the tab stop is set, and it's not.

Killing off a tab stop in the Tabs dialog box

To remove a tab stop using the Tabs dialog box, click the tab on the list below the Tab stop position box. This action selects that tab. Click the Clear button. It's gone!

Clicking the Clear All button in the Tabs dialog box removes all tabs from the ruler.

Setting Fearless Leader Tabs

One thing you can do in the Tabs dialog box that you cannot do with the ruler is set a leader tab.

A *leader tab* produces a row of dots when you press Tab. You see these tabs sometimes in indexes and all the time in tables of contents. Word gives you the choice of three different leaders:

Fearless dot leader tabs 147

Zipper line leader tabs- 147

U-boat underline leader tabs _____147

To set up a fearless leader tab, follow these steps:

1. **Position the toothpick cursor on the line where you want your leader tabs.**

   Suppose that you're asked by your city's government to index the phone book. You're starting the index in a new document in Word.

2. **Set a left tab stop on the ruler.**

   Choose the left tab stop from the Tab button, and then click the mouse on the number 3 on the ruler. This technique sets a tab stop 3 inches in from the page's left margin. A plump L appears on the ruler.

3. **Choose the Format⇨Tabs command.**

   The Tabs dialog box appears, as shown in Figure 13-8.

4. **Select from the Tab stop position list the tab stop you want to leaderize.**

   In this case, it's the tab stop set at 3 inches.

5. **Choose the style of fearless leader tab you want.**

   Click the appropriate style — dotted, dashed, or underlined, as presented at the beginning of this section. My personal favorite is the dotted underline, which you can select by pressing the Alt+2 key combination.

6. **Click Set.**

   You'll forget this step the first time you try this on your own. And you'll wonder why it didn't work. That's when you'll return here to reread this sentence.

7. **Click OK.**

8. **Type the text to appear before the tab stop:**

   `Last names beginning with the letter A`

9. **Press the Tab key.**

   Zwoop! The toothpick cursor jumps to your tab stop and leaves a trail of, well, "stuff" in its wake. That's your dot leader (or dash leader or underline leader).

10. **Type the reference, page number, or whatever:**

    `Letter A`

11. **Press Enter to end that line.**

You can adjust the tab stops after setting them if some of the text doesn't line up. *Remember:* To adjust the tab stops for more than one paragraph at a time, you need to select everything as a block. Refer to Chapter 6.

   ✔ In theater programs, the cast and actor information is often formatted with leader tabs. But in that case, it's usually a right tab that lines up the text:

   Horatio . . . . .Percival Sumter

   Lethargio . . . . .Robert Og

   Oreo . . . . .Billy Gully

   ✔ The word *tab* appears in one form or another 281 times in this chapter.

Chapter 14

Formatting Pages

- -

- -

*L*arger than a word! More cumbersome than a paragraph! Look, up on the screen! It's a sheet of paper! No! It's a window! No! It's a *page*.

In keeping the trend of going from small to big, the next step in the formatting circus is to format a page of information. Pages have a certain size and orientation, plus margins and page numbers. All that is covered here in a neat and tidy manner that entertains while it informs.

"How Big Is My Page?"

How many angels can dance on a sheet of paper? Well, it depends on the size of the paper, of course — not to mention the type of dance.

Most printing takes place on a standard, 8½-x-11-inch sheet of paper. That's what Word defines as a *page,* on which you can format margins and other page-formatting whatnot. But Word isn't burned to the frying pan on using only that size of paper. No, Word lets you change the paper size to anything you want — from a teensy envelope to a sheet of paper big enough to make the bed with.

The paper-size setting stuff is done in the Page Setup dialog box. The following instructions tell you how to change the size of the paper you're printing on.

1. **Position the toothpick cursor at the top of your document.**

   It doesn't have to be the top of your document. You can change the page size in the middle of your document if you like. Most of the time, however, you probably want the new page size for your entire document.

2. **Choose the File⇨Page Setup command.**

   The Page Setup dialog box appears.

3. **Make sure that the Paper tab is in front.**

   See Figure 14-1 to ensure that what you see on the screen is right. If not, click the Paper tab.

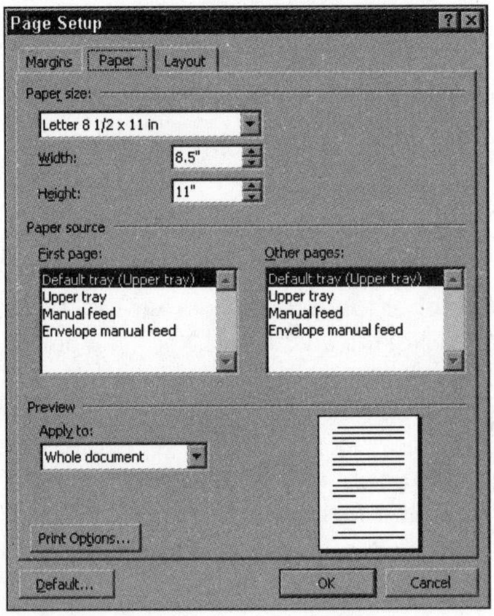

Figure 14-1:
The Page
Setup/Paper
dialog box.

4. **Click the Paper Size drop-down list.**

   The list drops down to reveal a slate of common paper sizes.

5. **Select a new paper size from the list.**

   For example, Legal 8 1/2 x 14 in is for legal-size paper. Other standard sizes are listed there as well.

   Most PC printers are capable of printing on several different sizes of paper. Weird sizes, though available on the list, may not be compatible with your printer — not to mention that you need that specific paper size to print on; Word can't make an 8½-x-11-inch sheet of paper another 3 inches longer.

   Select this new paper size by clicking it with your mouse.

6. **Display the Apply To drop-down list.**

Select `Whole document` to have the new paper size apply to your entire document. Choosing `This point forward` applies the new paper size to the current page (where the toothpick cursor is) onward.

If you're using document sections, select the This Section option to have the new paper size apply to the current section. Sections are covered in Chapter 15.

7. **Click OK.**

Okay. Type away on the new size of paper.

✔ If you're printing on an odd-size piece of paper, remember to load that special paper into your printer before you start printing. Some smarter printers even tell you which size of paper they want to print on. Mine nags at me all the time for the proper-size paper. It's like a second wife.

✔ If the paper you're printing on isn't shown on the drop-down list, you can enter the measurements yourself. First select Custom Size from the Paper Size drop-down list. Then type the paper's width into the Width box and the height into the Height box.

✔ Keep an eye on the Preview window in the Page Setup dialog box. It changes to reflect the new paper size.

✔ Refer to Chapter 30 for information on printing envelopes. (There's a special command for doing that; no sense in finagling a new paper size here.)

The Wide and Narrow Choice

Word usually prints up and down on a piece of paper — which is how everyone is used to reading a page. However, Word can print sideways (or longways) on a page as well. In this case, the page's orientation is changed; rather than up and down, the paper is printed sideways.

The technical, I'm-an-important-word-processing-expert terms for the two paper orientations are Portrait mode for the up-down paper and Landscape mode for sideways. A portrait picture is usually taller than it is long to accommodate our faces — unless someone has large ears on a juglike head. Landscape is for those lovely oil paintings of seascapes or lakes and trees that are wider than they are tall.

To make Word print the long way on a sheet of paper — in Landscape mode — do the following:

1. **Choose File➪Page Setup.**

The Page Setup dialog box appears. Make sure that the Margins panel is forward if it's not already, as shown in Figure 14-2.

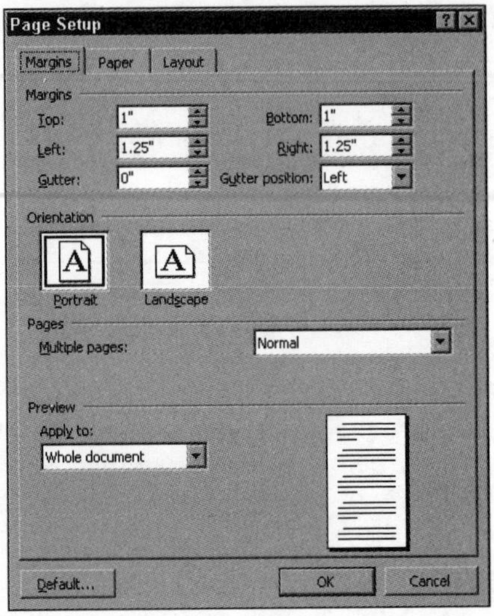

Figure 14-2:
The Page
Setup/
Margins
dialog box.

2. **Choose Portrait or Landscape from the Orientation area.**

   The sample document and the tiny icon change to reflect the document's perspective.

3. **Click OK.**

✔ Printing in Landscape mode may require you to adjust the document's margins; see the next section.

✔ Avoid printing standard documents in Landscape mode. Scientists and other people in white lab coats who study such things have determined that human reading speed slows drastically when people must scan a long line of text. Reserve Landscape mode for printing lists, tables, and items for which normal paper is too narrow.

✔ As with changing the paper size, you can have Landscape or Portrait mode apply to an entire document, from a certain point forward, or to a selected section within your document. See the preceding section for more information.

✔ It's possible to change orientation in the middle of a document; for example, to have one page in a long document print in Landscape mode. To do that, you must take advantage of Word's section-formatting commands. You start a new section, change the page orientation for that section only, and then start another section when the page orientation needs to change back. See Chapter 15 for more information on creating sections in your document.

Marginal Information

Every page has margins. They provide the air around your document — that inch of breathing space that sets off the text from the rest of the page. Word automatically sets your margins at 1 inch from the top and bottom of the page and 1¼ inches from the left and right sides of the page. Most English teachers and book editors want margins of this size because these people love to scribble in margins (they even write that way on blank paper). In Word, you can adjust the margins to suit any fussy professional.

To change the margins, follow these steps:

1. **Position the cursor where you want the new margins to start.**

   If you're changing margins for part of your document, it's best to set the new margins at the top of the document, the top of a page, or the beginning of a paragraph (or the beginning of a new formatting section). If, on the other hand, you want to change the whole document, where you place the cursor doesn't matter.

2. **Choose the File⇨Page Setup command.**

   The Page Setup dialog box appears. Click the Margins tab if it's not up front (as shown in Figure 14-2).

3. **Enter the new measurements for the Top, Bottom, Left, and Right page margins.**

   Type the new values in the appropriate boxes. For example, typing a value of **1"** in all the boxes sets all margins to 1 inch. Entering a value of **2.5"** sets a 2½-inch margin. You don't need to type the inch symbol (").

   The Preview window shows you how your margins affect text on the page.

4. **Choose Whole Document, This Point Forward, or This Section from the Apply To drop-down list.**

   • **Whole Document** changes the margins for your whole document, bonnet to boot.

   • **This Point Forward** means that the new margins take place from the toothpick cursor's position, onward.

   • **This Section** means that the margins apply to only the current section. (See Chapter 15 for more information on sections.)

5. **Click OK.**

   Your new margins are enforced.

   ✔ Margins are a page-wide formatting command (which is why they're covered in this chapter). To set the indents for a single paragraph, you need to use a paragraph-formatting command. See Chapter 12.

✔ If you want to print on 3-hole paper, set the left margin to 2 or 2.5 inches. This setting allows enough room for the little holes, and it offsets the text nicely when you open up something in a 3-ring notebook or binder.

✔ Keep in mind that most laser printers cannot print on the outside half-inch of a piece of paper — top, bottom, left, and right. This space is an absolute margin; although you can tell Word to set a margin of 0 inches right and 0 inches left, text still does not print there. Instead, choose a minimum of .5 inches for the left and right margins.

✔ Likewise, many ink printers have a taller bottom margin requirement. If you attempt to print outside that area, a dialog box appears, informing you of your offense.

✔ The Gutter margin applies more to documents printed on two pages and intended to be bound in a book-like format. The Gutter position item lets you select whether the gutter appears on the left side or top of the page. No need to put your mind in the gutter.

✔ The Pages area of the dialog box lets you set up how Word is printing your document. The Normal item (as shown in Figure 14-2) means that you're printing pretty much the same page format for the entire document. Other items on the drop-down list let you select different ways of laying out the page: Mirror Margins item is used for printing pages to be bound together.

The 2 Pages Per Sheet item is nifty: Choose Landscape from the Paper Size panel and then click 2 Pages Per Sheet. Notice in the Preview window how Word splits a sheet of paper down the middle with pages on either "side." This feature is fun for creating a brochure or greeting card.

✔ If your homework comes out to three pages and the teacher wants four, bring in the margins. Set the left and right margins to 1.5 inches each. Then change the line spacing to 1.5. Refer to the section in Chapter 12 about changing line spacing. (You can also choose a larger font; check out the section in Chapter 11 about setting your text size.)

Page Numbering

Please sing the refrain from the word-processing anthem:

Your word processor will number your pages for you.

Your word processor will number your pages for you.

Your word processor will number your pages for you.

Memorize it. Live it.

Word can number your pages for you. There is no need to do it yourself. No matter how many pages you have or how much you add to or delete your text, Word keeps it all straight. There's nothing for you to do, other than tell Word where on the page to stick the page number. Please, oh please, don't manually number anything in a word processor!

Where to stick the page number?

The question is not "*Can* Word put a number on your page?" but rather "*Where* should the number go?" If you follow these steps, you can direct Word to put the page number just about anywhere on the page (well, anywhere *logical*):

1. **Choose the Insert⇨Page Numbers command.**

   The Page Numbers dialog box, as shown in Figure 14-3, appears.

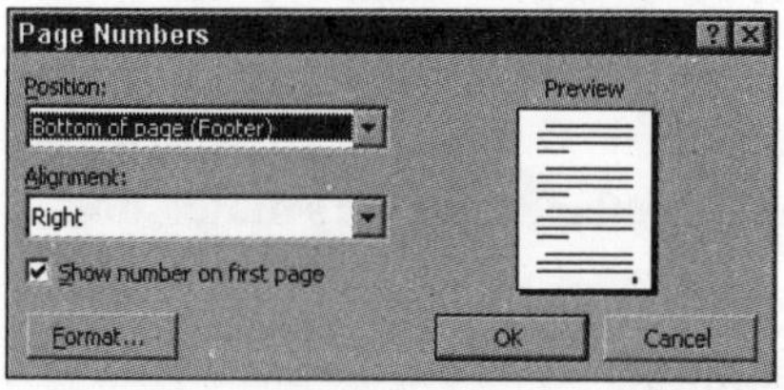

Figure 14-3:
The Page
Numbers
dialog box.

Page Numbers

Position:
Bottom of page (Footer)

Alignment:
Right

☑ Show number on first page

Preview

Format... | OK | Cancel

2. **Pick a position for the page number.**

   Word can stick the page number at the top or bottom of the page. Choose that position from the Position drop-down list.

   The page number can appear to the right or left or at the center, inside, or outside of your text. Choose the position from the Alignment drop-down list.

   Ponder this situation carefully and keep an eye on the Preview box.

3. **Choose OK.**

   The page numbers are inserted.

You can also create page numbering by sticking the page number command in a header or footer. See Chapter 15 for more information. (If you do end up putting the page number in a header or footer, you don't have to use the Page Numbers command.)

✔ If you want to get fancier page numbers, click the Format button in the Page Numbers dialog box. Doing so opens the Page Number Format dialog box. From there, you can select various ways to display the page numbers from the Number format drop-down list — even those cute little *ii*s and *xx*s.

✔ If you don't want a page number on your first page (the title page, for example), deselect the <u>S</u>how number on first page check box by clicking in it (refer to the Page Numbers dialog box, as shown in Figure 14-3). That action tells Word not to stick an ugly *1* at the bottom of your pristine title page.

Starting off with a different page number

To start numbering your pages with a new page number, heed the instructions in the preceding section to conjure up the Page Numbers dialog box. That must be done first because, obviously, there's no need to change page numbers when your document doesn't have them in the first place. Like, duh.

Follow these steps:

1. **Click the Format button in the Page Numbers dialog box.**

   Clicking this button opens the Page Number Format dialog box.

2. **Select the Start <u>a</u>t radio button.**

   Type in the box the page number you want to begin with. You can also press the arrows to wheel up and down. Whee!

3. **Click OK to close the Page Number Format dialog box.**

4. **Click OK to close the Page Numbers dialog box.**

You see the new page numbers reflected on the status bar's little nonsense line. Time to fool everyone into thinking that page 1 is really page 20!

✔ This procedure is something you may want to do for the second, third, or later chapters in a book. By setting a new page number, the page numbers in all chapters are continuous.

✔ You're changing only the page number that *prints,* not the actual number of pages that print. The first item on the status bar, Page 20, does reflect the number of the page as you've changed it. However, the third item on the status bar, (1/5, for example) still shows the real page number and total page numbers that are in your document.

Starting a New Page

You can choose two ways to start a new page in Word: the horribly-wrong-yet-obvious way and the impressively neat way:

- **Horribly wrong:** Keep pressing the Enter key until you see the row o' dots that denotes the start of a new page. Yes, this technique works. But it's horribly wrong.

- **Impressively neat:** Press Ctrl+Enter. Voilà! New page.

Pressing Ctrl+Enter inserts a *hard page break* into your document, demanding that Word begin a new page On That Very Spot. This is the preferred way to start a new page.

In Normal view (refer to Chapter 2), the hard page break looks like a regular page break but with the addition of the words Page Break:

---Page Break---

In Print Layout view, the page break looks just like any other page break (refer to Figure 2-2).

Keep these things in mind when you're dealing with hard page breaks:

- You can also insert a hard page break by choosing Insert⇨Break from the menu. Choose Page break from the list and click OK. That's a load of steps, however, and Ctrl+Enter is what most people use all the time.

- The hard page break works just like a regular page break does, although you control where it lives in your document: Move the toothpick cursor to where you want the hard page break and press Ctrl+Enter.

- Pressing Ctrl+Enter inserts a hard page-break *character* in your document. That character stays there, always creating a hard page break no matter how much you edit the text on previous pages.

- You can delete a hard page break by pressing the Backspace or Delete keys. If you do this accidentally, just press Ctrl+Enter again or press Ctrl+Z to undelete.

- If you set hard page breaks, remember to use Print Preview to look at your document before you print it. Sometimes, the process of editing moves text around, making the hard page breaks unnecessary and awkward. Refer to Chapter 9 for more information on the Print Preview command.

✔ Don't fall into the trap of using hard page breaks to adjust your page numbering. You can use the power of the computer to alter your page numbers without having to mess with page formatting. See "Where to stick the page number?" earlier in this chapter.

Chapter 15

Formatting Documents

• •

• •

Document is an important word. It carries weight. Funny, you wouldn't think of a silly letter to your niece as something heavy, important, or legal sounding. But in Word, the big picture is the document. My wife keeps my honey-do list as a document on her computer. I suppose that means it must somehow be important.

As far as formatting is concerned, a document is not the same thing as a page. No, formatting a document is a *big picture* thing. In fact, much of the information in this chapter isn't necessary for most of the documents you create (the silly to-your-niece ones). But when you go nuts someday, or say the urge hits you to *really* flaunt your knowledge of Word, this chapter will be your boon companion.

All about Sections

Many of Word's formatting commands affect an entire document. For example, most of the page-formatting commands covered in Chapter 14 are typical document-wide commands: margins, paper size, orientation, and other whatnot. And the header and footers you can add to a document (covered in this chapter) also apply to a whole document.

If there ever comes a time when you need to change a document-wide format for a single page or group of pages, you need to break your document up into sections. Each section contains its own page formatting. So if you need to print one page in Landscape mode, you just create a new section for that page. Or, if your title page needs unique margins, you create a section just for it.

Sections are easy to create. They can simplify most document-long formatting hassles. The following sections tell you just about everything you need to know.

✔ A *section* is basically an area in your document whose page formatting is independent of the rest of your document.

✔ Text and paragraph formatting, as well as any styles you may create, don't give a hoot about sections.

✔ Sections are used to create many of the interesting and fun types of documents covered in Part IV of this book.

✔ The subject of sections is generally considered an advanced Word topic. Most people never use them. Only on rare occasions have I had the need to break up a document into sections. If you want, you can freely skip this information.

Creating a section

Breaking up your document isn't hard to do. Word has carefully placed all its breaking commands into a handy Break dialog box. To summon the dialog box, choose Insert⇨Break from the menu.

Figure 15-1 shows the Break dialog box. The items in the top group are text breaks; the bottom group contains section breaks.

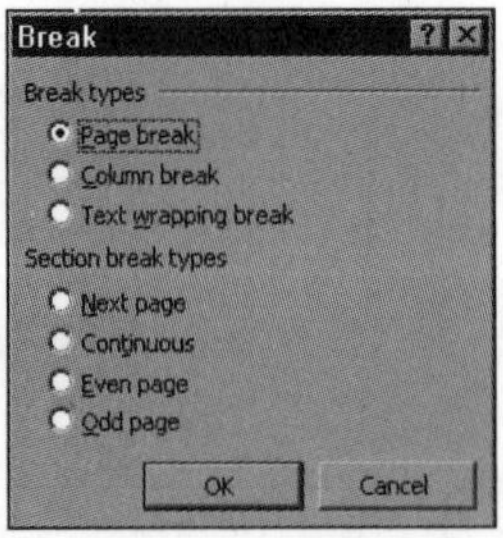

Figure 15-1:
The Break
dialog box.

Suppose that you're creating a title page on a new document. Before doing any typing, create the title page as follows:

1. **Choose the Insert⇨Break command.**

   The Break dialog box opens, as shown in Figure 15-1.

2. **Select <u>N</u>ext Page.**

The <u>N</u>ext Page option works like a hard page break; it inserts a page break *and* a section break into your document. This is the most common form of section break because most of the formatting items you're working with are at the page level.

3. **Click OK.**

In Print Layout view, the new section looks like a hard page break. In Normal view, the section break looks like this:

══════════════════════════════Section Break (Next Page)══════════════════════════════

The next step in the process is to move the toothpick cursor up to the first page (the title page in the preceding section) and format that page according to your needs.

✔ You can use the Continuous Section break to mix formatting styles within a page. For example, if you have columns of text sharing a page with regular text, the Continuous Section break is the ideal way to separate the individual formats. See Chapter 21 for more information.

✔ You can use the Even Page and Odd Page options to start the next section on the next even or odd page. For example, if the document you're writing will be bound, you may want certain sections to start on the right or left side of the bound hard copy. (I don't know anyone who uses these options.)

✔ Section breaks also provide a great way to divide a multipart document. For example, the title page can be a section; the introduction, Chapter 1, and Appendix A all can be made into separate sections. You can then use Word's Go To command to zoom to each section. Refer to Chapter 3 for more information on the Go To command.

✔ Refer to Chapter 14 for more information on starting a new page with a page break.

✔ You can also create a page break by pressing the Ctrl+Enter key combination.

✔ See Chapter 21 for information on a column break.

✔ I have no idea what a text-wrapping break is.

Deleting a section break

You can delete a section break with the Backspace or Delete keys. If you do this accidentally, you lose any special formatting you applied to the section. In this case, press the Undo shortcut, Ctrl+Z, before you do anything else.

Beware of creeping format! If you format a special page and then delete the section break, that special page formatting may "fall through" to the rest of your document. Always use Print Preview before you print to ensure that everything looks good. Refer to Chapter 9.

The Joys of Headers and Footers

In construction, a header is a buncha wood over a doorway or window. In baseball, a doubleheader is two games in a row (and a boon for seat cushion sales). In a document, a *header* is the text you see at the top of every page. The header's little brother is the *footer,* which is text that appears on the bottom of every page in a document. Word does 'em both.

- Headers usually contain things such as your name, the document name, date, page number, title, and phone numbers. ("Hurry! Buy now! Operators are standing by!")

- Headers can also be called "eyebrows." Weird, huh?

- Footers can include page numbers, a chapter or document title, and odor eaters.

- Footers are not the same thing as footnotes. See Chapter 22 for the low-down on footnotes.

Adding a header or footer

Headers and footers can make any document shine. You don't need to use them both; you can use just one or the other. Either way, the same command is used to add or play with them.

To add a header or footer, follow these steps:

1. **Choose <u>V</u>iew⇨<u>H</u>eader and Footer.**

   Word tosses you into a special version of Print Layout view that shows the Header and Footer areas of your document roped off. Also visible is the floating Header and Footer toolbar. Witness Figure 15-2 for an example.

 2. **Click the Switch Between Header/Footer icon to choose either the header or footer for editing.**

   Clicking the button switches you back and forth between the header and footer.

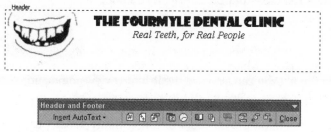

Figure 15-2:
A header
along with
the Header
and Footer
floating
toolbar
thing.

3. Enter your header or footer text.

Any text you type can be formatted using any of Word's text and paragraph formatting commands, including tabs (see Chapters 11, 12, and 13).

Word preformats the headers and footers in any document with center
and right tabs at the center and far right of the ruler. This allows you to
press the Tab key, type some text, and have the text automatically centered at the bottom (or top) of each page. This tab stop isn't required,
but it's mighty thoughtful of Microsoft to set it up that way.

4. Use the buttons on the Header and Footer toolbar for special items.

Hover the mouse pointer over each button to see a brief explanation of
its function (just like on the big toolbars!).

For example, you can press the Tab key and then click the Insert Page
Number button to put a page number in the center of a footer.

You can use the Insert AutoText drop-down list to put AutoText items
into the header or footer. The items inserted are updating "fields," which
reflect various aspects of your document, as shown in Figure 15-3. For
example, `Page X of Y` displays the current page number out of total
pages in the document.

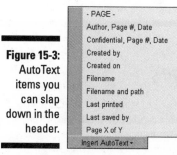

Figure 15-3:
AutoText
items you
can slap
down in the
header.

5. Click the Close button after you're done.

You're back in your document.

In Print Layout view, you can see the header or footer displayed in "ghostly gray" text. In Normal view, you cannot see any header or footer, even though it's still there. (You can also use the Print Preview command, as covered in Chapter 9, to see the header or footer.)

You can put anything in a header or footer that you can put in a document, including graphics (refer to Figure 15-2). This capability is especially useful if you want a logo to appear on each page. See Chapter 23 for information on Word and graphics.

✔ You don't have to go to page 1 to insert a page number in the header. Word is smart enough to put the proper number on the proper page no matter where you're editing the header in your document.

✔ In Print Layout view, you can quickly edit any header or footer by double-clicking its ghostly gray image.

✔ You probably want to put some text in front of the page number because a number sitting all by itself tends to get lonely. You can get really creative and type the word **Page** and a space before you click the # button, or you can come up with some interesting text on your own.

✔ Headers and footers are contained within any sections your document may have. If your document has more than one section in it, the header and footer's name appears with the section number, as in `Header-Section 2-`. Remember that any additions or changes to a header or footer in a section affect that section only.

✔ To insert the current date or time into the header or footer, click the Date or Time buttons on the Header and Footer toolbar.

✔ Don't forget to use the Switch Between Header and Footer button to alternately edit headers and footers.

Odd headers for odd pages, even headers for even pages

Word lets you put two sets of headers and footers in your document, if you like: one set for odd pages and another for even pages. For example, this book is formatted that way. The header on even pages contains the page number and the part title. The header on odd pages contains the chapter number and title and then the page number. You can do that too!

To force Word to accept two sets of headers and footers, obey these steps:

1. **Choose View➪Header and Footer.**

   This step displays any headers or footers in your document and also the Header and Footer floating toolbar thing (refer to Figure 15-2).

2. **Click the Page Setup button on the Header and Footer toolbar.**

   The Page Setup/Layout dialog box opens, as shown in Figure 15-4.

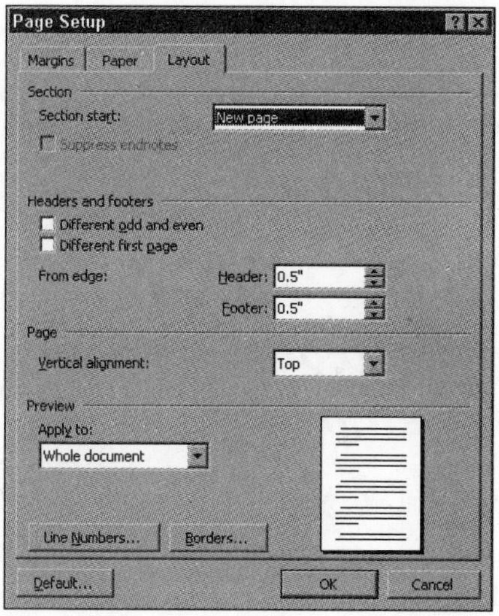

Figure 15-4:
The Page
Setup/
Layout
dialog box.

3. **Select the Different Odd and Even check box.**

   This step tells Word that you want two sets of headers and footers, one for odd pages and one for even pages. Notice how the Preview window changes to show two pages rather than one? Clever.

4. **Click OK.**

   You're returned to header/footer editing mode, but notice how the header or footer now says Odd Page or Even Page before it?

5. **Create the odd (or even) header or footer.**

   Refer to the preceding section for notes on making a header or footer.

6. **Create the even (or odd) header or footer.**

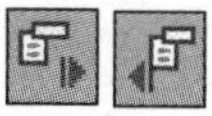

   Click the Show Next button to see the next footer in your document, or you can click the Show Previous button. These two buttons cycle you through the various odd or even headers or footers in your document.

7. **Click the Close button when you're done editing the headers and footers.**

   This odd–even stuff has nothing to do with the last number on your car's license plate or the last number in your address.

But I don't want a header on my first page!

To prevent the header or footer from appearing on the first page of text, which usually is the title page, you need to use the Page Setup/Layout dialog box as described in the preceding section. In the Page Setup/Layout dialog box, select the different first page check box; then click OK.

When you return to edit the headers and footers in your document, click the Show Previous button until you find the first header, titled First Page Header. Leave that header (or footer) blank. This procedure places an empty header on the first page; the header appears on all the other pages as ordered. You can also use this option to place a different header on the first page — a graphic, for example.

Multiple header and footer madness — beyond odd and even pages!

A header is a section-long thing. For most documents, which are one section, that's fine. But suppose for some reason that you need multiple headers in your document. Or, maybe you just need to turn the headers "off" for a section of text — if some graphic images appear in the middle of your document and you don't want your header interfering, for example. If so, you need multiple headers (starting headers, no headers, and then the starting headers again). To do that, you split your document into sections.

By using sections, you can have several different types of headers and footers floating throughout your document, one set for each section. The new section's headers and footers are completely different from the preceding (or next) section. And changing a header in one section doesn't affect any other section in the document. Refer to the section "Creating a section," earlier in this chapter, for more information on sections.

Chapter 16

Working with Styles

*T*here is a sad story of the perils of Doris. A lowly word processor, she works for William Morris. Then she writes and she formats. It's not very exciting, mostly because she spends more time formatting than writing. She toils away at the top of each page: Centered. Indented. Line spacing. Fonts. This isn't the kind of job that sweet Doris wants. There are formatting commands from Baroque to just plain. Too many commands, and it's driving Doris insane.

Lo, along comes Dennis, a wandering Word wizard. He types several commands, fingers flying like snow in a blizzard. A style he creates, which he magically applies. The formatting is done, right before Doris' eyes. "You did that with one motion, one command, one click. I just don't believe it. It's some sort of trick."

"No trick," counters Dennis. "It's simple, even fun. Just read Chapter 16 and then come back when you're done." For all Word's formatting commands — yeah, the whole dang doodle pile — can be stuffed into one single thing. That thing we call a style.

What Is a Style?

A *style* is nothing more than a collection of Word's formatting commands, all stuffed into a single box. So, when you want a paragraph that's indented and formatted in Courier, 10 point, you simply *apply* that style to the paragraph. Easy.

✔ Historically, styles were created to save formatting toil. As word processors grew more sophisticated and printers grew more fonts and Windows let you see things on the screen as they would print, the need for advanced formatting commands increased. To help you deal with all the formatting hoohaw, styles were created.

✔ All text in Word has a style. Unless you specify otherwise, Word uses the Normal style, typically Times New Roman, 12 point, left-aligned paragraphs. No indenting.

✔ Word doesn't demand that you use styles. They do, however, make formatting your documents easier.

Where Your Styles Lurk

In Word, styles can be found in one of two places: on the formatting toolbar and in the Style dialog box, obtained by choosing the Format⇨Style command.

You'll probably end up choosing styles from the toolbar. The Style dialog box is where you create and edit styles for your documents.

Styles on the toolbar

The easiest way to see and use the styles available in a document is to use the drop-down list on the Formatting toolbar — the one that says Normal — as shown in Figure 16-1.

You may need to arrange your toolbars to see the Styles drop-down list. See Chapter 29 for help.

The styles you see on the list are the ones you can use in your document. In Figure 16-1, you see the standard styles Word applies to every new document. There are four of them: the Normal style, which is applied to all text, and three heading styles.

The Clear Formatting item is simply a command that removes all formatting from whatever text is selected.

As you create new styles, they're added to the list.

If you modify an existing style, such as change the font, the style appears on the list with the modification. For example, if you change the font to Arial, a new item, Normal+Arial, appears at the top of the Style list. The font name (Arial, in this case) is added to the list. Of course, there are better ways to add items to the list, which this chapter endeavors to explain.

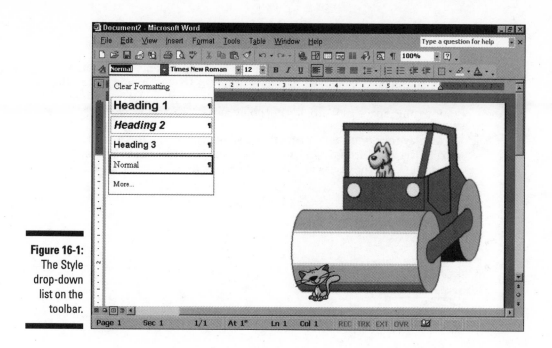

The way the styles appear on the list gives you a hint to their format. For example, the heading fonts are bold and of a specific size and weight, but the Normal font appears in 12-point Times New Roman.

A small paragraph mark (¶) beside a style name indicates a paragraph style. The formatting commands affect paragraphs as well as text.

An underlined A (a) next to a style name indicates a character style. The formatting commands affect only characters. There are no paragraph formatting commands.

- If more styles are available than can be displayed on the screen, a `More` item appears at the bottom of the drop-down list. Choosing that item activates the task pane, which is discussed in the next section.

- The standard styles are kept in a document template that Word uses for all new documents. The name of the template is NORMAL (or NORMAL.DOT), and it's discussed in the next chapter.

- The heading styles are not the same thing as headers and footers, covered in Chapter 15. Headers appear at the top of a page. Heading styles are used for chapter and section titles as well as for formatting Web pages.

Styles in the task pane

Most of what you do with styles happens in the task pane. So, if you've been avoiding the task pane in Word, now is the time to give up and accept the inevitable; despite the fact that the task pane occupies nearly one-fourth of your writing space in Word, it's *not* going away. Boo-hoo.

 To display the Styles and Formatting task pane, click on the AA button next to the Style drop-down list. Or, you can choose Format⇨Styles and Formatting. Lo, the Styles and Formatting task pane appears, looking something like Figure 16-2.

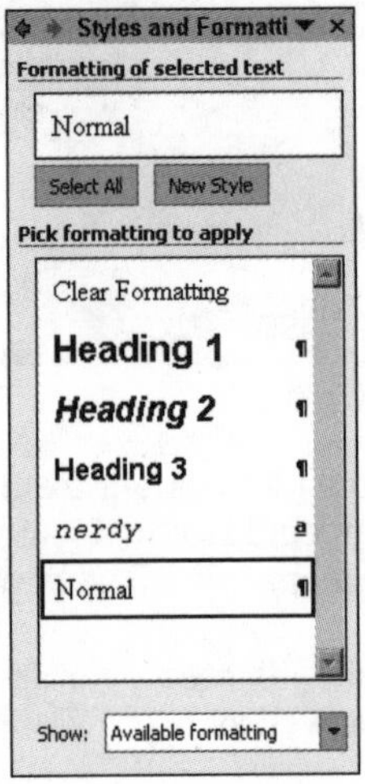

Figure 16-2:
The Styles
and
Formatting
task pane.

The Styles and Formatting task pane is *the* place to control, create, delete, or otherwise mess with the styles in your document. All the styles in your document appear there. The current style in use (the style of any selected text or where the toothpick cursor is a-winkin') appears in the top box. In Figure 16-2, it's the Normal style.

Point the mouse at a style on the list to see more information about that style. First, you notice a drop-down arrow thing, indicating the menu attached to each style (see Figure 16-3). Next, if you hold the mouse very still, a pop-up window appears, describing the style's specific formatting information. In Figure 16-3, the Heading 1 style is based on the Normal style *plus* various other formatting options.

✔ The Styles and Formatting task pane is the place where you create, edit, and work with styles.

✔ The Select All button selects all the text in your document, the same as the Edit⇨Select All or Ctrl+A commands. This way, you can apply a style to your entire document without leaving the task pane.

Style formatting information

Style name

Click to display
the style's menu.

Figure 16-3:
Getting
information
about a
style.

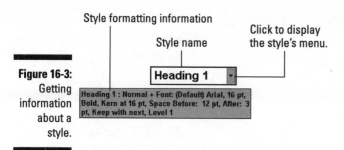

Heading 1

Heading 1 : Normal + Font: (Default) Arial, 16 pt,
Bold, Kern at 16 pt, Space Before: 12 pt, After: 3
pt, Keep with next, Level 1

✔ Refer to Chapter 6 for more information on selecting blocks of text.

✔ You use the style's menu to delete, modify, select, or update a given
style. Figure 16-3 shows you where to click. Information on using the
menu is covered later in this chapter.

✔ Feel free to close the task pane when you're done styling around.

Creating a New Style

I hate the Normal style. I suppose that they could have called it the Vanilla
style, but I'm one of the 25 percent of the population who likes vanilla ice
cream. And calling it the Boring style would show too much humor for a
Microsoft product. No, Normal is it. And Normal stinks.

The following sections show you how to create some new styles for your
document — something better than Normal.

According to those who keep track of such things, one out of every four ice
cream orders is for vanilla compared to one out of nine for chocolate.

Creating a style based on a paragraph you've already formatted

The easiest way to make up a whole new style is to use all your formatting
skills and power to format a single paragraph just the way you like. Then
create the style based on that formatted paragraph. Here's how:

1. **Type a paragraph of text.**

   Or, you can simply work with any paragraph of text already in your document. Basically, you just need something on the screen to see how your
   formatting works.

2. **Mark your paragraph as a block.**

   See Chapter 6 to find out how to mark a block of text.

3. **Format the block.**

   Select your character formatting. Select a font and select a point size to make the text big or little. See Chapter 11 for more information on character formatting.

   Stick to fonts and sizes for your character formatting; avoid bold, italics, or underlining unless you want them applied to *all* the text in the paragraph.

   Select the paragraph formatting. Choose Left, Right, Center, or Justified alignment, pick indents, and so on. See Chapter 12 for the full list of what you can do.

4. **Press Ctrl+Shift+S.**

   This key combination activates the Style drop-down list on the Formatting toolbar. The formatting information is highlighted inside the box.

5. **Type a new name for your style.**

   A brief, descriptive, one-word name does nicely.

   For example, if you create an indented paragraph that you want to use to list things, name the style List. Or, if you create a special musical style, name it Liszt.

6. **Press Enter.**

   The style is added to Word's repertoire of styles for your document.

The style you created now applies to the paragraph you typed (on which the style is based); any additional paragraphs you type also take on that style. And you can apply the style to other paragraphs.

✔ Give your style a name that describes the style's function. Names like Indented List or Table Body Text are great because they make it easy to remember what they do. Names like Ira or Gopple-bop are somewhat less desirable.

✔ The styles you create are available only to the document in which they're created.

✔ If you create scads of styles you love and want to use them for several documents, you need to create what's called a template. Chapter 17 covers this procedure in the section about creating your very own template.

✔ You may have to tweak some things in your style. If so, you need to use the Style and Formatting task pane. See the section "Modifying a style," later in this chapter.

Creating a style using the task pane

Using the Style dialog box to create a style is handy — as long as you're well versed with all Word's style commands, including some I introduce in the next part of this book. In any event, the following steps glide you through the trips and traps of using the Style dialog box to make up a style.

1. **Choose Format⇨Styles and Formatting.**

   The Styles and Formatting task pane appears (refer to Figure 16-2).

   Notice that you don't have to create a new paragraph or anything to format for this step. Basically, you just boldly march forth and build the style from scratch.

2. **Click the New Style button.**

   The New Style dialog box opens, as shown in Figure 16-4.

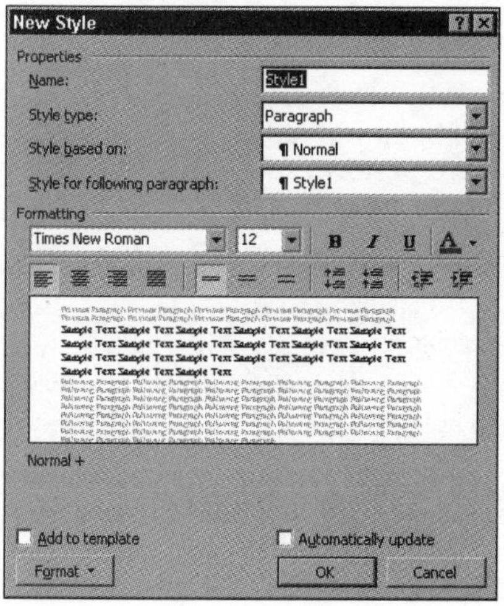

Figure 16-4: The New Style dialog box.

3. **Enter a name for your style into the Name text box.**

   This is the name that appears on the Style list, hopefully something memorable, something other than `Style1`. For example, type **Title A** for an A-level title in your document.

   Word warns you if you use a name already given to a style. Use another name.

4. **Choose the Style type.**

   Most styles are Paragraph, which means that the style covers all font and paragraph formatting options you can dream of, all of which apply to paragraphs as a whole.

Character styles are rare. I once I wrote a book where the commands to be typed had to appear in the Courier New font, bold and colored blue. So I created a character font with those formatting commands and named it Blue Text. Then, to format the special text, I selected it and applied the Blue Text character format.

The Table style is used for formatting tables; see Chapter 20. The List style is used for creating lists of items, such as the outlines in Word. It's best to become familiar with tables and lists before you create those formats.

5. Set the Style based on item.

To save time, you can use an existing style and build your new style on it. For example, if your new style is the same as the Body style but with smaller text, you can base your style on Body and then make the smaller text modification.

All styles are originally based on the Normal style.

The drop-down list contains a whole heck of a lot of styles. Scroll through the list to find a specific one, or just give up and use Normal.

6. Choose the Style option for the following paragraph.

This is a handy option, normally set equal to the name of the style you're creating. That way, all the paragraphs you type have the same style. This item can be used to perform some nifty formatting tricks; see the nearby sidebar, "The follow-me style," for more information.

7. Choose formatting options for your style.

The New Style dialog box contains a plethora of buttons and drop-down lists — common items you might be familiar with — which can help you instantly choose some basic formatting options. Use the preview window to help you make a selection.

If you need to get specific, such as choosing double underline or setting tabs, you need to use the Format button. Clicking that button displays a pop-up menu of Word's common formatting commands (similar to the commands on the Format menu). Choosing a command displays the corresponding dialog box where the various formatting options are set. Many of those dialog boxes are covered elsewhere in this book, but keep in mind that their settings affect the style you're creating and not any text in your document. (Not yet, at least.)

The New Style dialog box assumes that you *know* which formats you're putting into a style. If you don't know, you're better off using the techniques described in the preceding section, "Creating a style based on a paragraph you've already formatted."

8. Click OK to create the style.

The New Style dialog box goes away. The style you created appears on the Styles list.

TIP

The follow-me style

When I write a new chapter in a book, I start off with the Chapter Title style. The very next style I use is the Intro Paragraph style. Intro Paragraph is followed by Body, which is followed by Body, Body, Body, and on and on. There's no point in changing all those styles because Word can be told to switch styles automatically.

In the New Style dialog box (or Modify Style dialog box), locate the drop-down list labeled Style for following paragraph. The style shown on that list tells Word which style to switch to when you press the Enter key to end a paragraph. Normally, it's the same style, which makes sense for most of your work. But in situations where you *know* that the style will switch, you can demand that Word do the switching for you. You can edit the Chapter Title style so that the Intro Paragraph style is selected in the Style for following paragraph drop-down list. That way, pressing the Enter key after typing the chapter title switches the style over to Intro Paragraph. Very nice.

Creating a character-only style

Most of the styles you create in Word format are at the paragraph level. To create a style that contains lots of complex character formatting, you should create a character style. This type of style is flagged by an underlined *A* (**a**) on the Style list.

Suppose that all the mathematical formulas in your proposal for your flying car patent proposal must be in bold red text. You could just select that text and then use the Format⇨Font command to slap bold and red on the text (or use the toolbar). But that's too much work in this Age of Computers. Instead, you can create a character font that merely applies bold and red, but does so in one easy action.

To create a character-only style, follow the steps outlined in the preceding section. However, after Step 4, in the New Style dialog box, choose Character from the Style type drop-down list. This action gears everything in the New Style dialog box to accept only character and font-related formatting stuff; paragraph-level style stuff is no longer available.

Continue working the New Style dialog box, selecting various character options. When you're done, click OK to create the style.

- ✔ The special character styles don't affect any paragraph formatting. Selecting a character style changes only the font, style, size, underlining, bold, and so on.

- ✔ Hey! It's the 21st century and I want my flying car and I want it now!

✔ A section in Chapter 19 talks about creating that shocking white-on-black text. Refer to that section for information on creating a white-on-black character style.

✔ Also refer to the section about formatting theft, in Chapter 18, for a quick method of applying font formats.

Modifying a style

Styles change. Bellbottoms may come back. Again. And though my wife thinks I'm nuts, I believe my Chuck Taylors will very soon be a popular accessory for the upwardly savvy. Oh, but let me not get sidetracked.

Times New Roman — the bane of the Normal style — is a wonderful font . . . if you still wear an undershirt or bow ties and think that sushi is the name of the latest teenage pop singer. Still, Times New Roman is a workhorse used by everyone for almost everything. Maybe you want to put this font out to pasture and use a different font in your Normal style. If so, you can change it.

Here are the instructions for changing a style — any style, not just the Normal style.

1. **Summon the Styles and Formatting task pane.**

    Click the AA button or choose Format⇨Styles and Formatting from the menu.

2. **Point the mouse at the style you want to change.**

3. **Display the style's menu.**

   Refer to Figure 16-3 for where to click.

4. **Choose Modify.**

   The New Style dialog box appears, but it's called Modify Style because this style already exists. It works the same as the New Style dialog box (refer to Figure 16-4), but the settings you make now *change* the style rather than create a new style.

5. **Change the formatting for your style.**

   You're free to use any of the formatting options to change your style. You can even add new formatting options or a shortcut key (which is covered in the next section).

6. **Click OK when you're done.**

Close the task pane if you're done with that.

▶ Changing a style affects every dang doodle paragraph in your document that uses that style. The change is instantaneous, which is one of the advantages of using a style in the first place.

▶ In a way, changing a style is cool; if you need to indent the first line in every paragraph, just modify the style. When you click OK in the Modify Style dialog box, all the paragraphs magically change. Neat-o.

▶ If you do change the Normal style for good, you need to edit the NORMAL.DOT template. This is covered in Chapter 17.

Giving your style a shortcut key

Styles allow you the advantage of quickly formatting a paragraph of text. Style shortcut keys make formatting even better because pressing Alt+Shift+B to get at the Body style is often faster than messing with the Style drop-down list or dialog box — especially when you have a gob of styles you're messing with.

To give your style a shortcut key, follow these steps:

1. **Conjure up the Styles and Formatting task pane.**

2. **Display the style's menu thing (refer to Figure 16-3).**

3. **Choose <u>M</u>odify.**

   The Modify Style dialog box appears.

4. **Click the F<u>o</u>rmat button.**

5. **Choose Shortcut <u>k</u>ey from the menu.**

   A cryptic Customize Keyboard dialog box appears. Don't waste any time trying to explore here. Just move on to Step 6.

6. **Press your shortcut key combination.**

   Using Ctrl+Shift+*letter* or Alt+Shift+*letter* or Ctrl+Alt+*letter* key combinations is best, where *letter* is a letter key on the keyboard. For example, press Ctrl+Alt+B for your Body style shortcut key.

   Notice that the key combination you press appears in the Press New Shortcut Key box (see the middle left side of the dialog box). If you make a mistake, press the Backspace key to erase it.

7. **Check to see that the combination isn't already in use.**

   For example, Word uses Ctrl+B as the Bold character formatting shortcut key. This key combination appears under the heading `Currently Assigned To`, which shows up under the C<u>u</u>rrent keys box. Keep an eye on that box! If something else uses the shortcut key, press the Backspace key and go back to Step 5.

As an interesting aside, the key combination Ctrl+Shift+B also applies the Bold text format. My opinion: Feel free to use that combination for one of your styles because Ctrl+B is easier to type for Bold anyway.

If the key combination isn't used by anything, you see [unassigned] displayed under the Currently assigned to heading.

8. **Click the** A**ssign button.**

9. **Click the Close button.**

   The Customize Keyboard dialog box sulks away.

10. **Click the OK button.**

    The Modify Style dialog box huffs off.

    You can also close the task pane if you're done with it.

Congratulations; you now have a usable shortcut key for your style.

Deleting a style

You can delete any style you create. It's easy: Display the Styles and Formatting task pane, select the style, and choose Delete from its menu. You're asked whether you're sure that you want to delete the style. Choose Yes to delete it for real.

You cannot delete the Normal, Heading, or any other standard Word fonts.

Proper Style Application

You don't use a style as much as you *apply* it. The character and paragraph formatting carefully stored inside the style is applied to text onscreen, injected into that text or block like a stern shot of pickle juice. (Doesn't that make you want to squirm?)

Step-by-step, applying a style is easy:

1. **Decide what text you're applying the style to.**

   If it's a paragraph already onscreen, just stick the toothpick cursor somewhere in that paragraph. Or, you can select a block. Otherwise, the style is applied to any new text you type.

2. **Select a style from the Style drop-down list.**

   Or, if the Styles and Formatting task pane is visible, you can select the style from there, though that seems like a waste of screen space if you're merely selecting styles and not creating them.

✔ Remember the differences between paragraph and character styles. You cannot apply a paragraph style to just a single word in a paragraph; the style takes over the whole paragraph instead.

✔ You can also apply a style by using a shortcut key. Refer to the properly numbered instructions in the preceding section for the details.

✔ To apply a style to your entire document, choose Edit➪Select All. Then select the style you want for everything.

Using the Built-in Heading Styles

Three (or more) built-in heading styles are available in Word. You can use these styles if you plan on breaking up your text with different headings. Not that you have to, but doing so lends itself to certain advantages.

For example, this chapter has main headings, such as "Proper Style Application," and then subheadings, like "Giving your style a shortcut key." The main headings are formatted with the built-in Heading 1 style. The sub-headings are formatted with the Heading 2 style.

Granted, the heading styles are boring as they come out of the box. But you can change them to suit your document's needs. Refer to the section "Modifying a style," earlier in this chapter, for information on changing a style's look and smell.

The advantage to using the heading styles? The first is that you see the headings when you drag the elevator button on the scroll bar. Also, you can use the browsing buttons (below the vertical scroll bar) to hop through your document, stopping at various heading styles. All this is covered over in Chapter 3, if you're interested.

✔ Heading styles, like the Normal and Default Paragraph Font styles, cannot be deleted from your document.

✔ There are actually many heading styles Word can use, from Heading 1 on down through Heading 9. These mostly come into play when you use Word's outlining feature. See Chapter 26.

Managing All Your Various Styles

Styles can be like trading cards. And they should be! If you create a great style, it's nice to use it in several documents. This can be done without re-creating the style (and even without using a document template, which is covered in Chapter 17).

To trade or manage all the styles you have in Word, you need to use the Style Organizer. It's not the easiest thing to find:

1. **Summon the Styles and Formatting task pane.**

2. **Choose Custom from the Show list.**

   (The Show drop-down, or "pop-up," list is located at the bottom of the task pane.)

   The Format Settings dialog box appears, which you can mostly ignore.

3. **Click the Styles button.**

   Almost there; the Style dialog box shows up. Ignore it and. . . .

4. **Click the Organizer button.**

   Finally. The Organizer dialog box appears, with the Styles tab forward, as shown in Figure 16-5.

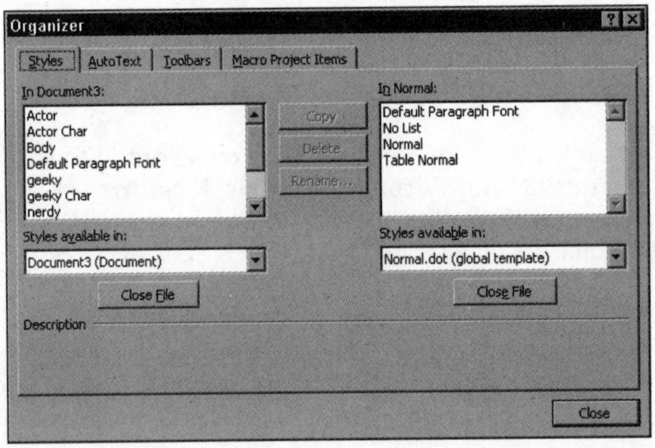

Figure 16-5:
The
Organizer
dialog box is
buried deep
within
Word's guts.

The purpose of the Organizer is to manage styles (and other things, but this chapter is on styles). You can do that by moving styles between various documents and document templates in Word.

For example, in Figure 16-5 you see on the left the styles available in your document, Document3. On the right are the styles that appear in the NORMAL.DOT document template. (NORMAL.DOT is a file that contains all Word's standard settings.)

Choose from either side of the dialog box the style you want to copy. After the style is selected, click the Copy button to copy it to the other side. That's how styles are swapped and shared between documents and templates.

To choose another document or template, click the Close File button. That button changes to the Open File button, which you can then use to open any Word document on disk. After it's open, a list of styles in that document is displayed in the window.

Click the Close button when you're done managing the styles.

 ✔ As you can see, the Organizer dialog box is also used to organize your AutoText entries, toolbars, and macros (which are an advanced topic not covered in this book). Just as with styles, you can copy AutoText entries or special toolbars from one document to another or between document templates in the Organizer dialog box.

 ✔ Also see Chapter 17 to find out just exactly what a document template is.

Chapter 17

Working with Templates

. . . .

. . . .

A *template* is a pattern you follow to create something. For example, the Department of Transportation uses these huge STOP templates that they lay down at intersections. The workers just spray paint over the template and a huge STOP appears on the roadway, hopefully near a stop sign somewhere. Hopefully, it's STOP and not POTS.

A Word template works like the big STOP template. It's basically a skeleton of a document to which you can add text (by typing, not spray painting). The template contains styles primarily, though it can also contain text and graphics and even its own toolbar. This chapter covers all that (except for the toolbar part, which is covered in Chapter 29).

Ode to the Document Template

Document templates are handy things to have. I use one for sending faxes, one for writing letters, one for writing plays, and so on. This book has its own Dummies Style template that contains all the text styles used in this book. Whenever I need to start a new chapter, I use the Dummies Style so that all the paragraph, heading, caption, and other styles match what my editor uses, which keeps her happy. I hope.

It's worth your time to create a template for every type of document you use regularly. The following sections tell you how.

✔ Unless you choose otherwise, Word uses the Normal document template, also known as NORMAL.DOT.

✔ See the section, "Understanding NORMAL.DOT," later in this chapter, for more information about NORMAL.DOT.

✔ My advice is to create your document *first* and then build the template based on the created document. Only if you're well versed with Word's formatting and style commands should you attempt to create a template from scratch. Even then, you most likely have to go back and "fix" things.

Using a Document Template

Word comes with a basketful of its own document templates, which helps you not only get an idea of how the templates can be used but also lets you take advantage of those predefined templates to quickly create common documents. To use a document template, follow these steps:

1. Summon the New Document task pane.

Word's templates are accessed through the task pane. You can summon the task pane by choosing File⇨New from the menu and then choosing the New Document item from the task pane's menu.

2. Click the General Templates item.

The Templates dialog box is displayed, as shown in Figure 17-1. This dialog box contains many panels full of templates, wizards, and whatnot. The General tab is shown in Figure 17-1 (which is where any templates you may create appear).

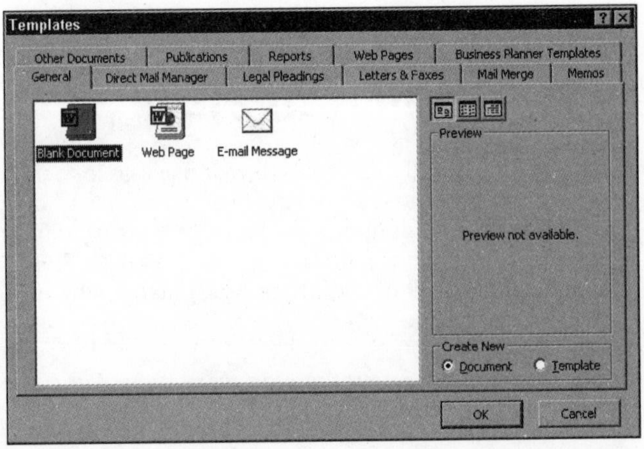

Figure 17-1: The Templates dialog box.

3. **Select a template.**

Templates are organized into categories, represented by the tabs in the dialog box. For example, click the Letters & Faxes tab. You see various templates and wizards displayed.

The *wizards* are programs that step you through the process of creating a new document.

Templates are special Word documents that contain various styles, plus maybe some text or graphics — enough to get you started. For example, the Professional Letter template in the Letters & Faxes tab has lots of fill-in-the-blank items, all in the proper position for a typical business letter.

The General tab's Blank Document template is the NORMAL.DOT template. That's the template Word uses whenever you start a new document. Boring.

4. **Click OK.**

Word starts up a new document, complete with that template's information, fonts, styles, and whatnot, all ready for use. You can take advantage of any styles stuffed into the template and view, use, or edit any text saved in the template.

✔ Opening a document with a template does not change the template; your new document is merely using the template's styles and any text it already has. Changing an existing template is covered later in this chapter.

✔ Refer to Chapter 18 for more information on wizards.

✔ Yes, Word can be used as your e-mail editor, as long as you're using Microsoft's own Outlook or Outlook Express program as your e-mail program. You can start a new e-mail message by choosing the E-mail Message template from the Templates dialog box (refer to Figure 17-1). Or, you can click the E-Mail button on the toolbar to start a new message. In this case, Word is merely being used as an e-mail *editor*. Because this is a basic word processing book, you need to refer elsewhere for information on how Outlook or Outlook Express works with Word in this manner.

✔ Some of Word's templates can also be used to create a Web page. Honestly, Word makes a lousy Web page editor. After all, if Word is such a good Web page creation tool, why does Microsoft need to develop and sell its Front Page program?

Creating Your Very Own Template

Building your own templates is easy — and useful. In the whole of word processing, you'll probably discover that you create lots of similar documents. Rather than start each one over from scratch, you need to create a new template and base your document on that template. All your styles are saved in the template, so there's no need to re-create them for the new document.

To create a template, follow these steps:

1. **Find a document to base the template on.**

   Although Word does let you create a template from scratch, it has been my experience that it's best to start with something. You can start with a document you've already created or just start creating a document.

   If you're creating a new document, all you need to put into it are the styles you plan on using, plus common text. For example, my Book template (for when I stop writing computer books and start writing "real" books) contains all the styles I need for writing books plus the word *Chapter* at the start of each page. That's because each document is a chapter and starting it with the text *Chapter* already in the template saves me valuable typing energy molecules.

   If you're using an existing document, save it to disk one last time just to be sure. Next, strip out all the text you don't want in the template. Delete all the graphics you don't want in the template. Edit the header and footer so that they contain only the items you need in the template.

   Figure 17-2 shows a sample template I created, complete with some text and graphics. Remember that the template needs to contain only the styles you need for that document, plus any text that is common to all documents. In Figure 17-2, only the text that stays the same is included; other text is added when the user opens the template to help him create a new document.

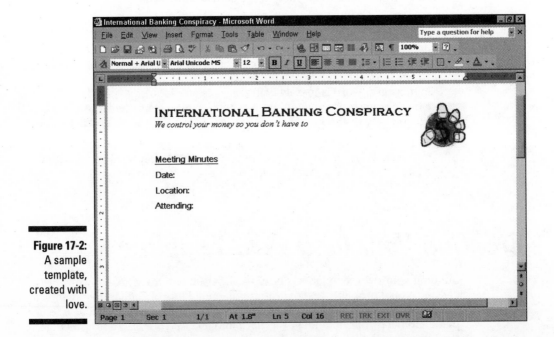

Figure 17-2:
A sample template, created with love.

2. **Choose File⇨Save As.**

The Save As dialog box appears. It's the same Save As dialog box that Word uses for saving anything. Refer to Chapter 8 if you need a refresher.

3. **Type a name for the document.**

The name goes into the File name box. Be descriptive.

You do not need to name the template using the word *template*.

4. **From the Save as type drop down list, choose** Document Template.

Ah-ha! This is the secret. The document must be saved as a Document Template. Choosing that item directs Word to save the document as a template in Word's special Templates folder. Word does all that work for you, but you must choose Document Template as the file type.

5. **Click the Save button.**

Your efforts are saved to disk as a document template, nestled in the proper place where Word keeps all its document templates.

6. **Close the template.**

Choose File⇨Close or click the X close button to close the template's window.

The reason for closing it is that any changes you make from now on are made to the template. If you want to use the template to start a new document, you need to choose that template from the Templates dialog box, as covered earlier in this chapter.

If you want to return to the template to modify it, see the next section.

Sticking the current date into a template

Any text you type into a template becomes a permanent part of that template. This situation isn't good news when you want to add the date to a template, because today's date may differ from the date you actually use on the template. Fortunately, there is a solution. Though the procedure is a bit cumbersome, the following steps enable you to set an updating date field in your template:

1. **Position the toothpick cursor where you want the date.**

2. **Choose Insert⇨Date and Time. The Date and Time dialog box appears.**

3. **Select from the Available Formats list the way you want your date to look.**

4. **Click to put a check by the Update automatically option.**

5. **Click the OK button.**

Your template now has a date field in it. (By the way, this trick works with any document, not just with templates.)

✔ Remember the purpose of a template: To store styles and often-used information in a single place.

✔ You can give a template any name, though if you choose the name of a template that already exists, Word warns you. This is standard file-saving stuff; just choose another name and be on your merry way.

Modifying a Document Template

Changing or editing a document template is identical to changing or editing any document. The difference is that you open a template rather than a document. It's a minor difference, but a big deal because templates, after all, are not really documents:

1. **Open the template by choosing <u>F</u>ile⇨<u>O</u>pen.**

   Yes, this is the normal Open command, and it displays Word's famous Open dialog box. Nothing new yet.

2. **In the Open dialog box, choose Document Templates from the Files of type drop-down list.**

   You would assume that Word would be smart enough to automatically zoom to the Templates folder, just as it did when you first saved the template. But, no. Word is stupid here. You must manually venture out to the Templates folder — or whichever folder you've saved the template to.

3. **Find the Templates folder.**

   Unless you've put the template somewhere else, you need to go to the Templates folder. Here's how:

   a. Choose drive C from the Look <u>i</u>n drop-down list.

   b. Open the WINDOWS folder.

   c. Open the Application Data folder.

   d. Open the Microsoft folder.

   e. Open the Templates folder.

   f. Open a beer.

4. **Open the template you want to edit.**

   Double-click its filename.

   When you open the template, it appears in Word just like any other document — though it's really a template. (Sneaky.)

5. **Make your changes.**

   You edit the template just as you would any other document. Bear in mind that it's a template you're editing and not a real document. Any style changes or text editing affect the template and are saved to disk as a template again.

6. **Save the modified template by choosing File⇨Save.**

   Or, choose File⇨Save As to assign the modified template a new name and maintain the original template.

7. **Close the template document by choosing File⇨Close.**

Any changes you make to a document template do not affect any documents already created with that template. The changes do, however, affect any new documents you create.

Understanding NORMAL.DOT

The Normal template is a special beast. Referred to as NORMAL.DOT (its old MS-DOS filename), the Normal template is where Word contains all the settings made for any new document you create with the Ctrl+N shortcut or by clicking the New button on the toolbar.

NORMAL.DOT appears in the New dialog box (refer to Figure 17-1) as the Blank Document template.

Knowing about NORMAL.DOT is important because you can change the Normal template if you want. For example, if you want to change the standard font and size (and whatever other formatting) Word uses when it opens a new document, simply make those changes to NORMAL.DOT. Change the font and margins for the Normal style. Then save NORMAL.DOT back to disk. That's it.

✔ Refer to the section "Modifying a Document Template," earlier in this chapter, for more information on how to find and change NORMAL.DOT.

✔ If you just want to change the default font, see the Chapter 11 sidebar "Changing the default font."

Attaching a Template to a Document

Documents have templates like people have last names. Mostly, the documents are born with their templates. You either choose the template from the Templates dialog box (refer to Figure 17-1) or just create a new document, in which case the NORMAL.DOT template is used. But what if you want to change templates?

You can't really change templates as much as you can reassign or *attach* a new template to a document. Here's how:

1. **Choose Tools➪Templates and Add-Ins.**

   The Templates and Add-ins dialog box appears, as shown in Figure 17-3.

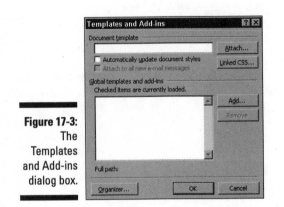

Figure 17-3:
The
Templates
and Add-ins
dialog box.

2. **Click the Attach button.**

   Word displays the Attach Template dialog box, which looks much like the Open dialog box, so I need not show an illustration of it here. Normally, this dialog box opens in the Templates folder, where you've probably stored a host of templates available for the plucking.

3. **Select the template you want to attach.**

   If the template isn't visible in the Attach Template dialog box, use the dialog box to browse to the folder containing the template.

4. **Click the Open button.**

5. **Click OK.**

   The styles (and toolbars and macros) stored in that template are now available to your document.

Note that attaching a template does not merge any text or graphics stored in that template. Only the styles (and toolbar and macros) are merged into your document.

Chapter 18

Formatting and Spiffing-Up Tricks

· ·

In This Chapter

▶ Reviewing your document's formats

▶ Playing with fields

▶ Using color text

▶ Centering a page on the up-and-down

▶ Having fun with click-and-type

▶ Borrowing a cup o' formatting

▶ Using the various AutoFormat commands and tricks

▶ Using Word's wizards

· ·

Nothing perks up a yawning document like some highly caffeinated formatting. This part of the book is dedicated to the formatting task, including the benefit of creating styles and using templates to make the job easier. Now it's time for some fun.

This chapter contains tips and tricks designed to make your formatting chores easier. The sections in this chapter are a grab bag of useful tidbits I've collected in my many years as a Word user. Some of these techniques may not appear useful to you right now, so flag this chapter for later consumption, when you're ready to absorb the knowledge nuggets that follow.

What's Going On with This Formatting!?

Ah, the mystery format! You're scanning through your latest masterpiece when you notice — right there, mocking you — a paragraph that doesn't seem to fit. Something's amiss with the formatting, but what? To see what's going on with a chunk of text, you could try to lodge the toothpick cursor in that paragraph and then select various formatting commands until you discover which way is up. Needless to say, this is an awkward way to discover your document's formatting.

A nifty trick to pull on any mystery part of your document is to press the Shift+F1 key combination. The mouse pointer changes to look like an arrow–question mark (see the margin).

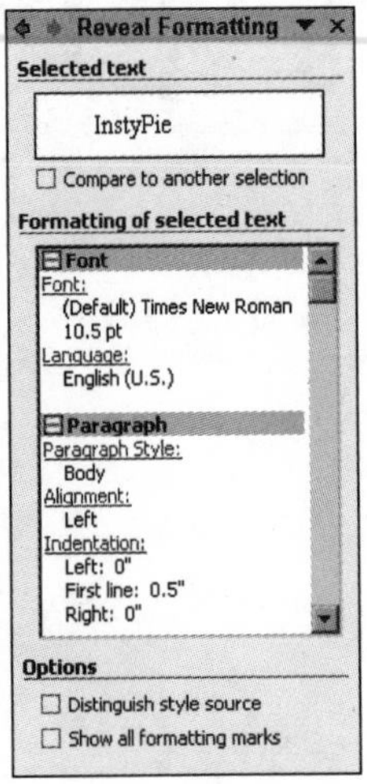

Figure 18-1:
Press
Shift+F1 and
click in your
text to see
what's up
with
formatting.

Now click any character in any word in any paragraph. Word describes exactly what the heck is going on with the formatting in the Reveal Formatting task pane, as shown in Figure 18-1.

You can continue to click text to check its formatting as long as you like. Close the task pane window when you're done.

✔ You can use the formatting summary to see what needs fixing or just to see how the formatting was done.

✔ The Shift+F1 key activates Word's point-and-shoot help. Click anything in Word's window to see help on that item.

Let Word Do the Work for You

Word can do many things for you, things that some users may do in other, less efficient ways. To help you with formatting chores, I've gathered tips on stuff that Word can make short work of. These are things many Word users may toil with in awkward ways. Why bother? Word can do it for you!

The joys of updating fields

A *field* is a special chunk of text you insert into your document. That chunk looks like real text, but what it really does is display special information: the current page or date, your name, and other stuff that may change. For example, Chapter 17 tells the story of how to stick an updating date field into a template. You can do similar tricks with other fields, and not just in templates but in any document you create.

The secret is the Insert⇨Field command. It displays the Field dialog box, as shown in Figure 18-2. The left side of the dialog box contains a scrolling list of fields (and there are quite a few); the right side of the dialog box changes, depending on which field you select in the list.

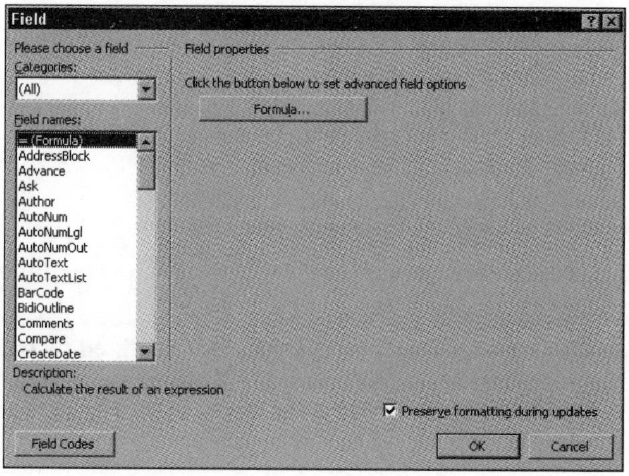

Figure 18-2:
The Field
dialog box.

For example, choose the Author field. Click OK. This technique sticks your name, or the name of the person or entity who registered Word, into your document. You see the author's name, but with a gray background:

```
Dan Gookin
```

The gray background is your clue that you've inserted a field and are not dealing with text directly.

- ✔ To see what's up with a certain field, click on that field name in the Field dialog box and refer to the Description area just below the scrolling list.

- ✔ One of the best fields you can use is the automatic page-numbering field. Unlike using the Insert⇨Page Numbers command, this field can be placed anywhere in your document. Choose Page from the Field names list to stick the current page number anywhere in your document.

✔ I also use the `PrintDate` field quite a bit. That way, the document prints with the current date.

✔ See Chapter 14 for information on sticking the page number in a more traditional spot in your document.

✔ Chapter 15 covers putting page numbers in a header or footer.

✔ You cannot edit text in a field. You can only delete it: Do so by selecting the entire field as a block and then pressing the Delete key.

Color your text

The easiest way to write more colorful prose is to color your text. In Word, color is a text formatting attribute just like bold, italics, or super big. Teenage girls can write in pink and bankers in green, and you can type angry letters to the editor in red.

To change text color, select the text as a block and then click the down arrow by the Font Color tool on the toolbar (see the margin). Clicking the down arrow displays a palette of colors. Choose a color, and your text takes on that color.

✔ Unless you have a color printer, don't expect your text to print in color.

✔ To remove colored text, select it as a block and choose Automatic from the Font Color tool's palette.

✔ The Automatic color is whichever text color is defined by the current style. For the Normal style, it's black. But if you're using a special style where the text color is fawn white, for example, choosing Automatic for the text color changes it back to fawn white.

✔ Colored text is much easier to find on the screen. For example, when I write, I color text purple if I plan on returning later to update it or if I need to check it again later. That makes the text easier to find when I'm reading or reviewing the document.

✔ If the Font Color tool already shows the color you want to paint your text, just click the tool to change the text color.

Don't forget these tricks!

Here are a few of the formatting tricks I mention in other parts of the book — this is the stuff I want to really drive home:

✔ Always use Ctrl+Enter to start a new page.

✔ Use tabs to line up your text. Never use spaces. One tab is all you need. If you're typing more than one tab, you need to reset the tab stops. See Chapter 13.

✔ Always use one tab between columns to line them up. That makes editing the information easier if you have to do it.

✔ If you need to change any page formatting in the middle of your document, you need to start a new section. See Chapter 15.

✔ Save your styles in a template! That way, you can use them for new documents you create without having to rebuild all your styles over and over. See Chapters 16 and 17.

✔ You can quickly undo any character formatting with the Ctrl+Spacebar key combination.

Centering a Page, Top to Bottom

Nothing makes a document title nice and crisp like having it sit squat in the center of a page. The title is centered left-to-right, which you can do by selecting Center alignment for the title's paragraph. But how about centering the title top-to-bottom? Word can do that too:

1. **Move the toothpick cursor to the start of your document.**

   The Ctrl+Home key combination moves you there instantly.

2. **Type and format your document's title.**

   It can be on a single line or on several lines.

   To center the title, select it and press Ctrl+E, the Center keyboard shortcut. Apply any additional font or paragraph formatting as necessary.

   Avoid the temptation to use the Enter key to add space above or below your title. Right now, the title sits by itself at the top of the page. That will be fixed in a jiffy.

3. **After the last line, choose Insert⇨Break.**

   The Break dialog box appears.

4. **Select the Next Page.**

   This step does two things. First, it creates a page break. Second, it creates a new section. That way, the page-centering command affects only the first section, which is the first page of the document.

5. **Click OK.**

   The new section appears on the screen.

6. **Move the toothpick cursor back to the title page.**

   You need to put the toothpick cursor on the page you want to format.

7. **Choose the File⇨Page Setup command.**

   The Page Setup dialog box appears.

8. **Click the Layout tab.**

9. **Choose** Center **from the** Vertical Alignment **drop-down list.**

    You can find this item in the bottom half of the dialog box.

10. **Click OK.**

 You may or may not see visual evidence onscreen that you centered a page. To be sure, click the Print Preview tool on the toolbar and, yes, you're a confirmed page centerer.

Click the Close button to return to your document from the Preview window.

Splash Around with Click-and-Type

The stereotype of the mad modern artist is of a person wearing a beret and standing before a huge, blank canvas with a bucket of paint. "Toss a little here," they say, throwing paint up in the corner. Then they get another bucket. "Toss it here," they say as they toss more paint in the middle. And so on. Soon they're charging $500,000 for their masterpiece and being feted by rich-yet-gullible Upper East Side leftist wannabes. But I digress.

You get a chance to be your own mad artist with Word's amusing and sometimes useful click-and-type feature. Like throwing paint on a canvas, click-and-type lets you splash text around your document wherever you want it — almost. Formatting rules be damned!

To use click-and-type, your document must be viewed in Print Layout view. Choose View➪Print Layout from the menu if none of this technique appears to work. Also, it helps to start on a blank page.

As you move the mouse pointer around the blank page, the cursor changes. The different cursor types tell you how text "splashed" on that part of the page is formatted.

Double-click with this type of pointer and you get an indented paragraph, left aligned on the page.

Double-click with this type of pointer to set a left-aligned paragraph. The paragraph is set on the page wherever you double-click.

Double-clicking in your document with this pointer creates a center-aligned paragraph at that very spot.

Double-clicking with this pointer sets Word up to do (can you guess?) a right-aligned paragraph. Wow.

✔ I prefer *not* to use click-and-type, primarily because I know all the other formatting commands. If you grow to understand and use click-and-type, more power to you. But for true control, the other formatting commands mentioned in this part of the book beat click-and-type hands down.

✔ If you really are splashing and dashing with click-and-type, consider changing the zoom level for your document, zooming out to make the whole thing easier to see. See Chapter 29.

Formatting Theft

Speaking of mad painters, the paintbrush tool on the Standard toolbar can be used to *paint* character styles, copying them from one bit of text to another in your document. Here's how:

1. **Jab the toothpick cursor in the middle of the text that has the formatting you want to copy.**

   The toothpick cursor must be in the midst of the word, not to the left or right (but it doesn't have to be in the exact middle, just "in the word"). If it's not, this trick won't work.

2. **Click the Format Painter button on the Standard toolbar.**

   You may need to rearrange the toolbars to see the Format Painter. See Chapter 29.

   The cursor changes to a paintbrush/I-beam pointer, as depicted in the margin. This special cursor is used to highlight and then reformat text in your document.

3. **Hunt for the text you want to change.**

4. **Highlight the text.**

   Click and drag the mouse over the text you want to change — "paint" it. (You must use the mouse here.)

   Voilà! The text is changed.

Mad modern artists can also make use of the following tips and tidbits:

✔ The Format Painter works only with character and paragraph formatting, not with page formatting.

✔ To change the formatting of multiple bits of text, double-click the Format Painter. That way, the format painter cursor stays active, ready to paint lots of text. Press the Esc key to cancel your Dutch Boy frenzy.

✔ If you tire of the mouse, you can use the Ctrl+Shift+C key command to copy the character format from a highlighted block to another location in your document. Use the Ctrl+Shift+V key combination to paste the character format elsewhere. Just highlight the text in your document and press Ctrl+Shift+V to paste in the font formatting.

✔ You can sorta kinda remember Ctrl+Shift+C to copy character formatting and Ctrl+Shift+V to paste because Ctrl+C and Ctrl+V are the copy and paste shortcut keys. Sorta kinda.

✔ Don't confuse the Format Painter with the highlighting tool, which is described in Chapter 27.

Using AutoFormat

Word's AutoFormat command has absolutely nothing to do with formatting in the sense of font or paragraph formatting. No, what AutoFormat really does is clean up your document, remove excess spaces, add spaces where needed, apply Heading formats to what it thinks are your document's headings, and other minor housekeeping chores. Yes, it removes the slop most of us add to our documents without thinking about it.

Before AutoFormat can do its job, you need to create the document's text. Write! Write! Write! Write your letter, memo, chapter, poem, whatever. Then follow these steps:

1. **Save your document to disk.**

   This step is most important, and saving your document is something you should be doing all the time anyway. So, save your file one more time before you use AutoFormat. Refer to Chapter 8 for details on saving documents.

2. **Choose Format⇨AutoFormat.**

   You may have to click the "show more" arrows at the bottom of the menu to find the AutoFormat command. The AutoFormat dialog box appears, as shown in Figure 18-3.

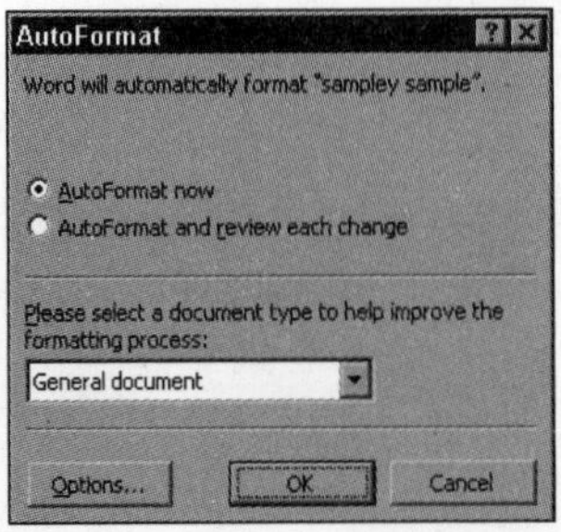

Figure 18-3:
The
AutoFormat
dialog box.

AutoFormat

Word will automatically format "sampley sample".

○ AutoFormat now
○ AutoFormat and review each change

Please select a document type to help improve the formatting process:

General document

Options...   OK   Cancel

3. Click OK.

Ook! Eep! Ack!

4. Formatting completed.

Word has carefully massaged and adjusted your document. You may find new headings, bulleted lists, and other amazing, whiz-bang things automatically done to your text.

Hey! AutoFormat created a list of helpful bullets right here in this text:

- If you like, you can choose AutoFormat and review each change option in the AutoFormat dialog box to see exactly what needs to be done before AutoFormat does its job.

- If your text is kinda boring, it doesn't appear as though AutoFormat did anything. Don't despair. AutoFormat is good at creating headings and bulleted lists, but it can't read your mind.

- You can always use the Undo command if you detest what AutoFormat did to your document. (Alas, there is no Detest command.)

- If you're interested in formatting your document automatically, refer to the section on wizards, later in this chapter.

Automatic Formatting As It Happens

Sometimes, Word can be so smart that it's scary. A long time ago, just having a program remind you to save before you quit was thought to be miraculous. But now . . . why, just the other day Word reminded me that I forgot to floss the night before and, boy, though that blackberry cobbler looked tempting, I am several stones over my ideal weight. Scary stuff.

Making the automatic formatting thing happen as you work

You must direct Word to be smart. The program cannot do it on its own. To take advantage of the many automagical things Word can do, follow these steps:

1. Choose Format⇨AutoFormat.

The AutoFormat dialog box exposes itself on the screen.

2. Click the Options button.

The AutoCorrect/AutoFormat dialog box appears, as shown in Figure 18-4.

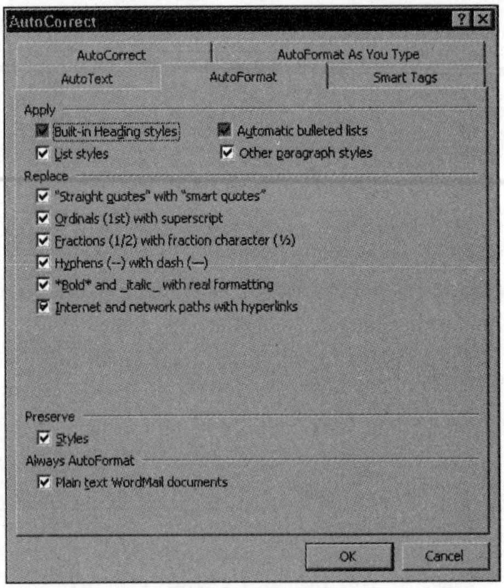

Figure 18-4:
The
AutoCorrect
dialog box.

3. **Because you don't know what the options do, check them all.**

   Hey! They *are* already all checked! Word comes out of the box with the AutoFormat options checked. If they're not checked, most likely someone has configured Word to work differently. Whatever. Make sure that all the options are selected and click to check any that aren't checked.

4. **Click OK and then click OK again.**

   Close both the dialog boxes you left hanging open. Now you're ready to start playing, beginning in the next section.

Automatic numbered lists

The best way to understand the AutoFormat-as-you-type adventure is to *live* it. Heed the following steps:

1. **Start a new document in Word.**

   The simplest way to do that is to press the Ctrl+N key combination. No messing around here.

2. **Type the following line:**

   ```
   Things to do today:
   ```

   Press the Enter key to start a new line. Then type

   ```
   1. Sell kidneys.
   ```

Now — prepare yourself — press the Enter key to end that line. You see something like Figure 18-5 on your screen.

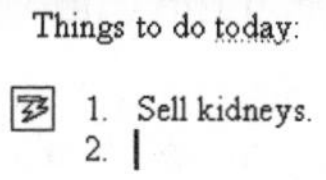

Figure 18-5:
Word
automatically
numbers a
list for you.

Things to do today:

1. Sell kidneys.
2. |

Not only does Word automatically give you a 2, but it also reformats the preceding line as indented text. Amazing. Stupendous.

3. Keep typing if you're pleased.

To stop the list from automatically numbering everything else in your document (all the way up to "Happily ever after"), press the Enter key twice.

If you're pleased, you can continue. Otherwise, if you're deeply unsatisfied, you can use the AutoCorrect Options icon floating near the freshly formatted text. If you point the mouse at that icon, it turns into a button you can click. If you click the button, a menu is displayed, as shown in Figure 18-6.

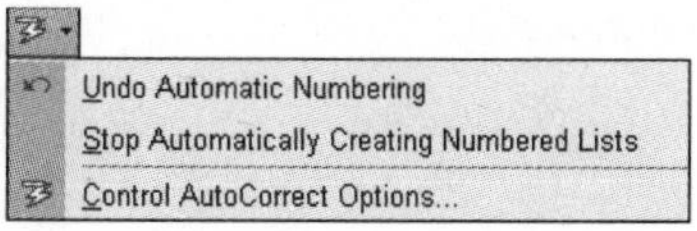

Figure 18-6:
Controlling
the
AutoFormat
options as
you type.

Undo Automatic Numbering
Stop Automatically Creating Numbered Lists
Control AutoCorrect Options...

Choose Undo Automatic Numbering if you would rather not number the list or would just like to do it yourself. This tells Word "Never mind!"

Choose Stop Automatically Creating Number Lists to permanently turn this option off. (You can turn it back on from the AutoCorrect/AutoFormat dialog box, as shown earlier in this chapter, in Figure 18-4).

The Control AutoCorrect Options item displays the AutoCorrect/AutoFormat dialog box.

Or, you can press the Esc key and continue typing your list.

> ✔ This trick also works for letters (and Roman numerals, too). Just start something with a letter and a period and Word picks up at the next line with the next letter in the alphabet and another period.
>
> ✔ You can also undo an AutoFormatted list by using the Undo command.
>
> ✔ I know that I've said earlier in this book not to press the Enter key twice to end a paragraph. Okay, I lied. You don't really have to press the Enter key twice to stop an automatic-formatting trick. You can press Enter and then Backspace. But Enter-Enter works just as well.

Automatic borders

In the old Smith-Corona days of yore, we would fancy up our documents by woodpeckering a line of hyphens, underlines, or equal signs. It brings back kind of a sentimental tear to the eye, especially for me, because I pressed the keys so hard that ripping the paper out of the typewriter often ripped the paper in two. Not with a word processor, though.

If you want a single-line border, from right margin to left across your page, type three hyphens and press the Enter key:

Word instantly transmutes the three little hyphens into a solid line.

Want a double line? Then use three equal signs:

Press the Enter key and Word draws a double line from one edge of the screen to the next.

Bolder line? Use three underlines:

As usual, the AutoCorrect Options icon appears, letting you change your mind or switch this option off. Also remember that you can press Ctrl+Z to undo this if, indeed, all you really want are three equal signs in a row.

Chickening Out and Using a Wizard

You're off to see the Wizard, the wonderful Wizard of Word. . . .

A *wizard* enables you to create a near-perfect document automatically. All you need to do is select various options and make adjustments from a handy and informative dialog box. Word does the rest of the work. This is so easy that it should be a sin.

To use a Word wizard, follow these steps:

1. **Choose File⇨New.**

   This command opens the New Document task pane.

2. **Click General Templates.**

   The Templates dialog box is displayed (refer to Figure 17-1, over in Chapter 17).

3. **Select a wizard.**

   A number of wizards come prepackaged with Word. Of course, none of them lives on the General panel. To find a wizard, click another tab, such as the Memo tab.

    Wizards live along with templates, though the wizards have the word *wizard* in their name and they sport a unique icon (see the margin). The Memos tab holds only the Memo wizard. (Other tabs have other wizards, which you can explore on your own.)

   Select the wizard by clicking it with your mouse. If you're lucky, a preview appears on the right side of the dialog box. How nice.

4. **Click OK.**

   Word hums and churns for a few minutes. It's thinking — no doubt a painful process. Give it time.

5. **Optionally, be enlightened by the Wizard dialog box.**

   The more advanced wizards quiz you, giving you a dialog box with a bunch of questions for you to answer. The wizard uses your answers to help create your document.

   Some wizards merely create a blank document for you to complete. Just fill in the sections that say something like {type the recipient's name here} with the proper information and you're on your way.

✔ Wizard. Wizard. Wizard. It's one of those words that gets weirder and weirder the more you say it.

✔ Even though a wizard created your document, you still must save it to disk after you're done. In fact, most wizards may just start you on your way. After that point, you work with the document just like any other in Word. Don't forget to save!

- ✔ Word has a special wizard menu item: <u>T</u>ools➪L<u>e</u>tters and Mailings➪ Letter Wi<u>z</u>ard. If you choose this command, follow your Office Assistant's advice and answer the various questions in the dialog box.

- ✔ Some wizards even fill in text for you. These are super-cheating wizards. The Stephen King wizard, for example, writes his books for him in less than a day.

Part III
Sprucing Up Your Document

The 5th Wave By Rich Tennant

"You want to know why I'm mad? I suggest you download my latest novel called, 'Why an Obsessive Control-Freak Husband Should Never Pick Out Bathroom Tile Without Asking His Wife First'."

In this part . . .

As the chapter numbers in this book get higher, the further away from basic word processing the subject drifts. Honestly, Part I is all about basic word processing, or, to be specific, text editing. Part II is about formatting, which is considered a must-have aspect of word processing. This part? Part III? Now the subject matter moves into an area traditionally dominated by desktop publishing programs. You have graphics, tables, lines, artwork, columns, lists, objects, and a whole salad bar of strange stuff, all of which Word can handle, but most of which is traditionally considered the domain of desktop publishing.

In a way, if I fancied myself a marketing person for Microsoft, I would consider changing Word's product name to Microsoft Idea rather than Microsoft Word. This program does a whole lot of things — some truly outrageous — most of which are well beyond the traditional role of a word processor. No, with all the junk they throw in, it's really about creating and expressing ideas more than just tossing words around. The chapters in this part tell you more.

Chapter 19

Borders, Boxes, and Shading

• •

In This Chapter

 Drawing a box around your text

 Boxing in a whole page

 Putting less than a box around your text

 Shading your text

 Printing white on black

• •

*T*here is a warm, fuzzy border between word processing and desktop publishing. Traditionally, word processors dealt with words and added some formatting to make things less ugly. Desktop publishing brought in graphics and design elements beyond the power of most word processors. Today, the distinction between the two isn't so clearly drawn.

As an example, ten years ago, being able to draw a box around your text was considered too advanced for a mere word processor. Ah, but Word is no mere word processor. This chapter covers the box-drawing topic, along with shading your text and adding pretty borders to everything.

Boxing Your Text

I surprised my wife when I told her that I actually took dancing lessons once. She wasn't so surprised when she found out I took only *one* dancing lesson and then quit. But I do remember some things.

I remember that the teacher said that anyone who walks heel-to-toe is able to dance. She also taught us the box step:

Step

There. Nothing to it. Heel-toe, no problem.

The following sections tell you how to box anything in your document, from mere words to paragraphs to full pages o' text.

Boxing in small bits of text or paragraphs

Word allows you to stick a box around any bit of text or paragraph in your document. For example, you can box in a title or draw a box around an "aside" paragraph or sidebar or put a box around a single word. No matter — whatever you're boxing up, follow these steps:

1. Choose the text you want to box.

It's best to select the text you want to put into a box: a word, a few words, several paragraphs, or an entire page.

If nothing is selected as a block, Word boxes in the paragraph the tooth-pick cursor is blinking in.

2. Choose the Format➪Borders and Shading command.

The Borders and Shading dialog box opens. Make sure that the Borders tab is chosen, as shown in Figure 19-1. (If not, click that tab with the mouse.)

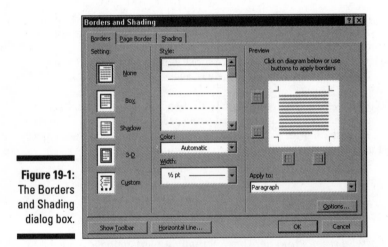

Figure 19-1:
The Borders
and Shading
dialog box.

3. Select the type of border you want from the Setting column.

Four preset, easy-to-use, pop-n-fresh border styles are available; don't bother with the Custom style until you fully figure this out. Just click the style of paragraph border you want. My favorite is Shadow.

Optionally, you can choose a line style from the Style list.

The Color drop-down list sets the border color. (The Automatic color is black or whichever text color is defined by the style.)

The Width drop-down list sets the line width.

Observe the Preview window to see how the border affects your text.

4. **Choose Text or Paragraph from the Apply To list.**

   Word is unusually smart with this step. If you select only one word or any bit of text less than a paragraph, Word assumes that you want to box in only that text. Even so, you can choose Paragraph or Text from the list.

5. **Click OK.**

   Your text now has a box around it.

Putting a border around pages of text

You can not only rope titles and paragraphs but also put a border around each page in your document. That may sound hokey, but if you're making a newsletter or award or something cheesy like that, the border can come in handy.

To stick a border around your document, choose Format⇨Borders and Shading and then click the Page Border tab. I'm not including a figure here because this panel looks and operates just like the Borders panel; see the preceding section for more information.

Fixing a page border that doesn't wrap around the entire page

Sometimes, for some unknown reason (probably because Word hates you), the page border doesn't wrap around the entire page. Actually, the problem has to do with your printer. I think. Well, whatever. There is a way to make a border wrap around all your text on the page, despite what Word thinks of you.

The solution lies in the Options button in the Border and Shading dialog box. Click that button to display yet another dialog box. Locate the Measure from drop-down list and choose Text from that list. Click OK to close the Options dialog box. Click OK to close the Border and Shading dialog box. Your border shall now appear!

The only difference you find on the Page Border panel is the Apply To drop-down list, in the lower-right corner. Before you click OK, you need to tell Word which parts of your document need a page border. Then click OK.

- ✔ Select Whole Document from the Apply To list to have a border on every page.

- ✔ Other options on the Apply To list deal with sections in your document. For example, if you want to border only one page out of many, you need to make that page its own section. Refer to Chapter 15 for more information on creating a section break in your document.

Making partial boxes

Borders don't have to be boxes. In Figure 19-2, the newsletter's title is created with only top and bottom borders. This too can be done in the Borders and Shading dialog box:

Figure 19-2:
Top and bottom borders in a newsletter heading.

ALIEN WATCH

They've landed!   *No one is safe!*   *We're doomed!*

They're breeding us for food!   Beware of lentils!
3 out of 10 elementary school teachers are aliens!   They run the government!
Could the next knock on your door be an alien—with a pod???   We survived Y2K, now this?

Vol. 4, Area 51   **December 1, 2001**

1. **Keep your eye on the Preview window.**

   This window is where you can preview how your boxing-in skills work.

2. **Choose None from the Setting list.**

   It's best to start with no lines anywhere.

3. **Select a line style from the Style list.**

   You can choose from several styles and double- or single-line patterns, some of which are shown in Figure 19-2.

   You can also mess with the Color and Width doohickeys if you feel like it. Oh, play, play, play. What's the point in doing any work?

4. **Click on the top button in the Preview part of the dialog box.**

   This step tells Word to put the line above your text. You can also click above the "text" in the Preview window to place a line there.

The Bottom, Left, and Right buttons around the Preview window can also be used to place lines on specific sides of the text.

5. **Stick another line on the bottom of your text.**

   Choose a line style and then click the bottom button.

6. **Click OK after you finish lining in your text.**

   The box is now missing two sides, so it's really not much of a box at all and will probably spill all its contents if you tip the page the wrong way, so be careful.

Using the Border Button on the Toolbar

If you ever need to slap down a quickie border on your paragraph (or in a table), you can take advantage of the Border button on the toolbar and its handy palette o' options.

Just click the down arrow by the button, and you see a selection of line positions — top, bottom, outside, and so on (see Figure 19-3). Pick one from the list and whichever paragraph the toothpick cursor is on, or whatever text is selected, it grows that line.

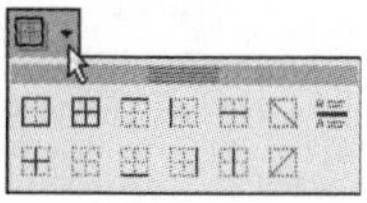

Figure 19-3: A palette of borders, courtesy of the Border button.

✔ The palette only sets the border's position. The border line style is whatever has been previously selected in the Borders and Shading dialog box.

✔ So, if you don't like the line style, choose Format➪Borders and Shading from the menu to change it.

✔ To remove all borders from a paragraph, click the Border button on the toolbar and click the No Border button.

✔ The Border button on the toolbar affects only text, not the entire page. For that, see "Putting a border around pages of text," earlier in this chapter.

Giving Your Text Some Shade

The neatest Border dialog box effect of them all is shading. You can shade words, sentences, paragraphs — any block of text — and weird parts of your document, like a title, as Figure 19-4 shows. You can shade in gray, color, and patterns with or without a border around it. It's a veritable smorgasbord of scribbles to junk up your text with. Heed these steps:

Figure 19-4:
A sample bit
o' text with a
border and
shading.

Golem Films Presents
Maude Just Wants Her Pills

A New Level in Terror

Brought to you by the people who produced last year's smash, "Acid Drool"

1. **Mark your text or title as a block.**

   Refer to Chapter 6 for efficient block-marking instructions.

   If you want the shaded area to cover more than the title line, highlight the lines before and after the title. That creates a "buffer" of shading around the text.

2. **Choose Format⇨Borders and Shading.**

   The Paragraph Borders and Shading dialog box appears, but. . . .

3. **Make sure that the Shading panel is up front.**

   If it's not, click the Shading tab with your mouse. The Shading panel jumps to the front, as shown in Figure 19-5.

4. **Select a shade from the Fill palette.**

   The first three rows of the palette (below the No Fill choice) give you shading options for your text in percentages of black, from white to all black in various increments. Then comes the rainbow of colors and, naturally, the More Colors button, which displays a whole palette of zillions of colors, some visible only to certain mollusks, from which you can choose.

   The best values to select for shading your text are gray. I'm fond of the 20 percent gray value because it prints nicely without wiping out the text.

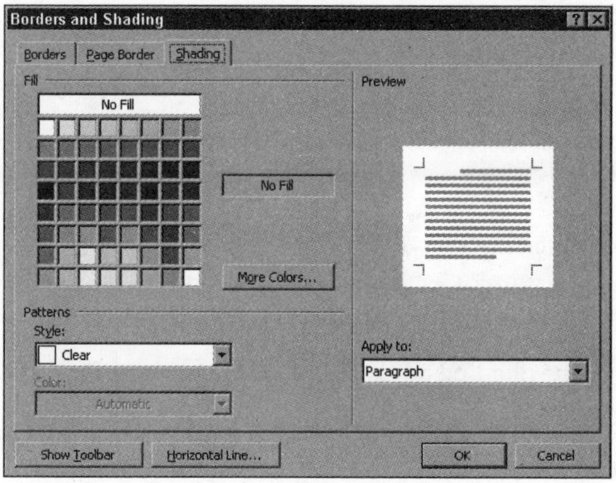

Figure 19-5:
The Shading
part of the
Borders and
Shading
dialog box.

Try to avoid using the patterns. Though some of them may look like gray-fills, they are really ugly. I suppose that someone somewhere may find them useful, but for shading text, they're probably not what you need.

5. Click OK.

Your text appears shaded onscreen. Everyone will wonder how you did it.

✔ Nope, just because you visited the Border dialog box doesn't mean that you have to put a border around your text.

✔ You can't print color shading unless your printer can print in color. Duh.

✔ If the shading stinks (and we're all allowed a little latitude for screwing up here), you can remove it. Just follow the steps I just outlined, but select None instead in the Shading panel in Step 4. Oh, and you can always use Ctrl+Z, the Undo command, to chicken out of anything.

✔ Shaded titles look best when they're at the top of your first page — not on a page by themselves.

Creating That Shocking White-on-Black Text

After shading, the next most-fun thing to do is print white text on a black background. This procedure is a very bold move and stands out prominently in your text — like being hit in the face with a cinder block. So don't use this technique casually.

This line for head transplant patients only.

To produce white-on-black text, you must do two things. First, you must create a black background; second, you must create white-colored text. Here is how you create a black background:

1. **Mark your text as a block.**

   It's best to start with text you've already written. At some point here, you will have black text on a black background, which you cannot see. If you already have the text written, it's easier to see after you're done. (See Chapter 6 for block-marking instructions.)

2. **Choose Format⇨Borders and Shading.**

   Ensure that the Shading tab is selected, as shown in Figure 19-5.

3. **Click the black square in the Fill area.**

   That's the first square in the fourth column; you can see the word Black in the box to the right of the color grid.

4. **Click OK to exit the Borders and Shading dialog box.**

Now you don't see anything onscreen because you have black text on a black background. (Actually, with the block highlighted, you see what looks like a large white block floating over a black block. Don't freak!)

With the block of text still highlighted, you need to change the text color to white. This step is done by using the Text color tool on the formatting toolbar.

1. **Click the Font Color tool on the toolbar.**

   A drop-down palette appears.

2. **Choose White.**

   It's the last square in the palette, to the lower right. (If you point the mouse at the square long enough, a bubble with the word *White* appears.) Click that square to color your text white.

   You can now unhighlight your block. The text appears onscreen and printed in white letters on a black background.

   ✔ Word is (actually) smart about displaying white-on-black text, especially when that text is selected. You never "lose" the text on the screen.

   ✔ I don't recommend reversing vast stretches of text. White text on a black background prints poorly on most computer printers. This stuff is best used for titles or to highlight smaller blocks of text.

   ✔ If you have trouble printing the white-on-black text, you may need to modify your printer settings. In the Print dialog box, click the Properties button. If your Printer Properties dialog box has a Graphics tab, click it. Choose the proper option to ensure that your printer prints in graphics mode. Then click OK to close the Printer Properties dialog box.

Chapter 20

Building Tables

*H*ow would you make a table? Armed with the proper power tools, safety equipment, instructions, and enough wood, sure, you could do it. Maybe you could carve the table from a solid cube of maple. Or maybe you're not Martha Stewart and you opt to buy your table at a hardware store unassembled or unpainted or — what the heck — break down and buy it at a furniture store, all ready to go. Chairs, too. But then there's Word, where making a table is as easy as dragging your mouse. Won't that make Martha jealous!

Word doesn't just have a Table command. No, it has a whole Table *menu* full of commands, settings, and controls for creating very nifty, handy, and neat tables in your document. No skills are needed, no confusing instructions written in Chinglish, and no need to scour the brambles for sticks or driftwood. Look! Up on the menu! It's Table Man, Ma, and he's here to rescue us!

Why Use Tables?

And so the debate rages: Should you stick information into a table or just use a bunch of tabs to line things up?

Okay, it's not a debate. It's probably nothing you've ever thought about, but it's ponderable.

If you have short bits of text you need to align in columns, use tabs:

Husband	Reason for Divorce
Brad	Drinking
Alex	Roger
Roger	Still married

This type of table works great for simple or brief lists. But when you have larger bits of text, you need to create an official table in Word. This chapter tells you how to go about that.

- ✔ Use a table whenever you have information that can be organized into rows and columns.

- ✔ Each cubbyhole in a table is called a *cell.* Into the cell, Word lets you put text (any amount) or graphics.

- ✔ Cells can have their own margins, text, and paragraph formats. You can even stick graphics into cells.

- ✔ Unlike working with tabs, Word's tables can be resized and rearranged to fit your data. In other words, if you plan on modifying the information later, it's best to use a table as opposed to a brief list formatted with tabs.

- ✔ Alas, Word does not have a handy Chair command (although rumor has it that Microsoft is working on barstools).

Splash Me Down a Table

Tables are "drawn" into your document using the handy Table and Borders button. Basically, you draw the table first and then fill in the rows and columns later. And it doesn't matter whether text is already in your document; drawing the table moves any existing text out of the way to make room for the table.

To splash down a table in the middle of your document, follow these steps:

1. Click the Tables and Borders button.

 After you click the button (shown in the margin), the Tables and Borders tool palette appears, floating over your text. See Figure 20-1. This palette contains buttons for building tables as well as options from the Borders and Shading dialog box (refer to Chapter 19).

Figure 20-1:
The Tables
and Borders
palette.

If you weren't previously in Print Layout view, Word switches you there automatically. (You cannot splash down tables in Normal view.)

2. **Ensure that the Draw Table button is "on" in the Tables and Borders palette.**

   The Draw Table button should be active (looking like it's selected), unless you've done something else between this step and the preceding step (which would have been naughty of you). If the Draw Table button isn't on, click it.

   The mouse pointer changes to a pencil, which I call the *pencil pointer*.

3. **Drag the mouse to "draw" the table's outline in your document.**

   Start in the upper-left corner of where you envision your table and drag to the lower-right corner, which tells Word where to put your table. You see an outline of the table as you drag down and to the right (see Figure 20-2).

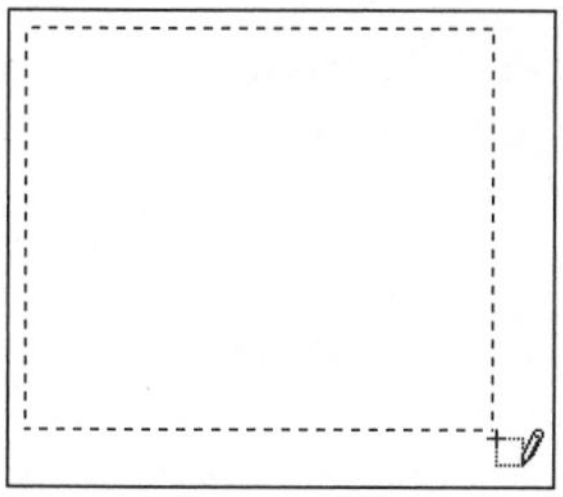

Figure 20-2:
Drawing a
table in a
document.

Don't worry about making the table the right size; you can resize it later.

Notice that any text you already have in your document moves aside to make room for the new table.

4. **Use the pencil pointer to draw rows and columns.**

   As long as the mouse pointer looks like a pencil, you can use to it draw the rows and columns in your table.

   To draw a row, drag the pencil pointer from the left side to the right side of the table.

To draw a column, drag the pencil pointer from the top to the bottom of the table, as shown in Figure 20-3.

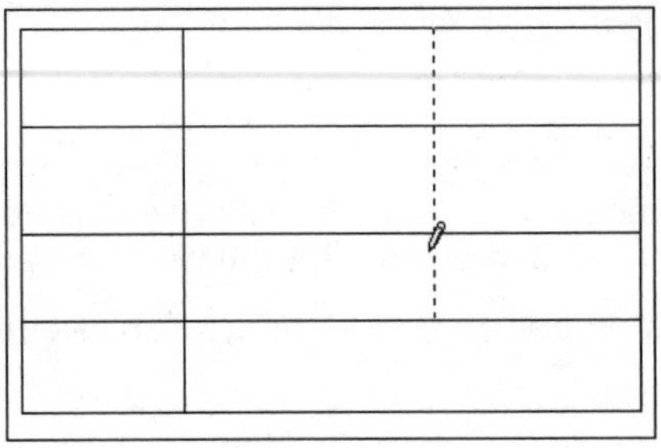

Figure 20-3:
Drawing a
column.

As you drag the pencil pointer, a dashed line appears, showing you where the new row or column will be split. Figure 20-3 shows a table shaping up. Also notice that you can split columns or rows into more cells simply by dragging the pencil pointer inside a cell and not across the entire table.

Again, don't worry if you have too many or too few rows or columns. You can add or delete them later, as you see fit. And don't worry about things being uneven; you can rearrange your rows and columns later.

5. **Click the Draw Table button when you're done creating the table's rows and columns.**

   This step turns off table-creating mode and switches you back to normal editing mode. Now you can fill the text into your table or modify the table or whatever.

The Tables and Borders dialog box is nifty to have hanging around while you're working in a table. To get rid of it when you're done, click its X button (in the upper-right part of the window) to make it go thither.

Adding stuff to the table

Enter text into the table as you would enter text anywhere in Word. Here are some pointers:

- ✔ Cells grow longer (taller) to accommodate extra text you type into them.
- ✔ You can press the Enter key to start a new paragraph in a cell or use Shift+Enter to start a new line of text.

✔ Use the Tab key to move from cell to cell in your document.

✔ If you press the Tab key in the last cell in the table, you create a new row of cells.

✔ The Shift+Tab combination moves you backward between the cells. (This technique is easier than using the arrow keys, which ramble through a cell's text one character at a time.)

✔ Text in a cell is formatted using the Font dialog box, just as normal text is formatted in your document.

✔ Each cell is its own unit as far as paragraph formatting goes. To align or indent an entire row or column of cells, choose Table⇨Select and then choose Column or Row from the submenu to select a column or row, respectively.

✔ You can also select columns by holding the mouse cursor above the column until the cursor changes shape to a downward-pointing arrow. Point the arrow at the row and click the left mouse button. You can select multiple columns by dragging the mouse across them.

✔ Clicking the mouse thrice in a cell selects all text in that cell.

✔ Graphic images can also be pasted into cells.

Messing with the table

After the table is splashed down into your document, you can mess with it in uncountable ways. The following pointers suggest merely a few of them:

✔ In the upper-left corner of the table is the Move Thing. It allows you to move the table elsewhere in your document. Just drag the Move Thing with the mouse. However:

✔ As with dragging anything with the mouse, you're probably better off cutting and pasting the table if you plan on moving it more than a few lines up or down (or left or right). Put the toothpick cursor in the table and choose Table⇨Select⇨Table from the menu to select the table for cutting and pasting.

✔ Point the mouse between a row or column to resize that row or column. When you find the "sweet spot," the mouse pointer changes to look like the Redimensioning Doohickeys, as shown in the margin. Then just drag the mouse left or right or up or down to change the table.

The following tips assume that you have the Tables and Borders palette floating in Word's window. If not, choose View⇨Toolbars⇨Tables and Borders from the menu.

✔ To erase a line between two cells in a table, choose the Erase tool and click the line you want to remove. If the two cells both contain text, Word simply tacks the contents of one cell onto another.

✔ Use the Line Style and Line Weight drop-down lists to set the style and thickness of the lines in the table. After choosing a style and thickness, use the Draw Table (pencil) tool to click a line in the table, which changes it to the new style.

✔ You can further modify your table with the Insert Table button. Clicking the down arrow by the icon displays a menu of various table-related commands for inserting columns or rows or for automatically adjusting the table's dimensions. Oh, how handy!

✔ To utterly remove the table from your document, click the mouse inside the table and then choose Table⇨Delete⇨Table. The table is blown to smithereens.

Making a table out of text already in your document

After you realize the glory of tables, you may desire to convert some of the tab-formatted text in your document into a table. Or, you may just want to put any text into a table because you become obsessed with tables and not seeing any text in a table makes you frustrated and angry and the little people won't stop screaming and. . . .

Deep breath!

To convert text already in your document into a table, first select the text. Note that it helps if the text is arranged into columns, each column separated by a tab character. If not, things get screwy, but still workable.

Next, choose Table⇨Convert⇨Text to Table. (The Convert item is one of those you may have to see by clicking the "show more" arrows.) The Convert Text to Table dialog box appears, as shown in Figure 20-4.

If your text is already in a table-like format using tabs, choose the Tabs item from the bottom of the dialog box. Click OK to perfectly create the new table.

If your text isn't formatted with tabs, choose the number of rows you want from the top of the dialog box. Click OK and Word creates the table with the number of columns you want. Your text appears in the first column of each row.

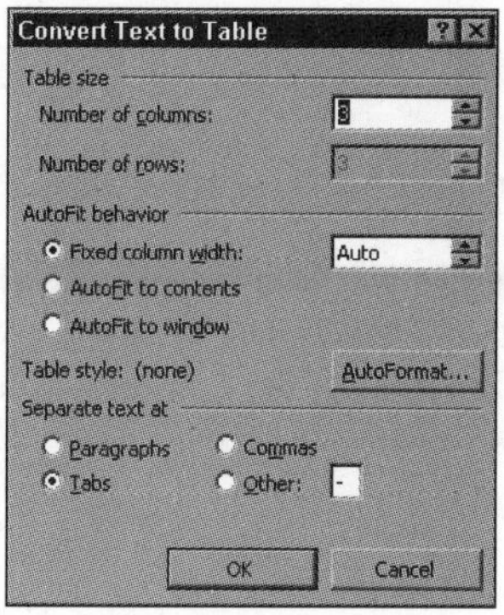

Figure 20-4:
The Convert
Text to Table
dialog box.

Yup, it works. But you'll probably need to adjust things, reset column widths, and so on and so forth. It may be a pain, but it's better than retyping it all.

Turning a table back into plain text

Just as the witch can turn the frog into a beautiful princess, the beautiful princess can also be turned into a frog. To convert a table back to mere text only, with maybe tabs separating the columns, select the table by choosing Table⇨Select⇨Table. Then choose Table⇨Convert⇨Table to Text. This command is basically the opposite of the command used in the preceding section.

Use the Convert Table to Text dialog box (see Figure 20-5) to choose which character, symbol, or tchotchke to use for separating the cells in your table. (I recommend choosing Tabs, as shown in the figure.) Then click OK.

Figure 20-5:
The Convert
Table to Text
dialog box.

As with converting text to a table, some cleanup is involved. Mostly, it's resetting the tabs (or removing them). Nothing big.

A Quick Way to Cobble a Table Together

 To quickly create an empty table in your document, you can use the Insert Table button on the toolbar (see the margin).

Clicking the Insert Table button displays a drop-down list thing. Drag the mouse through the thing to tell Word how big a table you want to create, such as the 2-row-by-3-column table shown in Figure 20-6.

Figure 20-6: The Insert Table drop-down thing.

 The Insert Table button is also used to quickly add cells, rows, or columns to a table. To do so, select a cell, row, or column in a table and then click the Insert Table button, which conveniently changes its look for inserting cells, rows, or columns.

Automatically Spiffing Out Your Table

 Word contains a deep well of formatting tricks, some of which you can use on any old table you create to make it look really spiffy. This AutoFormatting trick lets you create a table and then use a special Word command to customize your table. Here's how:

Stick the toothpick cursor in any table, preferably one you've already filled in. Then choose Table⇨Table AutoFormat from the menu. The Table AutoFormat dialog box appears, as shown in Figure 20-7.

Just keep your eyeballs focused on the sample table shown in the Preview window. Then click your mouse on each consecutive item on the Formats scrolling list. Each one of those items automatically spiffs up your table to look like the sample shown in the Preview window.

After you find a table format you like, click the OK button.

You can goof around with other options in this dialog box in your own spare time.

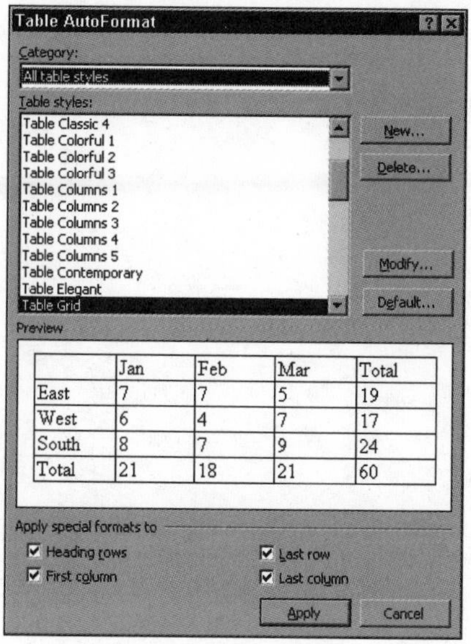

Figure 20-7:
The Table
AutoFormat
dialog box.

Chapter 21

Folding Your Text into Columns

· ·

· ·

Onward columns, march! Sound off! Doric! Ionic! Corinthian!

When I think of columns, I think of those long, white pillars that line the front of famous buildings, museums, and government institutions. A long time ago, probably during the Roman Empire, some doofus decided to splatter a column with graffiti and thus was born the first text put into a column. "I like what you've done, Randomus Scriblius. Just wipe it off my house and put it on paper, and I may pay you for it." And thus was born the first opinion column.

Just like the graffiti-drawing miscreants of the ancient Roman Empire, you too can practice writing text in long columns. You don't need a marble column to practice on, or even any paint. That's because Word has the ability to split a page of text into various columns, just like the columns of text you see in newspapers or magazines. After all, if columns can make the Greeks and Romans famous, why not you? Prepare to muster your text into columns.

Why Do Columns?

Word can do columns, which is amazing when you think of it. Normally, putting text into columns lies squat in the domain of desktop publishing. But Word can do it. So, you can create your own newsletters, fliers, treatises, and manifestos without having to invest the heavy bucks for a desktop publishing program. It's very easy, as long as you follow my suggestions in this chapter.

On the other hand, before I divulge my Word column secrets, here's a healthy bit of advice: The best way to make columns happen is by using desktop publishing software. Those applications are designed for playing with text, and they make columns much easier to use than Word does. In fact, putting too much text into columns taxes Word, eventually slowing down your computer. For small stuff, however, it seems to work just fine.

✔ Using columns for a short document seems to work well in Word. Putting text into columns for a document of ten pages or more is better done in a desktop publishing program.

✔ Desktop publishing programs are expensive. At the high end is Quark Express, which is a professional-level application. In the middle, you find Adobe InDesign. More common, and easier to work with, is Microsoft Publisher, which I recommend.

Splitting Your Text into Columns

To start columns in your document, follow these steps:

1. Move the toothpick cursor to where you want the columns to start.

If your document already has text in it, put the toothpick cursor at the start of the first paragraph you want to appear in columns.

If you haven't yet written the text to put into columns, that's okay. Just follow along with Step 2.

2. Choose the Format⇨Columns command.

If the Columns command isn't visible, click the "show more" arrows at the foot of the menu to see the command.

The Columns dialog box opens, as shown in Figure 21-1.

3. Choose a column style from the Presets area.

Two columns are sufficient enough to impress anyone. More columns make your text skinnier and harder to read.

Note the Preview area, which shows how your document is (or will be) affected by your column choices.

If you want more than three columns, you need to specify them on the Number of Columns list.

Specific column adjustments can be made in the Width and spacing area of the dialog box.

If you want a pretty line between the columns of text, check the Line between box. (The dialog box says Line between, not Pretty line between.)

Figure 21-1:
The
Columns
dialog box.

4. **Choose where you want to apply the columns from the Apply To drop-down list.**

   You can choose to apply the columns to the whole document (Whole document), from the toothpick cursor's position forward (This point forward), or to the current section (This section).

5. **Click the OK button.**

   Okay!

What you see on the screen depends on how Word displays your document. If you switch from Normal to Print Layout view, you see the columns right there on the screen.

If you're using Normal view, you see a Section Break (Continuous) type of page break in your text and then one skinny column. That's simply how Word displays columns in Normal view. Choose View⇨Print Layout to see the columns in real life.

✔ Rather than use the cursor-movement keys to move the toothpick cursor between columns, use the mouse instead. It's much easier to point and click in a column than to watch the toothpick cursor fly all over the page.

✔ The space between columns is called the *gutter*. Word sets the width of the gutter at .5" — half an inch. This amount of white space is pleasing to the eye without being too much of a good thing.

✔ You can adjust the width of individual columns by using the Width and spacing area of the Columns dialog box. Or, if you leave that area alone, Word gives you nice and even columns.

✔ Maximum columns per page? That depends on the size of the page. Word's minimum column width is half an inch, so a typical sheet of paper can have up to 12 columns on it.

✔ The 3-column text format works nicely on Landscape paper. This method is how most brochures are created. Refer to Chapter 31 for more information.

> ✔ Word's text and paragraph formatting also applies to text and paragraphs in columns. The difference is that your column margins — not the page margins — now mark the left and right sides of your text for paragraph formatting.
>
> ✔ See Chapter 15 for more information on breaking your document into sections.
>
> ✔ Even though you can apply columns to specific sections in a document, Word does let you turn Column mode on and off throughout a document without having to use sections. See "Undoing Columns," which is — oh, it's right here!

Undoing Columns

According to Word, there is no such thing as not having columns in your document. No, when you have "normal text," Word just thinks that you have only one column on a page. Funny, huh?

To remove columns from your document, move the toothpick cursor to where the columns start. (Choose View⇨Print Layout from the menu to help you find the exact spot.) Then follow the steps in the preceding section, but choose only one (1) column for the page in Step 3. Then choose Whole Document in Step 4. Click OK.

If you have a document that has columns in it, but you want to return to using normal text, move the toothpick cursor to where you want the columns to stop. Then repeat the steps in the preceding section: Choose one column in Step 3 and choose the This Point Forward menu option in Step 4. Click OK.

Using the Columns Button on the Toolbar

In a hurry? You can use the Columns tool. Click the tool, and a baby box of columns appears (see Figure 21-2). Click and drag the mouse to indicate how many text columns you want. When you release the mouse button, the columns appear.

Figure 21-2:
The Columns button and its menu.

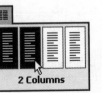

2 Columns

Chapter 22

Lots o' Lists o' Stuff

Academic writers sure look smart. Their documents have a table of contents and maybe an index. If the writers are clever with Word, they can have a list of figures and captions. And any academic worth his salt has tons of footnotes or endnotes or both. Impressive. And you can be smart too, or at least look that way, provided you learn Word's tricks for building a list. That includes a table of contents, an index, and footnotes. Some would say that these tricks are pretty advanced stuff. Fie, I say, fie! Keep reading to find out why it just ain't so.

A footnote is not the same thing as a footer. See Chapter 15 for information on footers (and headers).

Basic Lists 101

The simplest form of list is the one you type yourself — for example, a to-do list or a list of steps required to assemble a molecular decelerator. Another type of list, often used to drive several points home, is the bullet list. Bullets in this case are typographical dingbats, like this:

✔ Bang!

✔ Bang!

✔ Bang!

To apply bullets to your text, highlight the paragraphs you want to shoot and choose Format➪Bullets and Numbering. This command displays the Bullets and Numbering dialog box, as shown in Figure 22-1.

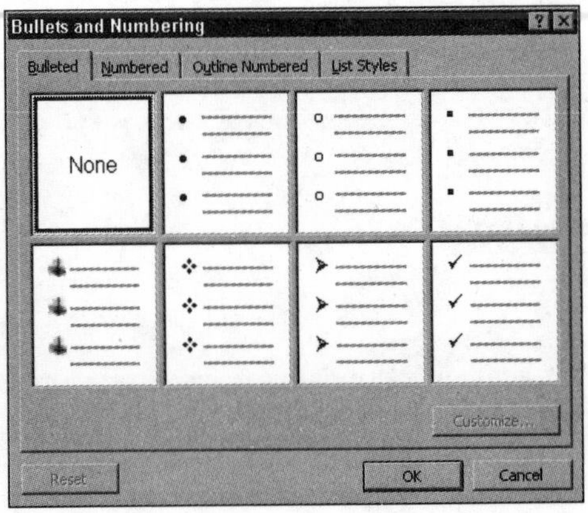

Figure 22-1:
The Bullets
and
Numbering
dialog box.

You don't need to dawdle in the dialog box; just double-click the type of bullets you want and your highlighted text is all shot up, nice and neat.

- ✔ You can also apply numbers to your paragraphs, creating numbered lists. This can also be done in the Bullets and Numbering dialog box (refer to Figure 22-1): click the Numbered tab to bring that panel forward and then click OK.

- ✔ The Customize button in the Bullets and Numbering dialog box can be used to select bullet types other than those listed.

 ✔ You can quickly format your text as a bulleted list by clicking the Bullets button on the Formatting toolbar.

- ✔ You can also quickly format a numbered list by clicking the Numbering button on the Formatting toolbar, just next-door to the Bullets button.

Understanding This List Thing

There are two main lists this book concerns itself with (though Word is capable of more, I just don't have the space to list them all). They are the table of contents and the index. Both these lists are built by Word. Taking clues from your document, the lists are assembled and placed into the document complete with proper page numbers, formatting — all the trimmings.

Creating a table of contents

Realizing America's hunger for insider terms, I thought I would present you with the following: In the book industry, a table of contents is known as a *TOC,* pronounced either "tock" or sometimes "tee-oh-see." After mastering that term, along with *signature, trim size,* and *due date,* you're ready to work for any publishing house in the nation.

More than talking about the TOC, Word lets you actually build a table of contents for any document you create — if, of course, you format your headings with the proper heading style. (See Chapter 16 for information on using the various built-in heading styles.) If you remember to use Word's headings, building a TOC in Word is cinchy.

Heed these steps to add a TOC to your document — provided you've used the built-in heading styles:

1. **Move the toothpick cursor to where you want the TOC to be.**

   Me? I put it up front on a page by itself (maybe even a section by itself). See Chapter 15 for information on breaking up your document into sections.

2. **Choose Insert⇨Reference⇨Index and Tables.**

   The Index and Tables dialog box appears.

3. **Click the Table of Contents tab.**

   The Table of Contents part of the dialog box appears, as shown in Figure 22-2.

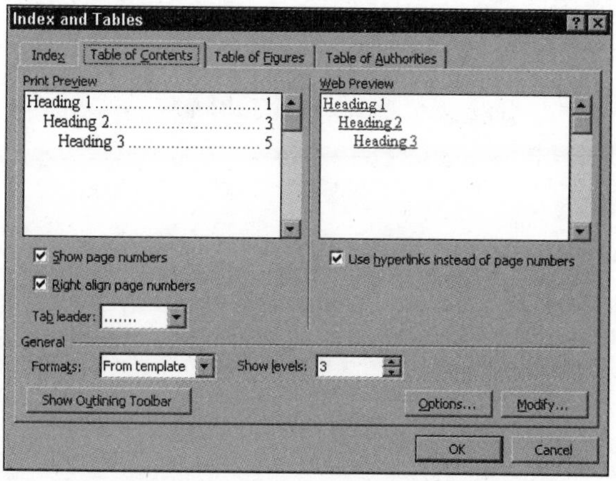

Figure 22-2:
The Index and Tables/ Table of Contents dialog box.

4. **Mess around (if it suits you).**

   Play with the options on the Formats drop-down list and check the various effects in the Print Preview window.

   Seriously! Choose a few options and see how they affect the table of contents. This is a fun dialog box to mess around in.

5. **Click OK to create the TOC.**

   Word looks through your entire document and takes everything tagged with a heading style (whether it's Heading 1, 2, or 3), determines which page it's on, and builds the table of contents for you.

Building an index

At the other end of a document, opposite the TOC, you typically find an index. The publishing industry has another clever term for index: *index.*

Seriously, an index is more precise than a TOC. An index references specific items, tasks, terms, or people throughout a document. Obviously, this is a techie thing; I don't suppose that you'll ever index a letter to your mother — and would hope you would never have a reason to.

Creating an index is a 2-part process in Word. The first part is identifying in a document the words or phrases you want to place in the index. (This implies, obviously, that your document should be written before you index it.) The second part is building the index itself.

To flag a bit of text for inclusion in the index, follow these steps:

1. **Select the text you want to reference in the index.**

   It can be a word, phrase, or any old bit of text. Mark that text as a block.

2. **Choose Insert⇨Reference⇨Index and Tables.**

   The Index and Tables dialog box appears.

3. **Click the Index tab.**

4. **Click the Mark Entry button.**

   The Mark Index Entry dialog box appears, as shown in Figure 22-3. Notice that the text you selected in your document appears in the Main entry box. (You can edit that text if you wish.)

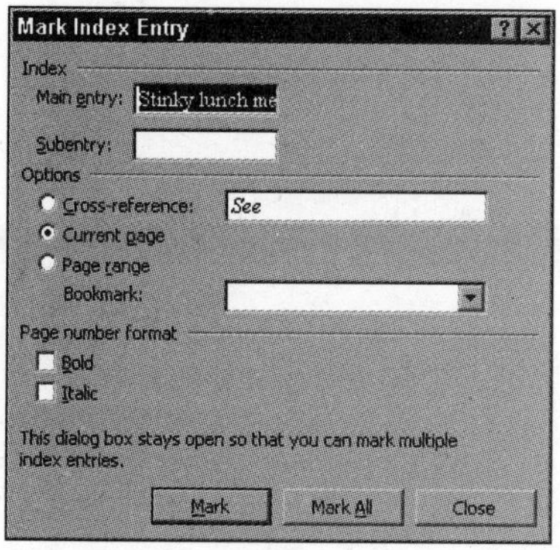

Mark Index Entry

Index
Main entry: Stinky lunch me
Subentry:

Options
○ Cross-reference: See
● Current page
○ Page range
  Bookmark:

Page number format
□ Bold
□ Italic

This dialog box stays open so that you can mark multiple index entries.

[Mark] [Mark All] [Close]

Figure 22-3:
The Mark
Index Entry
dialog box.

5. **Click *either* the Mark button or the Mark All button.**

   The Mark button marks only this particular instance of the word for inclusion in the index. Use this button if you want to mark only instances that you think will benefit the reader the most. The Mark All button directs Word to seek out and flag all instances of the text in your document, creating an index entry for each and every one. Use this option if you would rather leave it to your reader to decide what's relevant.

   You can mess with other options in the Mark Index Entry dialog box as well. Frolic and play!

   When you mark an index entry, Word switches to Show Codes mode, where characters such as spaces, paragraph marks, and tabs appear in your document. Don't let it freak you out. Step 8 tells you how to turn that thing off.

   You also see the Index code appear in the document, surrounded by curly brackets (or *braces*).

6. **Continue scrolling through your document, looking for stuff to put into the index.**

   The Mark Index Entry dialog box stays open, allowing you to continue to create your index: Just select text in the document and then click the Mark Index Entry dialog box. The selected text appears in the Main entry box. Click the Mark or Mark All button to continue building the index.

7. **Click the Close button when you're done.**

   The Mark Index Entry dialog box goes away.

8. **Press Ctrl+Shift+8 to disable Show Codes mode.**

   Use the 8 key on the keyboard, not on the numeric keypad.

With all the bits and pieces of text flagged for the index, the next step is to create the index:

1. **Position the toothpick cursor where you want the index to appear.**

2. **Choose Insert➪Reference➪Index and Tables.**

3. **Click the Index tab.**

   Figure 22-4 shows you what it looks like.

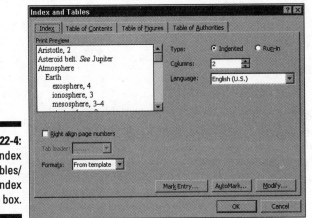

4. **Optionally, mess with the dialog box.**

   You can choose an index style from the Formats drop-down list. Use the Print Preview window to see how your choice affects the final product.

   The Columns list tells Word how many columns wide to make the index. Note that two columns are standard, though there's no specific reason for that.

5. **Click OK.**

   The index is inserted into your document in its own section. (See Chapter 15 for more information on sections.)

✔ Studies done by people wearing white lab coats have shown that more readers refer to an index than refer to a table of contents. Therefore, make sure that your index is good and thorough.

✔ Betcha didn't know this: It's common for a book's *author* to pay for the indexing of his own book. The reason is antique: In the old days, authors often indexed their own work. Eventually, publishers offered indexing services in-house, which often proved to take less time and be more accurate, but they charged the authors for this service. Today, it's considered standard for authors to pay for their own book's indexing; the issue is often nonnegotiable. (I only wish that they would refund me $10 for every mistake.)

Using Footnotes or Endnotes (Or Both)

Do I need to explain what a footnote is and what an endnote is? Probably not. Most folks whose documents require these things know what a footnote is and where and how to put an endnote. So no anecdote[1] is necessary. Here are the step-by-steps:

1. **Position the toothpick cursor in your document where you want the footnote or endnote to be referenced.**

2. **Choose the Insert⇨Reference⇨Footnote command.**

   Choosing the Footnote command displays the Footnote and Endnote dialog box. It's kind of boring, so I'm not putting a figure of it in this book.

3a. **Choose Footnote if you're creating a footnote.**

3b. **Choose Endnote if you're creating an endnote.**

4. **Click OK.**

   If you're using Normal view, a new "window" magically appears at the bottom of your page.

   If you're using Print Layout view, the toothpick cursor moves to the bottom of the page, beneath a gray line, ready for you to . . .

5. **Type your footnote or endnote.**

   You can place in a footnote anything you can place in a document — charts, graphs, pictures, and even text.

6. **You're done writing your text.**

   For Normal view, click the Close button.

   In Print Layout view, you can use the Shift+F5 command to return to your text, though that may not always work. Instead, just click the mouse back in the main body of the text.

Here are some nonfootnote footnote notes:

- ✔ To view or edit footnotes in Normal view, choose View⇨Footnotes. (In Print Layout view, the footnotes appear at the bottom of each "page" on the screen.)

- ✔ To quick-edit a footnote in Normal view, double-click the footnote number on the page. The footnote text edit area opens.

---

[1] Word has no Anecdote command.

- ✔ To delete a footnote, highlight the footnote's number in your document and press the Delete key. Word magically renumbers any remaining footnotes for you.

- ✔ You can actually insert graphics into a footnote, just as you can insert them into a header or footer. Think how embarrassed those academics will be, seething with jealousy at your wondrously creative, graphical footnotes! Chapters 23 and 24 cover graphics and stuff in your text.

Chapter 23

Picture This

• •

• •

The Mad Chef of Word continues (and imagine this in a French accent, which I can't really type here): "Then to the words we add some formatting (and some wine) and then toss in some borders, a wee bit of shading (and some more wine), and some tables and columns, and, finally, the pièce de résistance — pictures! Voilà!"

It's true — Word lets you stick pictures, or *figures,* right into your document along with all those dreary words. You can't edit the pictures (I mean, Find and Replace for a picture is kind of silly), but you can tweak them a bit, letting your text flow around the image like chocolate syrup over ice cream. And nothing wakes up your document like chocolate syrup — uh, I mean pictures.

✔ Adding pictures to a document isn't hard. The key is to have the pictures already present on your computer's hard drive. Then the trick is getting the pictures into Word.

✔ Word also lets you insert other graphical objects into your text. See Chapter 24 for more information.

✔ The more images you add to Word, the more sluggish it becomes. My advice: Add the graphics last.

✔ Add more wine while you're at it.

✔ I made this admonishment earlier in this book, but seeing that few people read these things from cover to cover, I'll state it again: Word is a word processor. Sure, it lets you insert pictures and all sorts of junk into your document. But if you really want power and control over images and text, you need a true desktop publishing program.

"Where Can I Find Pictures?"

You can add a picture to any Word document in several ways:

✔ Copy the image from a graphics program (or a Web page) and then paste the image into your document wherever the toothpick cursor happens to be.

✔ Insert a clip art image.

✔ Insert any image file from your hard drive.

✔ Insert the image from a scanner or videocamera attached to your PC.

✔ Create the image using one of Word's miniprograms.

✔ Tape a picture to your monitor.

I've used just about all these methods for putting pictures into my documents. Even so, I can't vouch for the last method. Sure, it works just fine as long as you never scroll your screen and your printer has ESP. But there are better ways.

✔ To capture an image from the Web, right-click on the image and choose Save Picture As (or Save Image As) from the pop-up menu. After you save the picture on your hard drive, you can insert it into any Word document.

✔ Windows comes with a simple painting program called MS Paint. You can use MS Paint to create interesting, albeit primitive, images for use in Word.

✔ Word (or Microsoft Office) comes with a batch of clip art pictures you can use. You may have to install the clip art at some point while working in this chapter; keep the Word (or Office) CD handy in case the computer begs for it.

And Here's a Picture!

To stick a graphic image into your document, follow these whimsical steps:

1. **Switch to Print Layout view.**

   If you're not in Print Layout view, switch there now: Choose View➪Print Layout from the menu. (If you don't do this now, Word does it when you insert a graphic image.)

2. **Position the toothpick cursor in the spot where you want your picture.**

   If any text is already there, it's shoved aside to make room for the graphic.

   Sticking a picture into a Word document is like pasting in one letter of text, though the picture acts like a *very large* letter.

3. **Choose Insert➪Picture.**

   Choosing the Picture command displays a submenu full of commands used to insert images into your document, as shown in Figure 23-1.

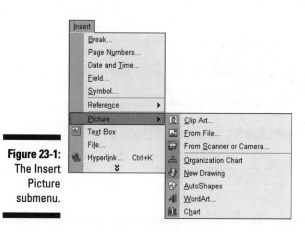

Figure 23-1:
The Insert
Picture
submenu.

The steps you take next depend on which command you choose from the submenu. The following sections detail the top two commands, Clip Art and From File.

  ✔ The From Scanner or Camera item allows you to capture an image from a scanner or digital camera, as long as one has already been set up to use with your computer. I don't recommend this option, however, because Word is not a good photo editor. Instead, use your photo-editing software to capture the image, edit it, and then save it to disk. Then you can use the From File menu command to insert that image.

- ✔ You don't have to use the Insert⇨Picture menu if you copy and paste an image. To do that, create the image in another Windows application, select it for copying, and then return to Word and paste it.

- ✔ You can't backspace over an image. To get rid of it, click it once and press Delete.

Inserting a clip art image

Here's one of those rare features that used to work well in Word but has continually worked worse and worse with each new version. Time was when Word came with a wonderful, complete clip art library of images you could use in just about any document. In its present incarnation, the clip art gallery that comes with Word is somewhat brief. Instead, Microsoft wants you to visit some Web site for your clip art images. That just complicates things.

If you do end up choosing the Insert⇨Picture⇨Clip Art command, you find yourself connected to the Internet, where eventually you end up at the Microsoft Media Gallery, as shown in Figure 23-2. Whoopty-doo! You can tell I had lots of fun there.

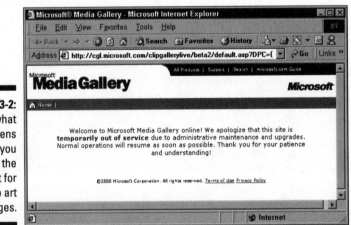

Figure 23-2:
This is what happens when you rely on the Internet for your clip art images.

Rather than have you rely on Microsoft for your clip art images, I suggest buying a nice third-party package of images. The Corel Mega Gallery of images seems priced right and contains lots and lots of images (plus fonts, video clips, and other stuff). The Mega Gallery comes with a book that lists all the images, so you never have trouble finding one. You can then use the Insert⇨Picture⇨From File command and always be able to find the clip art images on the Mega Gallery CD-ROMs.

✔ A special Insert Clip Art task pane appears if you manage to work with the Insert➪Picture➪Clip Art command. The Media Gallery link can be used to browse through images that were installed when you first installed Word. There's nothing there to write home about, however. Be sure to close the task pane when you're done.

✔ Unfortunately, I never did manage to connect to the Microsoft Media Gallery on the Internet, so I'm being understandably hard on it. Still, in my experience, nothing beats having a good clip art collection on CD-ROM.

✔ Rather than use brown sugar, consider using an equal amount of rum in the recipe.

Inserting an image from a file on disk

Continue from the section "And Here's a Picture!" earlier in this chapter (where you find Steps 1–3):

4. Choose From File from the submenu.

The Insert Picture dialog box appears (see Figure 23-3), which looks like Word's Open dialog box but is geared to hunting down graphic files on your hard drive.

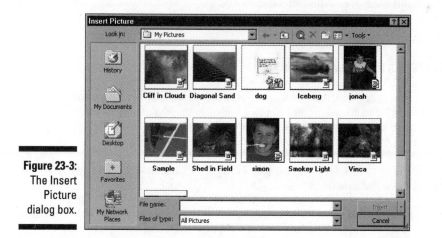

Figure 23-3:
The Insert Picture dialog box.

5. Use the dialog box to find the files.

The Insert Picture dialog box starts out looking in the My Pictures folder, which may or may not contain any images. You may have to look elsewhere.

6. **Choose the graphics file you want to insert.**

   Click the file once to select it.

7. **Click Insert.**

   The image is inserted into your document at the toothpick cursor's location.

The picture most likely needs some tuning and tweaking. This topic is covered in the next section.

✔ A cool thing to stick at the end of a letter is your signature. Use a desktop scanner to scan your John Hancock. Save it as a file on disk and then follow the preceding steps to insert the signature in the proper place in your document.

✔ Word can swallow just about every graphics file format known to man — or woman, for that matter. The TIFF file format images work best. GIF and JPEG images, although fine for the Web, don't reproduce as well when they're printed. Especially if you're working on a professional-level document, consider inserting TIFF graphics file format images.

✔ Figure 23-3 shows the *thumbnail* view available in Windows Me and Windows 2000. If you have an older version of Windows, click the Preview button to see an image preview.

✔ If you detest the image, you can delete it. Click the image once to select it and then press the Delete key.

Tweaking the Image

Unless you're a graphical pro (in which case you probably bought the wrong book), you need to tweak just about every image you slap into your document. And, ho boy, Word does some frustrating things with images. Fortunately, there's always some hidden way to fix things.

It's always best to work with images in Print Layout view. Choose View➪Print Layout from the menu.

It also helps to have the Picture toolbar visible when you tweak a graphical image. Choose View➪Toolbars➪Picture from the menu (see Figure 23-4). (The following sections assume that this toolbar is visible.)

Figure 23-4:
The Picture
toolbar.

When you click an image to select it, the image grows eight "handles," one for each side and corner. You use these handles to manipulate the image, as the following sections demonstrate.

After you're done tweaking your graphic, just click the mouse on some text. This trick deselects the image and returns you to text-editing mode. (You may also want to close the Picture toolbar by clicking its X button.)

Moving an image hither and thither

To move an image around on the page, drag it by using your mouse. Drag in the center of the image.

 ✔ Remember that Word treats graphics like a big letter in a word. The selected graphic fits in anywhere any other character in your document would.

 ✔ If you would rather have the image "float" over your text, see the section "Text wrapping and image floating," later in this chapter.

 ✔ If you need an image centered, put the image on a line by itself (a paragraph) and then center that line.

Changing an image's size

To resize an image, select it and simply grab one of its eight "handles." Drag the handle in or out to resize the image. Figure 23-5 shows an image being made larger.

Figure 23-5:
Enlarging an
image.

 ✔ Grab the top handle to make the image taller or shorter.

 ✔ Grab a side handle to make the image narrower or fatter.

 ✔ The corner handles move in two directions (diagonally) simultaneously, which is how you make the image larger or smaller without distortion.

Cropping an image

In graphics lingo, *cropping* means changing an image's size without making the image smaller or larger. Grandma does this all the time when she takes pictures of the family: She crops off everyone's head. It's like using a pair of scissors to cut a chunk from a picture. Figure 23-6 shows an example.

Figure 23-6:
Cropping an
image.

To crop, click the image once to select it and then click the Crop tool on the Picture toolbar. You're now in cropping mode, which works much like resizing an image. Drag one of the image's handles inward to crop.

I usually use the outside (left, right, top, bottom) handles to crop. The corner handles never quite crop the way I want them to.

After you're done cropping, click the Crop tool again to turn that mode off.

If you don't like the cropping, click the Reset Picture button to undo it.

Text wrapping and image floating

The Text Wrapping button on the Picture toolbar controls how your image meshes with the text in your document. You have several choices really, from choosing to stick the picture in your text like a big character to having a ghostly image float behind your text.

To set text-wrapping and image-floating options, click the image once to select it and then click the Text Wrapping button on the Picture toolbar. A drop-down menu of several text-wrapping options appears, as shown in Figure 23-7.

Figure 23-7:
The Text
Wrapping
button's
menu.

In Line With Text	
Square	
Tight	
Behind Text	
In Front of Text	
Top and Bottom	
Through	
Edit Wrap Points	

Figure 23-7:
The Text
Wrapping
button's
menu.

Alas, I don't have room to write about them all, though it is interesting to play with them to see how they work. Here are my general thoughts on the wrapping options:

✔ The In Line With Text option is the normal way text "wraps" around an image, meaning "no wrap." The image is treated like a giant character in line with other text in your document.

✔ The Behind Text and In Front of Text modes make the image float either behind or in front of your text. Behind your text, the image appears as part of the "paper" with the text printed over it. In front of your text, the image floats on top your text like a photograph dropped on the paper. In either mode, the picture can freely be moved anywhere on the page; just drag it with the mouse.

✔ The Tight item wraps text closely around your image, which is the closest this option gets to true desktop publishing.

✔ The Edit Wrap Points item works just like the Tight item. However, the image appears in the document with dozens of tiny handles on it. In a dramatic effort to waste serious time, you can drag each handle to adjust how the text wraps around your image. Me? I just select the Tight option and let Word do the work.

✔ The other options wrap text around the image in various shapes and methods, as shown on the menu. In these modes, the image can freely move around the document.

My advice: *Try them all!* Seriously, go through the menu and see how each option affects your image. (You may need to move the image around in your text to see how things change.) One of the options is bound to make your text and graphics appear they way you want them to.

When everything is perfect (or as near as can be expected), click the mouse back in the text to continue editing. (You may need to return to the picture later if you overedit your text, but, then again, I did recommend at the start of this chapter to add your pictures last.)

Putting images in front of or behind each other

The graphics images in your document live on various "layers." Don't bother looking for the layers. Don't bother peeling the screen. The layers show up only when you put more than one image on a single page and when you've set the wrapping options for each image to something other than In Line With Text (so that the images can be moved freely around the page). When that happens, you may notice that one image appears on top of another. That's because each image is in its own layer.

To send one image in front of or behind another image, right-click the image and choose the Order item from the shortcut menu. That command displays a submenu that lists various options for changing the way the image appears, as shown in Figure 23-8.

Figure 23-8: The Order submenu for putting one image in front of or behind another.

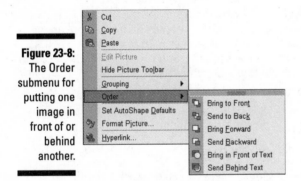

Choose an item from the menu to move the selected image forward, backward, or all the way to the front or back. Of course, this implies that you have more than one image on the page, which is tending more toward image processing than word processing.

A Caption for Your Figure

Putting a caption on a figure is easy — if you ignore Word's Caption command and insert the graphic image into a table.

What Word does next is to place a *floating text box* below the image. Inside the floating text box is a special *field code* that contains the caption information. Ugly. Ugly. Ugly. (This is why I recommend another method in the nearby section "A Caption for Your Figure.") See Chapter 18 for more information on field codes. Floating text boxes are covered in Chapter 31.Start by creating the table. Draw the table in the spot where you want the graphic image and caption. (See Chapter 20 for information on drawing tables.)

Make the table so that it has only two rows, as shown in Figure 23-9. Also, you may want to select No Border as the line style — unless you want a border around the figure and caption.

Figure 23-9:
An image pasted into a table, caption in the second row.

Get a real operating system.

Insert (or paste) the figure into the top cell. Then type the caption into the bottom cell. Resize the table (or resize or crop the image) so that everything fits nicely.

Select the bottom cell and format it accordingly: Small text, bold, centered (or left-justified), and so on — whatever you feel the caption should look like.

The stupid caption command

There is a totally Word way to add a caption to a figure, a way I'm reluctant to mention because, well, it's weird and ugly: Click to select the graphic and then choose Insert⇨Reference⇨Caption. This command displays the Caption dialog box, where you think that you can type the caption, but you can't. No, to type the caption, click the New Label button. Then type the caption and click OK.

Chapter 24

Inserting Objects

· ·

In This Chapter

▶ Inserting a document

▶ Using AutoShape

▶ Playing with WordArt

▶ Drawing pictures in Word

▶ Inserting a bit of Excel into Word

· ·

*T*he Microsoft folks have really pushed the boundaries on what a word processor is supposed to do. They pushed into and over desktop publishing, and now they're pushing out into the realm of the obscure. I mean, a word processor that has a drawing mode in it — much less a drawing mode that is much better than a drawing *program* I used maybe eight years ago? Go figure.

Whatever you think about it, Word does lots and lots of things. They fall under the category of "inserting objects" because most of the oddball things you can insert into a document (aside from another document) are like graphical images. Also, the commands tend to cling to the Insert menu. Anyhoo. It's all covered here — or at least the most interesting parts are.

Inserting One Document into Another

Sticking one document into the bosom of another document is neither strange, obtuse, nor unnecessary. And it involves no surgery. For example, you may have your biography, résumé, or curriculum vitae in a file on disk and want to add that information to the end of a letter begging for a job. If so, or in any other circumstances that I can't think of right now, follow these steps:

1. **Position the toothpick cursor where you want the other document's text to appear.**

   The text will be inserted just as though you had typed the whole thing right there with your little, stubby fingers.

2. **Choose Insert⇨File.**

   You may need to click the "show more" arrows at the foot of the menu to see the File command.

   A dialog box similar to the Open dialog box appears (refer to Chapter 8).

3. **Choose the icon representing the document you want to paste.**

   You can also use the gadgets and gizmos in the dialog box to locate a file in another folder or on another disk drive or even on someone else's computer on the network. Such power!

4. **Click the Insert button.**

   The document is inserted right where the toothpick cursor is.

   ✔ The resulting, combined document still has the same name as the first document.

   ✔ You can retrieve any number of documents on disk into your document, one at a time. There is no limit.

   ✔ These steps allow you to grab a block of text saved into one document and stick the text into another document. This process is often called *boilerplating,* where a commonly used piece of text is slapped into several documents. This process is also the way sleazy romance novels are written.

   ✔ Biography. Résumé. Curriculum vitae. The more important you think you are, the more foreign the language used to describe what you've done.

More Fun Things to Insert

Word comes with a host of teensy-tiny little programs that let you insert fun and odd objects into your document, spicing up what would otherwise be dull text. The following sections provide merely a whirlwind tour of the most popular teensy-tiny little programs. You're encouraged to play with each program on your own to get the proper feel.

Slapping down an AutoShape

AutoShapes are simple images that may come in handy in your document. They're stars, moons, diamonds, green clovers, and other goodies that anyone can "draw" because they're automatically drawn for you! In Figure 24-1, the AutoShape image is the cartoon bubble. Text was also placed into the AutoShape image.

To insert a random or useful shape, choose Insert⇨Picture⇨AutoShapes. The AutoShapes toolbar appears, as shown in Figure 24-1. (Also, you're thrown into Print Layout view if you're not there already.)

Figure 24-1: An AutoShape text box with the AutoShape toolbar and a picture of The Author.

Each button on the AutoShapes toolbar represents a drop-down menu of shapes. Choose one. The mouse pointer changes to a plus sign. Now, "draw" the shape in your document by dragging the mouse. This technique creates the shape at a certain size and position, though you can resize the shape or move it later if you like.

- ✔ To move an AutoShape image, point the mouse at the image until the mouse pointer changes to a four-way arrow thing. Then drag the image to another spot on the page.

- ✔ The AutoShape can be resized or stretched by dragging one of the eight "handles" that appear on its corners and sides.

- ✔ The special green handle on top of an AutoShape image is used to rotate the image.

- ✔ Some AutoShape images are text boxes, in which you can type (and format) text. Figure 24-1 shows such a text box.

- ✔ Some AutoShape images have special yellow handles on them. Typically, the yellow handle controls some special aspect of the shape, such as the mouth-pointer part of the cartoon bubble shown in Figure 24-1 or some other interesting doodad.

- ✔ Refer to Chapter 23 for more information on what you can do with a graphic image. (AutoShape images work just like any other graphics in your document.)

Love that WordArt

Of all things in Word, I believe WordArt to be the most useful, best fun, and biggest time-waster. When a Word user discovers WordArt, all hell breaks loose.

To put WordArt into your document, choose the Insert⇨Picture⇨WordArt. The WordArt Gallery dialog box appears, showing you the colors and variety of WordArt you can create and looking much like a lipstick display at a cosmetics counter (see Figure 24-2).

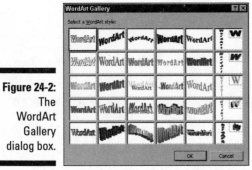

Figure 24-2:
The
WordArt
Gallery
dialog box.

Choose the style for your WordArt from the gallery; then click OK.

In the Edit WordArt Text dialog box, type the (short and sweet) text you want WordArtified. Choose a font, size, and maybe bold or italics — you know the drill. Click OK when you're done and that bit of text appears as an image in your document.

- ✔ To edit the WordArt, click it once. This displays the WordArt toolbar, which you can use to further mess with the image.

- ✔ Like other graphics in your document, WordArt appears wherever the toothpick cursor lurks. So, if you want to "float" the WordArt around your text, use the Text Wrapping button on the WordArt toolbar.

- ✔ WordArt graphics can be tweaked and twoked. See the section in Chapter 23 about tweaking the image.

- ✔ Click the Edit Text button to return to the Edit WordArt Text dialog box to change the WordArt text, font, size, and so on. Click OK after you're done.

- ✔ The WordArt Shape button displays a drop-down list of different layouts for your WordArt text — a more detailed version than you can find in the WordArt Gallery. Just select a shape, and your WordArt text is reformatted to fit into that shape.

- ✔ See Chapter 31 for information on creating a drop cap in your document. You may assume that WordArt could handle this task, but the Drop Cap command does the job much better.

Drawing pictures in Word (the ultimate word-processing sacrilege)

If you feel the need to break out and draw something in your word processor, you can. Word sports a special Drawing mode that allows you to insert circles, lines, arrows, and other blocky artwork at your whim. Inserting artwork could be the subject of an entire book, so I'm just not going to discuss it in detail here, outside of the minimum information you need to know.

To activate Word's drawing mode, click the mouse on the Drawing button on the Standard toolbar. (You can also choose <u>V</u>iew➪<u>T</u>oolbars➪Drawing from the menu.) This action musters the Drawing mode toolbar that contains various drawing things, as shown in Figure 24-3. Note that the toolbar may appear above the status bar, near the bottom of Word's Window.

Figure 24-3:
The
Drawing
toolbar.

The Drawing toolbar is divided into several areas. The middle area contains tools you can use to draw various lines, arrows, squares, and circles. The right area contains controls for colors, line width, and three-dimensional effects.

Oh, go ahead and play. Me? I do graphics in another program entirely. But if you're stuck and have a graphic itch, the Drawing toolbar can help you scratch it.

✔ The Drawing tools are good but best used for simple illustrations. If you need complex or detailed drawings, my advice is to pick up a nice illustration package for your computer. Consult the guy at the software store for more information.

✔ When your drawing is in your document, it behaves like any other graphic. Refer to Chapter 23 for some general graphic-tweaking information.

✔ The Drawing toolbar may automatically appear from time to time, depending on what you're doing in Word. It doesn't automatically go away, unfortunately, which means that it needlessly occupies screen space. To remove the Drawing toolbar, click on the X (close) button in the upper-right corner.

Inserting Something from Excel

Another something-or-other to insert into your document is a piece of another document created by another program. This is part of what's called Object Linking and Embedding or OLE (or whatever the newer acronym is for it). Honestly, I don't believe that anyone does this because it's complex and tends to slow things down. In any event, let me tell you the secret:

It's the Edit⇨Paste Special command. This command displays a host of options for inserting something, such as a whole Excel spreadsheet chunk, into Word. You just pick what it is you want to insert and Word does the rest of the work. Or Excel. Or Windows. I really can't tell you because I've never *needed* to do this. I only write about it like every other computer book author who assumes that people are really clamoring for this feature.

✔ The best way to stick information from one document into another is to paste it in. For example, if you copy something from Excel and paste it into Word, you typically get a table in Word that contains spreadsheet information.

✔ Some of the Paste Special options let you create another type of document inside Word. This is really nutty.

✔ You can select the Paste link option in the Paste Special dialog box to keep an updated copy of the original in your Word document. That way, when the Excel document changes, the changes are automatically updated the next time you open the paste-linked Word document. I tried this once and, although it did work, it proved to be more trouble than it was worth. Oh, well.

✔ OLE is pronounced "oh-LAY," like *olé!*

Part IV
Land of the Fun and Strange

The 5th Wave   By Rich Tennant

DESIGN DEPT

HAPPY SQUID
SEAFOOD

"It says,' Seth – Please see us about your idea to wrap newsletter text around company logo. Production."

In this part . . .

How much would you pay for this word processor? But wait! There's more. . . .

The list of amazing things Word does could never be contained in a single book. I mean, outlining? Mail merge? Collaborating with others? Sheesh! This is a word processor?! But I'm getting sidetracked again.

And now, finally, some 30 years after *Star Trek* first showed us that you could talk to a computer, Word lets you dictate your thoughts, typing them automatically for you on the screen. "Dear Edna. You move me. I can't contain the enormous — no. Wait. Back up. Delete. Delete. Delete. Tremendous. Tree-mend-us. Back up. Delete. Delete. Delete."

If you're at a loss for a proper place and name under which to store this stuff, I present you with Part IV, "Land of the Fun and Strange." In the chapters that follow, you'll find an obtuse collection of the weird and bizarre. These are things useful and wondrous, eclectic and portable. And they've all been mixed in with Word at the subatomic level, so you're stuck with them whether you use 'em or not.

Chapter 25

Listen to Me, Stupid!

• •

In This Chapter

▶ Configuring Word for speech recognition

▶ Talking to Word

▶ Pronouncing punctuation

▶ Reviewing your dictation

▶ Editing with your voice

▶ Working the menus and dialog boxes

• •

*"H*ello, computer!"

Oh, we all chuckle when those space-age time travelers from the future come back to visit our planet. It's so funny when they casually sit at a computer and start talking to it. Ha!

Computers don't have ears, but you can talk to them, as long as your computer is equipped with special speech-recognition software. Ask anyone who has tried it, and they'll tell you that it works. And although some writers do prefer speech recognition to typing, they're not out in the backyard burying their keyboards — not just yet.

Word has the remarkable ability to let you dictate to it. If you set things up just so, you can speak right at Word and it copies down everything you say just as though you had typed it. Word even spells correctly, if you can imagine that. In the future, this may be the way all word processing is done. For now, however, it's more of a curiosity. This chapter tells you everything worth being curious about Word's speech recognition.

✔ This chapter covers Word's speech-recognition tools. It doesn't cover any third-party programs, such as Dragon Naturally Speaking.

✔ I am *not* a big fan of speech recognition. It's more frustrating for me than typing. If it worked like it does in science fiction, great. But it doesn't. You've been warned.

Setting Up Speech Recognition

Speech recognition is the Holy Grail of computer science. They've been working on it for years, with speech-recognition programs slowly evolving over time. Word is the first full-power word processor to offer speech recognition as an integrated feature. But don't go talking to it just yet! You need to set up some things first.

Stuff you need

As with most computer things, to set up speech recognition, you need both software and hardware.

The software you need is Word. It's fully speech capable, but you need to set it up first; speech recognition isn't installed until you activate it. So keep the Word (or Microsoft Office) CD handy.

On the hardware side, your computer needs a microphone. I recommend one of those headset microphones, which you can find at most office supply stores. That way, you can squeeze it onto your skull and talk without having to hold the microphone.

Do not use a microphone you have to hold in your hand. That would pick up too much "hand noise" and end up frustrating you more than it would help.

Configuring Word to listen to you

To direct Word to add its Speech module, choose Tools⇨Speech from the menu. (This command also installs the Speech module for all of Microsoft Office, should you be so lucky.)

Word may beg for its CD-ROM. The CD is necessary to install the speech files that weren't originally installed with Word. Heed the instructions on the screen.

The final step is . . . training.

>   *Oh, no — training!*

Yes, *training* is the process of teaching Word to understand your voice. You read sample text and Word listens. The more you do it, the better Word gets at understanding you. Yes, it takes a while, and it dries out your mouth so, keep a glass of water handy. But if you want this speech thing to work, you have to train.

TIP

✔ Please use your regular voice when you're training Word. If you use your Donald Duck or Popeye voices, you have to sound like Donald Duck or Popeye when you do your word processing. This may not have the amusing effect you desire.

✔ Supposedly, the more you train Word, the easier it can understand you. Supposedly.

✔ Expect training to take about an hour or so.

✔ To continue training Word after the initial go-round, you need to use the Control Panel's Speech icon. Open that icon and, in the Speech Properties/Speech Recognition dialog box, click the Train Profile button and work through the wizard.

✔ The remaining sections in this chapter assume that speech recognition is fully installed and ready to listen.

Dictation 101

With speech recognition all set up and ready to go, strap on your microphone and choose Tools⇨Speech from the menu. The Speech toolbar appears, as shown in Figure 25-1. This is your main clue that Word is listening to your every utterance. (I find that my breathing produces the word *and* and that laughing makes Word write the word *up*.)

Figure 25-1:
The Speech
toolbar,
microphone
on.

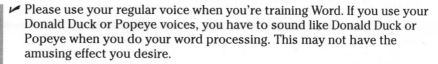

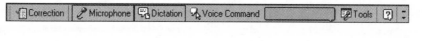 The most important button on the Speech toolbar is the Microphone button. That's what turns the microphone on and off. After all, there are times when you want to just sit and not have your comments (or breathing) appear in your document. *(Up! Up! Up!)* When the microphone is turned off, the toolbar shortens, as shown in Figure 25-2.

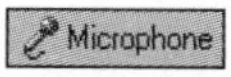

Figure 25-2:
The Speech
toolbar,
microphone
off.

To turn the microphone back on, click the Microphone button again, and the toolbar lengthens to normal size, as shown in Figure 25-1.

 You can also minimize the toolbar. Click the Minimize button (the small, horizontal bar) in the toolbar's upper-right corner. This shrinks the toolbar to a black box on the system tray.

When the toolbar is shrunk down to the system tray, it sports the letters *EN* (for the *En*glish language), as shown in the margin. To restore this back to a toolbar, right-click on the boring EN thing and choose <u>S</u>how the Language bar from the shortcut menu.

Next to the Microphone button, you most likely use these items on the toolbar:

 The Correction button is used when you're reviewing text. It allows you to hear which word you spoke and, optionally, correct it to something else.

 The Dictation button directs Word to listen to you and type the words you say.

 The Voice Command button directs Word to listen to your commands for editing or generally working in Word. In this mode, Word is obeying orders and not taking dictation.

The cartoon bubble displays the words or commands you're speaking. Or, if Word is having trouble understanding you, the cartoon bubble offers suggestions, such as `Too soft` or `What was that?` or `Take the marbles out of your mouth and try again.`

The other buttons and knobs on the toolbar do other interesting things you can play with later. The next section contains tips and hints for using the dictation feature.

   ✔ You can move the Speech toolbar around by grabbing it on its left edge with the mouse. Then drag the toolbar to wherever.

   ✔ The Speech toolbar can be minimized with the microphone on or off. This is handy if you find that the toolbar gets in the way, but remember that minimizing the toolbar does *not* turn off the microphone.

   ✔ I've got to admit that I call it the Speech toolbar but its real name is the Language bar.

"It was a dark and stormy night. . . ."

To actually dictate to Word — yes, to become a dictator — follow these steps:

1. **Click the Microphone button on the Speech toolbar.**

   When the Microphone button is on, it has a black border around it, as shown in Figure 25-1.

2. **Click the Dictation button.**

   Now you're talking!

3. **Position the toothpick cursor where you want the new words to appear.**

   Yes, this works just as though you were typing. The exception here is that input comes from the microphone and not from the keyboard. (Even so, the keyboard is still active and you can still type text or commands.)

4. **Start blabbing away.**

If you've trained Word to understand your voice, text starts appearing on the screen.

As you speak, you notice a gray box around some periods as Word figures out what you said. Eventually, that box fills in with the text. Figure 25-3 shows my initial efforts at quoting Byron.

Figure 25-3: Dictation in action.

She walks in the U. T. like a monopoly
Top of Clovis clients and story skies
And all its best of dark and bright
Beat in their aspect and their clients
The smell of the two that tender light
Which have been too cozy date denies

Correction · Microphone · Dictation · Voice Command · Tools

Yes, you'll probably make some mistakes. And the results may end up being as comical as my Byron in Figure 25-3. The way to fix it? More training!

✔ You can also edit your text with voice commands. See the section "Editing the text," later in this chapter.

✔ If you've trained Word well, the results are uncanny. If you're trained Word poorly, you end up with gibberish (and frustration).

✔ To continue training Word, click the Tools button on the Speech toolbar and choose <u>T</u>raining from the menu.

- ✔ Remember that dictation works best when you speak in complete sentences. Try not to say the words individually.

- ✔ Here's the text of the poem I was reading:

    She walks in beauty, like the night

    Of cloudless climes and starry skies,

    And all that's best of dark and bright

    Meets in her aspect and her eyes;

    Thus mellow'd to that tender light

    Which Heaven to gaudy day denies.

- ✔ If you read this poem and Word translates it into something funny, feel free to e-mail me the results at dgookin@wambooli.com. I'll post them at this Web page:

    `www.wambooli.com/fun/humor/Byron/`

Periods, commas, tabs, and the Enter key

Most punctuation marks and special keys can be spoken. For example, you can say "period" to put a period at the end of a sentence. Saying "enter" starts a new line. Table 25-1 lists a bunch of punctuation marks you can pronounce and have Word interpret them as punctuation marks and not as the words themselves.

Table 25-1	Pronounceable Punctuation
Saying This	*Gives You This*
Asterisk	*
At sign	@
Backslash	\
Cent sign	¢
Close paren	)
Comma	,
Dash	—
Dollar sign	$

Saying This	*Gives You This*
Enter	New line (like pressing the Enter key)
Equal sign	=
Exclamation point	!
Greater than	>
Hyphen	-
Less than	<
New line	New line (like pressing the Enter key)
Open paren	(
Percent sign	%
Period	.
Plus sign	+
Question mark	?
Slash	/
Tab	Tab (like pressing the Tab key)

There are probably more secret words you can pronounce in addition to the ones in the table. The best way to discover a new one is to try speaking it; follow the symbol name with "sign" to see whether that helps.

My advice is to keep one hand on the keyboard and another on the mouse. That way, you can use the mouse to fix things or choose options as you speak. You can use your hand on the keyboard to type characters rather than pronounce them.

Did I Really Say That?

Correction If you're reviewing your text and need confirmation of a word you spoke, put the toothpick cursor on that word and click the Correction button (as shown in the margin). Word plays back the word you spoke, which you hear over the computer's speakers. A pop-up menu then appears, as shown in Figure 25-4, from which you can choose another word or phrase to correct.

Figure 25-4:
The
Correction
feature lets
you tell
Word what
you *really*
meant to
say.

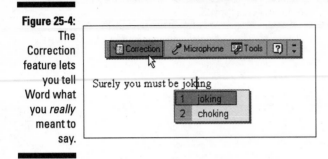

You can also correct words by right-clicking on them with the mouse. When you do, a list of similar-sounding words appears at the top of the shortcut menu. To replace the word, choose a new one from the list.

Issuing Voice Commands

Sit! Heel! Beg! Roll over!

Seriously, you may find that Word understands the voice commands far better than it understands your attempts to dictate science fiction. You will also find, unfortunately, that editing with voice commands is far slower and more frustrating than using the keyboard or the mouse.

To switch to command mode, ensure that the Microphone is on and click the Voice Command button, as shown in the margin. The Speech toolbar enters command mode, which has a limited vocabulary geared toward editing your text.

Editing the text

I know of no one who edits text exclusively with voice commands. It's just too efficient to use the keyboard and mouse. But if you're curious, slam the Speech toolbar into Voice Command mode and try out some of the basic editing commands.

For basic cursor movement, try the following commands:

Say This	*To Move the Cursor Like this Key*
Up	↑
Down	↓
Left	←
Right	→
Home	Home key
End	End key

Delete text using the "Backspace" or "Delete" voice commands.

To select text, say the word *select* followed by the text you want to select: "Select word," "select sentence," "select line," or "select paragraph."

Ramblings and rumblings on voice recognition (that you don't have to read)

With all the computing power and software know-how they can muster, someday computer scientists will perfect voice recognition. No training will be required. You just sit down and start dictating, and the computer will type for you, all spelled and punctuated properly. Even so, no matter how good voice recognition gets, I don't believe that computers will ever lose their keyboards or mice.

For one, it's much too easy to edit using the keyboard and mouse. I can fly the toothpick cursor to the top of the page with one key command faster than I can ever say "up" 20 times. Menus, dialog boxes, options, and editing — these were all designed with the mouse and keyboard in mind. And no matter how perfect your dictation and how well the computer understands you, editing will always be involved.

The second point is that thinking, speaking, and writing are all different mental activities. For example, I typically think of something to write,

mutter it several times to get the feel, and then, finally, type it out with my fingers (muttering along with my typing). I just can't imagine doing all that out loud. It's a totally different paradigm, just as reading a book is mentally different from reciting poetry or singing.

Finally, Word itself will have to change if voice recognition is to ever take over. A word processor is a computing device that requires keyboard input. That's the way it was originally designed, and that's the aspect of Word that Microsoft engineers have been honing for nearly 20 years. If there is to ever be a "voice-recognition processor," it should be built from the ground up with voice recognition in mind. In other words, if they continue to cobble voice recognition into Word, attempting to merge these two approaches, the result will be extremely messy. That's probably not the best way to take word processing into the 21st century.

Accessing menus and dialog boxes

Shouting out menu names and commands is easy. Start by switching the toolbar over to Voice Command mode. Then just say the menu name and then the item. For example, say "Format, font" to access the Format⇨Font command. This command displays the Font dialog box.

You work your way through a dialog box by saying the command or label in the dialog box. For example, in the Font dialog box, say "bold" to activate the bold option. To change the font size, say "size" followed by the new size value.

To close a dialog box, say "Okay." To cancel, say "Cancel" or "Escape."

Chapter 26

Working with an Outline

. . . .

In This Chapter

▶ Creating an outline in Word

▶ Adding topics and subtopics

▶ Adding a text topic

▶ Rearranging topics in an outline

▶ Viewing the outline

▶ Printing the outline

. . . .

*T*he daring young man on the flying trapeze had better have a net. Without a net, he could have a short career. And audiences forgive a guy when he falls. Really! Enjoy the show, folks! He's got a net!

The daring young man (or woman) on a flying word processor had better have an outline. I wouldn't write a book without one. Sure, with short papers and documents, you have no need for an outline. (Are you listening, Dr. Tremaine?) But for anything with more than two thoughts, an outline is a blessing. May you read this chapter and be blessed.

Word's Outline Mode

An outline in Word is just like any other document. The only difference is in how Word displays the text on the screen. I'll give you a hint: Outline mode makes solid use of the heading style — which is terrific because so much of Word assumes that you're using the heading style.

To create a new outline, follow these steps:

1. Start a new document.

Press Ctrl+N or click the New button on the toolbar.

2. Switch to Outline view.

Ah. The secret. Choose View⇨Outline or click the Outline View button crowded into the lower-left corner of the window. See Figure 26-1 (though this figure has lots of text in it that you don't see on your screen right now).

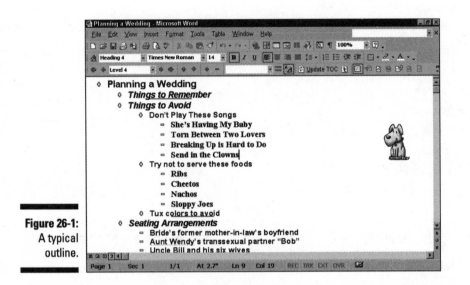

Figure 26-1:
A typical
outline.

Two amazing things happen: First, you get to see the Outlining toolbar, which replaces the ruler on Word's screen. The Outlining toolbar helps you work with and organize your outline. Second, a hollow minus sign appears before the toothpick cursor. This minus sign means that you're typing a topic in the outline and that the topic has no subtopics.

3. You're ready to start your outline.

All the outlining details are covered in the next few sections. In the meantime, I offer some general facts:

✔ Word's outlining function is merely a different way to look at a document. It's possible, but not really necessary, to shift back into Normal or Print Layout view when you're working on an outline.

✔ Don't worry about fonts or formatting while you're creating an outline. Word uses the Heading 1 through Heading 9 styles for your outline. That's okay.

✔ All Word's normal commands work in Outline mode. You can use the cursor keys, delete text, spell check, save, insert oddball characters, print, and so on.

Adding topics to your outline

An outline is composed of topics and subtopics. The main topics are your main ideas, with the subtopics describing the details. You should start your outline by adding the main topics. To do so, just type them out.

In Figure 26-2, you see several topics typed out, each on a line by itself. Pressing Enter after typing a topic produces a new hollow hyphen, at which you can type your next topic.

Figure 26-2:
Level-one
topics.

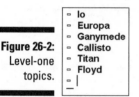

- Io
- Europa
- Ganymede
- Callisto
- Titan
- Floyd
- |

✔ Press Enter at the end of each topic. This tells Word that you're done typing information for that topic and want to move on to the next topic.

✔ Pressing Enter creates another topic at the same "level" as the first topic. To create a subtopic, see the next section.

✔ A topic can be a single word, a few words, a complete sentence, or a big paragraph. However, your main topics should be short and descriptive, like in a book's table of contents.

✔ You can split a topic by putting the toothpick cursor somewhere in its middle and pressing the Enter key. That way, *Pins and Needles* can be split into two categories (beneath the *Sharp things* topic, of course).

✔ To join two topics, put the toothpick cursor at the end of the first topic and press the Delete key. (This method works just like joining two paragraphs in a regular document.)

✔ It doesn't matter whether you get the order right at first. The beauty of creating your outline with a word processor is that you can rearrange your topics as your ideas solidify. My advice is just to start writing things down now and concentrate on organization later.

✔ An outline can be the plot to a novel, a speech you're giving, a recipe, an itinerary, a product development cycle — just about anything that requires more than one thought.

✔ Remember that a topic line should be an individual thought or idea. If your topic is

    liver and fava beans

you should split it in two:

```
liver
fava beans
```

Use the Enter key to split a topic.

Working with subtopics

Outlines have several levels. Beneath topics are subtopics, and those subtopics may have sub-subtopics. For example, your main topic may be "Things that make me itch," and the subtopics would be what those things actually are.

You don't really *create* subtopics in Word as much as you *demote* main topics.

To create a subtopic, simply type your subtopic at the main topic level. Put the toothpick cursor on the topic and click the Demote button on the Outline toolbar.

Instantly, the text in the topic moves over a tab stop and the style changes to the next heading style. Both these actions visually indicate that you're working on a new topic level.

To see which level topic you're viewing, use the Outline Level drop-down list. You can also select a level from the list to instantly promote or demote the current topic to any other level in the document.

✔ You can continue creating subtopics by pressing the Enter key at the end of each subtopic — just as you created new main-level topics. Word keeps giving you subtopics, one for each press of the Enter key.

✔ Notice that the main topic (the one the subtopic lives in) grows a + symbol. That's the sign that a topic has subtopics. More on that in the section "Viewing Your Outline," a bit later in this chapter.

✔ You can also demote a topic by pressing the Alt+Shift+→ key combination.

✔ Unlike when you're creating main topics, you can get a little wordy with your subtopics. After all, the idea here is to expand on the main topic. For example, if you're writing a speech, a subtopic would contain a more detailed sketch of your talk — maybe not the talk itself, just more details.

✔ To make a subtopic back into a topic, you promote it. Put the toothpick cursor on the topic and press Alt+Shift+← or click the Promote button.

✔ To make any topic a main-level topic, click the Promote to Heading 1 button.

> ✔ See "Viewing Your Outline" for information on looking at different parts of your outline while hiding other parts.

> ✔ You can create a sub-subtopic simply by repeating the preceding steps for a subtopic. In fact, Word lets you organize on a number of levels. Most outlines, however, typically have maybe four or five levels max.

Adding a text topic

If you feel the need to break out and actually write a paragraph in your outline, you can do so. Although it's perfectly legit to write the paragraph on the topic level, what you should really do is stick in a text topic using the Demote to Body Text button. Here's how:

1. **Press the Enter key to start a new topic.**

   Do this just as you would create any new topic on a line by itself.

2. **Click the Demote to Body Text button.**

   Or, you can press Ctrl+Shift+N. What this step does is change the style to Normal (which is what the keyboard shortcut key does). In your outline, however, that style allows you to write a paragraph of text that isn't a heading. So you can write an actual bit of text for your speech, instructions in a list, or dialogue from your novel.

> ✔ The Body Text style appears with a tiny, hollow square by it, unlike topics that have hollow plus or minus signs by them.

> ✔ If you change your mind, you can promote or demote your body text to a topic or subtopic. Refer to the preceding section.

Rearranging topics

Just like shuffling the stack of 3 x 5 cards my high school teachers urged me to use when outlining, reorganizing your topics in a computer outline is a cinch. And it's more fun, too, because you're using a computer and not something that has your mother's recipes on the back side. (And, boy, was she mad!)

To move any topic in your outline, put the toothpick cursor in that topic and then click one of the following buttons:

> ✔ Click the Move Up button (or press Alt+Shift+↑) to move a topic up a line.

> ✔ Click the Move Down button (or press Alt+Shift+↓) to move a topic down a line.

> ✔ Click the Promote button (or press Alt+Shift+←) to move a topic left.

> ✔ Click the Demote button (or press Alt+Shift+→) to move a topic right.

The mystery of the master document

One concept close to outlining is Word's master document feature. It's rather interesting, and quite useful if you plan on using Word to cobble together several chapter-size documents into a longer novel. Alas, it's a bit technical and I'm rapidly running out of room in this book for technical things.

Basically, a master document works like an outline. The master document contains, rather than subtopics, links to other documents on disk. That way, you can stitch together a larger document out of several smaller documents. The master document can print everything, in order, with page numbers, headers, footers, and even a master table of contents and index. The buttons on the right side of the Outlining toolbar carry out these tasks.

You can also use the mouse to move topics around: Drag the topic by its plus or minus sign and drop it off at the new location. Personally, I don't use this technique because my outlines are rather complex and moving topics in this manner becomes unwieldy.

Viewing Your Outline

Unless you tell Word otherwise, it displays all the topics in your outline, from top to bottom — everything. But this display really isn't part of the glory of outlining. What makes outlining on a computer special is that if you want to step back and see the Big Picture, you can do so.

To see specific levels, use the Show Level drop-down list. For example, to see all the first-level topics in your outline, choose Show Level 1 from the list. All subtopics and text topics are hidden.

If a topic has subtopics, not only does it have a hollow plus sign by it, but you also see a fuzzy line extending out over the last part of the topic name. I haven't met anyone yet who knows exactly what the fuzzy line is supposed to mean.

If you want to see your outline in more detail, choose Show Level 2 or Show Level 3 from the list. Each item on the list displays the outline only up until that level; higher levels remain hidden.

To see the entire outline, choose Show All Levels from the list.

✔ You can open or close individual topics by double-clicking the hollow plus sign with the mouse.

✔ Open or expand a topic with the Expand button on the toolbar or by pressing Alt+Shift+Plus (the plus key on the numeric keypad).

✔ Collapse a topic with the Alt+Shift+Minus key combination. (Use the minus key on your keyboard's numeric keypad.)

✔ If you have wordy topic levels, you can direct Word to display only the first topic line by clicking the Show First Line Only button.

✔ Another great way to view the outline is to click the Show Formatting button. This button shows or removes the formatting from the outline, which (with the formatting removed) lets more text appear on the screen.

✔ As your outline nears perfection, you can copy parts of it and paste them into other, new documents. This method is the way some writers create their books and novels; the document is merely a longer, more complete version of what starts as an outline.

Printing Your Outline

Printing your outline works just like printing any other document in Word. But because it's an outline, there is one difference: Only those topics visible in your outline are printed.

For example, if you want to print only the first two levels of your outline, choose Show Level 2 from the Show Level drop-down list. This action hides all subtopics and when you print your outline, only the first and second topics are printed.

If you want your entire outline to print, choose Show All Levels before printing.

The outline shortcut key summary box

When I'm typing, I like my hands to remain on the keyboard. Because of this preference, I discovered the following key combinations that work when playing with an outline. Try them if you dare:

Key Combo	Function
Alt+Shift+→	Demote a topic
Alt+Shift+←	Promote a topic
Alt+Shift+↑	Shift a topic up one line
Alt+Shift+↓	Shift a topic down one line
Ctrl+Shift+N	Insert some body text

Key Combo	Function
Alt+Shift+1	Display only top topics
Alt+Shift+2	Display first- and second-level topics
Alt+Shift+#	Display all topics up to number #
Alt+Shift+A	Display all topics
Alt+Shift+Plus (+)	Display all subtopics in the current topic
Alt+Shift+Minus (–)	Hide all subtopics in the current topic

Chapter 27

Collaboration Tricks

● ●

● ●

*F*or the most part, writing is something you do by yourself. However, there are times when you need (or want) to share your work with others — for example, you want to make sure that your proposal is upbeat and inoffensive, so you run it by someone else. In these instances, you can use some of Word's collaboration tools to help you and your writing partners (or overlords or editors or whomever) communicate.

This chapter covers the Word tricks and techniques that let you happily work with others. This way, you and your comrades can cooperatively work on a new antigovernment manifesto, but when the state police come, they'll arrest just one guy.

✔ This book does not cover online collaboration, where you can meet on the Internet to mutually mangle a document.

✔ I really wish that Microsoft would release the geniuses who designed these collaboration tools over to the Word mail merge department. These collaboration tools are fun to use and actually make sense, unlike mail merge, which was probably designed by drunken monkeys in strait-jackets.

Making Comments

Word's comments are like sticky notes for your text, though physically they look more like cartoon bubbles. This is the first of Word's various text-markup commands. You can use them to communicate with others (or your-self), offering suggestions, ideas, editing, or general advice.

Adding a comment

To a comment into your document, follow these steps:

1. Position the toothpick cursor where you want to make a comment.

You can also select a block of text if your comment concerns some spe-cific sentence or phrase.

2. Choose Insert⇨Comment.

You may need to click the "show more" arrows at the bottom of the menu to find the Comment command.

A cartoon bubble appears with the text `Comment:` in it (see Figure 27-1).

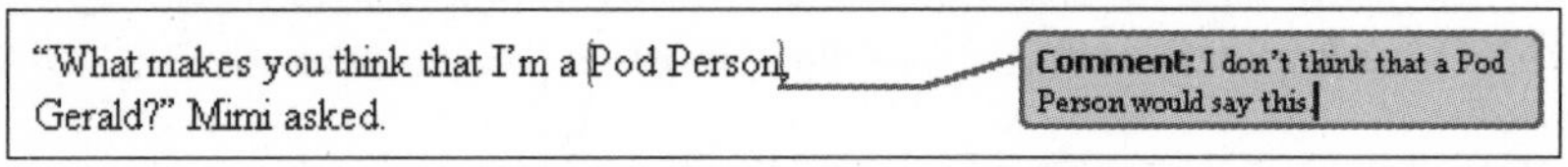

Figure 27-1:
Inserting a
comment
into your
text.

"What makes you think that I'm a Pod Person, Gerald?" Mimi asked.   **Comment:** I don't think that a Pod Person would say this.

It's best to use Print Layout view to best see the comments. If you're using Normal view, the comments appear as large, colored parentheses in your text. The comment text is added in the reviewing pane at the bottom of the document window.

3. Type your comment.

The cartoon bubble expands to contain all your comments — and they can be quite large, though short and to the point is best.

4. When you're done, just click in your text and keep writing.

The comments stay visible in your text unless you hide them, which is covered in the next section.

Repeat these steps to add more annotations to the text.

✔ You can edit the comments as you edit any text in Word.

✔ Comment text has its own style: `Comment Text`.

✔ The comments also print, unless you direct Word not to print them. To do so, in the Print dialog box, choose Document from the Print <u>w</u>hat drop-down list (in the lower-left part of the dialog box.) Or, if you want to print the comments, choose Document showing markup from the list.

✔ You can see how the comments are printed by using the File⇨Print Preview command. See Chapter 8 for the details.

✔ To see the comment text appear in Normal view, simply point the mouse at the colored parentheses. The comment appears in a pop-up bubble on the screen. (Then again, I don't recommend Normal view for this particular Word trick.)

✔ Astute readers may notice that inserting a comment also displays the Reviewing toolbar.

✔ You can summon or hide the Reviewing toolbar by choosing <u>V</u>iew⇨<u>T</u>oolbars⇨Reviewing from the menu.

✔ You can also insert a comment by clicking on the New Comment button on the Reviewing toolbar.

✔ It's also possible, and entirely nerdy, to insert an audio comment: Click the down arrow by the New Comment button and choose Voice Comment from the menu. (You're on your own from here because I don't have enough space in this chapter to write about voice comments.)

Hiding comments

To dispense with the comments, and indeed all document markups, choose <u>V</u>iew⇨<u>Ma</u>rkup from the menu. This command hides the comments (and other document markups).

You can also hide the comments by using the Reviewing toolbar: Choose <u>C</u>omments from the <u>S</u>how drop-down list (see Figure 27-2). This action removes the check mark by the <u>C</u>omments item and hides the comments in your document.

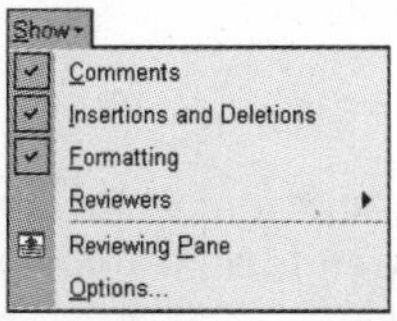

Figure 27-2: The Show menu.

Show ▾
☑ Comments
☑ Insertions and Deletions
☑ Formatting
Reviewers ▸
Reviewing Pane
Options...

(Likewise, to show a document's comments, you can choose Comments from the Show drop-down list.)

You can also choose Original or Final from the Display for Review drop-down list, which is the first item on the Reviewing toolbar. The Original and Final items are geared more for tracking document changes (covered later in this chapter), but they can also be used to hide comments.

Reviewing all comments

 To see all a document's comments at once, click the Reviewing toolbar's Reviewing Pane button, which, like its name says, displays the reviewing pane. This action opens a frame below your document window that lists each comment, who made the comment, the comment's date and time, and then the comment itself.

To close the reviewing pane, click the Reviewing Pane button again.

Another way to review comments is by using the Next and Previous buttons on the Reviewing toolbar.

 Click the Next button to have Word instantly jump to the next comment in your document.

Click the Previous button to have Word instantly jump back to the more recent, previous comment in your document.

Deleting a comment

To delete a comment, first select it. All you need to do is click the mouse in the comment's cartoon bubble. This action makes the bubble's color turn a shade darker. That's all you need to do to select the comment.

After the comment is selected, right-click it and choose Delete Comment from the pop-up menu.

 You can also click the Delete Comment button to delete a selected comment.

Nonprinting Text

Another way to stuff secret messages into your document is to use Word's hidden text format. As Chapter 11 states, the hidden format makes text invisible in Word. The text doesn't show up on the screen, and it doesn't print. But you can still see it! Keep reading. . . .

To hide text — any text — in your document, select the text as a block and hide it: Choose Format➪Font. In the Font dialog box, click the Hidden option in the Effects area. This action hides the text onscreen and when it's printed, but leaves all the other text (and paragraph) formatting intact. Click OK to apply the hidden text format.

Meanwhile, back in your document, the text you selected is gone! Whew!

Show ▾ To see the hidden text, use the Show command. Click the Show button on the toolbar or press Ctrl+Shift+8 (the 8 key on the keyboard, not on the numeric keypad). These keystrokes display the hidden text with a dotted underline.

> ✔ To globally unhide text, select your entire document with Ctrl+A, open the Font dialog box, and remove the check mark by the Hidden text attribute. Click OK. But be warned! If any comments are in the hidden text, they're deleted when you do this.

> ✔ Refer to Chapter 6 for more block-marking instructions.

> ✔ This technique is also good for hiding sensitive parts of a document. For example, you may want to print a report both internally and publicly. Making the internal information hidden ensures that it doesn't print on the public document.

Whip Out the Yellow Highlighter

Word comes with a text highlighter that lets you mark up and colorize the text in your document without damaging your computer monitor.

To highlight your text (onscreen, electronically, of course), click the Highlight button on the Formatting toolbar. Click!

 Now you've entered Highlighting mode. The mouse pointer changes to something I can't describe verbally but can picture in the left margin. When you drag the mouse over your text, that text becomes highlighted — just like you can do with a highlighter on regular paper. It's amazing what those whiz kids at Microsoft come up with. . . .

To stop highlighting text, click the Highlight button again or press the Esc key.

> ✔ To unhighlight your text, click the down arrow by the Highlight button and choose None as the highlight color. Then drag over your highlighted text to unhighlight.

> ✔ To remove highlights from your entire document, press Ctrl+A to select all your text and choose None from the Highlight button's drop-down list.

✔ You can also highlight a block of text by first marking the block and then clicking the Highlight button. See Chapter 6 for all the proper block-marking instructions.

✔ The highlighted text prints, so be careful with it. If you don't have a color printer, highlighted text prints black on gray on your hard copy.

✔ In addition to the None color for erasing highlight marks, you can choose any of the highlight colors available on the Highlight button's drop-down list. And to think that an office supply store would charge you an extra $1.20 for each color.

Sharing Work with Revision Marks

Every writer jealously guards his text. It's enough that someone must edit — some lowly editor who seethes with jealously over the fact that the noble writer is the one who gets all the fame and glory even though it's the editor who deserves the credit. Oh, editors can be nasty. *[Hey! — Ed.]* But other writers can be worse.

Revision marks are a way of tracking changes made to your document by evil people. Okay, maybe not evil, but people who change things without first making suggestions. To help protect yourself against such intrusion, you can use one of Word's many revision-tracking tools. The following sections outline two ways you can put them to use.

Tracking changes between two versions of the same document

Go ahead and put away the magnifying glass. When someone else returns your Word document to you, it's a cinch to have Word compare the "new" document with your pristine original. Word flags any changes, displaying them for you right on the screen. Here's how:

1. **Make sure that you have the edited (newer) document loaded and on the screen.**

   The original document should be saved to disk. That's okay for now; you don't need to open it. Just open the edited document and have it on the screen in front of you.

   Yup. The newer and original documents should have two different names. That's best.

2. **Choose Tools⇨Compare and Merge Documents.**

   An Open dialog box appears, though it's named Compare and Merge Documents and not Open.

3. **Find the original document on disk.**

    Use your finely honed Open dialog box skills to find and select the original document on disk.

4. **Click the Merge button.**

    Word thinks long and hard. What it's doing is comparing the document on the screen with the older copy on your hard disk.

5. **Peruse the changes.**

    Snoop over the changes made to your pristine prose by the barbarian interlopers!

What you're looking at is your original document, not the edited copy. (Check the name on the title bar.) Remember that!

New or added text appears underlined and in another color.

In Print Layout view, deleted text appears as a small triangle, with an underline leading to the right margin where the deleted text appears. In Normal view, the deleted text appears in ~~strikethrough~~.

Yes, it is annoying to read. Oui, oui!

✔ Astute readers will note that merging a document in this manner automatically displays the Reviewing toolbar, handy for reviewing the changes to your document, as covered in the next section.

✔ Each "reviewer" is given their own color on your screen. For example, on my screen I see the revision marks as red. Had a second reviewer gone over the text, those comments would appear in a second color, and so on for other reviewers.

✔ If you want to thumbs-up-or-down each revision, refer to the next section "Reviewing the changes."

✔ To see the changes as they appear according to the edited document, choose Original Showing Markup from the Display for review drop-down list (the first item on the Reviewing toolbar).

✔ To hide the revision marks, choose Final from the Display for review drop-down list.

Reviewing the changes

There is no sense is showing blind obedience to any editor or critic! If you're a budding writer, it's time for you to learn a new term: STET. It's Latin, and it means *to stand*. When you STET an edit, you're telling the editor that you reject the change that was made and wish the item to stand. Now, please keep in mind that the editor is there to guide you and, under most circumstances, wants to see your text read better than it probably did originally. Still, STET is a handy order to give.

To STET the changes in your text, you have several choices. First, right-click on any revision. From the pop-up menu, you can choose either the Accept or Reject commands; Accept Insertion and Accept Deletion confirm that the change that was made is something you want. Reject Insertion and Reject Deletion are the STET commands; they tell Word to restore the text to its original, intended state.

 To quickly find the next markup, use the Next button on the Reviewing toolbar.

 The Previous button takes you back to the preceding markup.

 The Accept Change button can be used to grant your approval to any edit.

 The Reject Change button is used to, well, STET.

 If you're in a real hurry, you can use the drop-down menus beneath either the Accept Change or Reject Change buttons to choose either the Accept All Changes in Document or Reject All Changes in Document commands, respectively. It's kind of a global admission that either, yes, the editor is right or, no, STET STET STET.

> ✔ If you goof, you can click the Undo button in the Accept or Reject Changes dialog box.
>
> ✔ Going through this process removes all the revision marks from your document. If you want to re-review the revisions, you have to repeat the steps in the preceding section for comparing two documents.
>
> ✔ Don't forget to save your revised text back to disk.

Tracking changes as you make them

Suppose that *you* are the editor! Ha! Crack an evil smile as you attempt to scissor and paste someone else's labors. Gads! That must be fun!

Please be gentle as you edit. Don't go nuts! To help, you can activate Word's revision-tracking feature, which lets you see your markups on the screen as you make them.

Activate markup mode by clicking on the Track Changes button on the Reviewing toolbar. Or, you can double-click on the TRK acronym on the status bar. Either way, revision tracking is armed and ready.

Now edit!

Any text you add appears underlined. Deleted text is immediately banished to the right margin. Or, if you're using Normal view, deleted text is shown in ~~strikethrough~~.

Have fun.

Chapter 28

Working with Documents

● ●

In This Chapter

▶ Making a new folder for your stuff

▶ Changing folders

▶ Using Word's Find command

▶ Opening, saving, or closing groups of files

▶ Working with non-Word documents and text files

● ●

*T*he more work you do in Word, the more documents you create — piles of files. And if you don't clean up or organize those piles, then just like manure in a barnyard, you're going to be hip-deep in files in a few weeks. Maybe sooner.

This chapter tackles the subject of files — using and organizing them. It's more of a Windows chapter, so I'll be brief on the file-management part. Still, you can do lots of file management right in Word, without ever having to mess with Windows, the Big Momma Operating System.

Also covered: importing and exporting files. No international license required or bribes to pay!

Creating a New Folder

To keep organized, you may need to create new folders for your new projects. For example, if you've just started your plan to manipulate the world's economy through brain waves, you're going to need a new folder to put all those memos and letters in. Here's how you do that:

1. **Summon the Save As dialog box with File➪Save As.**

   Obviously, having something to save first helps, such as that first letter to the Federal Reserve Bank.

2. **Click the Create New Folder button.**

   The New Folder dialog box appears.

3. **Type a name for your new folder.**

Be descriptive. Be creative. Be short and sweet. Be to the point. (Try really hard to achieve this goal if you're a lawyer.)

Have the folder name reflect its contents.

4. **Click OK.**

Through the magic of the computer, your new folder is created. Further magic: Word automatically opens the folder and displays its contents. It's empty.

5. **Continue saving your document.**

You don't really have to save a document every time you create a folder. You can click the Cancel button in the Save As dialog box to return to your work. The next time you go to save a document (or open one, for that matter), you're using the new folder you just created.

✔ You can create new folders in the Save As dialog box but not in the Open dialog box. I mean, like, duh. If you created a new folder in the Open dialog box, there wouldn't be anything in the folder for you to open. Some people. . . .

✔ You can get lots of mileage from a folder named Junk or Misc.

Using Another Folder

If you go into a folder-creating frenzy, you need to be able to access those folders whenever you want to see the documents they hold or to save a new document in a specific folder. Here's how you go about it:

1. **Summon the Open command with File➪Open.**

Or press Ctrl+O. Soon, the Open dialog box swings into full view.

2. **First, see which folder you're using.**

The folder's name appears in the Look In drop-down box at the top of the dialog box. Normally, it's the My Documents folder, which is where Word wants to save stuff.

If you're already in the folder you want to be in, skip to Step 6 (meaning that you're more or less done).

3. **Select the disk drive you want from the Look In drop-down list.**

If you select a floppy drive, ensure that you have a disk in the drive before you select it.

If you only have one hard drive, C, select it as well. Looking for your folder from the top down is best.

Because most folders are kept in the My Documents folder, you can always click the big My Documents button on the left side of the Open dialog box. That zooms you to that folder, pronto.

4. **Select your folder from those listed in the dialog box.**

   You may have to scroll through the list to find the folder you want.

5. **Keep repeating Step 4 until you find the folder you're looking for.**

   For example, you may have to open My Documents, and then Projects, and then Memos to finally see the documents stored in the Memos folder.

6. **Open your document.**

   Click the Open button.

   ✔ Some folders contain other folders. To see their contents, double-click the folder's name in the Open dialog box.

   ✔ Also see Chapter 8 for more information on using the Open dialog box.

   ✔ Each disk in your system has its own set of folders. If you can't find the folder you want on one disk, try another. For example, scope out hard drive D if drive C turns out to be a dud.

Finding Files in Word

Finding files is really a Windows function. It's what Windows does best, but Word can also locate your wayward documents. Too bad finding socks or a clean shirt isn't this easy:

1. **Summon the task pane.**

   Choose View➪Task Pane if it's not visible.

2. **Choose Search from the task pane's menu.**

   You see the menu by clicking the downward-pointing triangle near the upper-right corner of the task pane. The Search command is the third item on the menu.

   Lo, the Basic Search task pane appears, as shown in Figure 28-1. In its Basic Search mode, the task pane helps you find files based on any text they contain.

3. **Type in the Search text box the text you're looking for.**

   For example, I wrote a touching poem awhile back, and all I can remember was that it contained the word *dermatitis*.

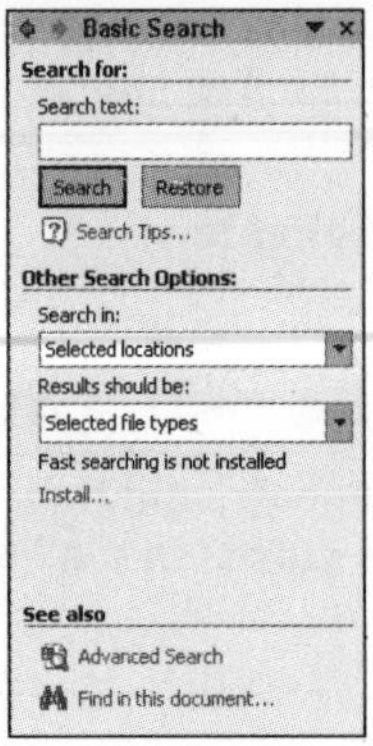

Figure 28-1:
Use the
Basic
Search task
pane to look
for files.

4. **Click the Search button.**

   The Search Results panel appears. Then everything sits still for a while as Word scours the hard drive.

   Scour. Scour. Scour.

   Eventually, you see a scrolling list of folders and documents Word found that match the information you searched for. Or, if nothing was found, no files are displayed; try again using some other bit of text, or just give up now and cook yourself some yummy noodles.

5. **To open a file, choose it from the list.**

   The file opens and, well, there you are. (You can use the Find command after the document is open to locate the text again, if you need to do so. See Chapter 5.)

To perform another search, you need to click the Modify button. That returns you to the Basic Search task pane from the Search Results task pane.

✔ If you want to restrict the search to certain folders or disk drives, use the Search in drop-down list to customize where you want Word to look.

✔ You can also use the Results should be drop-down list to choose which types of files Word looks for. Normally, Word searches for all Microsoft Office file types, though you can narrow it down to only Word files by removing various check marks.

✔ To find a file based on its name, use the Find command in Windows Explorer. Alas, this command varies with each version of Windows, and because this isn't a Windows book, there's no point in going through all those steps here. Just go out and buy a good book on Windows, preferably one that's written by Dan Gookin. Thanks.

Deleting a file in Word

Previous versions of Word sported a handy (yet potentially deadly) Delete command. In addition to working with files, creating new folders, and finding stuff, Word let you mercilessly venture out to your disk and kill off files in a rage of wanton destruction. Since that time, this feature has been downplayed, though it's still possible to delete files in Word.

The secret to deleting files is to use the Open or Save As dialog box. Those dialog boxes actually behave like mini-Windows Explorer windows.

For example, you can rename a file in the Open dialog box by selecting that file and pressing the F2 key — just as you would in Windows Explorer. Likewise, you can delete any file by selecting it and pressing the Delete key on your keyboard.

So, deleting files in Word is entirely possible. Yet I do have an admonishment: Never delete any file you did not create yourself. That will keep you out of trouble.

Working with Groups of Files

The Open dialog box enables you to work with files individually or in groups. To work with a group of files, you must select them with the mouse, which you do by following the typical Windows procedure for selecting several items in a group:

1. **Press the Ctrl key and click each document you want to select.**

   The item becomes highlighted.

2. **Repeat Step 1 for each additional item you want in your group.**

   Et cetera.

You can select a group of files in only one folder. However, if you follow the instructions in "Finding Files in Word," earlier in this chapter, you can select files from all over your hard drive.

Opening files

Here's how to open more than one file at a time using the Open dialog box:

1. **Select the file or group of files that you want to open from those shown in the Open dialog box's window.**

2. **Click the Open button.**

   The files open, and Word places each in its own document window.

3. **Work away!**

There is a limit on the number of files Word can work with at once. No, I don't know what the maximum number is — but you will! You'll see some odd error message about not enough memory or "heap" space or something bizarre. Don't panic. Close a few windows — maybe even quit Word — and start over.

Saving a gang of documents simultaneously

To save a multitude of documents all at once, you can switch to each window and incant the File⇨Save command. Or, you can be sneaky and do the following:

1. **Press and hold the Shift key — either one.**

2. **Choose File⇨Save All.**

   Normally, you choose the Save item. But if you press the Shift key before choosing the File menu, it magically becomes the Save All menu item.

   There is no prompting, and no wait-and-see. Everything is just saved to disk as fast as your PC can handle it.

✔ If a file has not yet been saved, you're prompted to give it a name. For more information, refer to the section in Chapter 8 about saving a document to disk the first time.

✔ I use the File⇨Save All command whenever I have to get up and leave my computer — even for a short moment, such as when the phone rings or when aliens land outside and demand Bisquick.

Closing a gang of documents simultaneously

You can conjure up a Close All command just like the Save All command. The difference is that you choose the Close All item from the menu; just press the Shift key (either one) before you click the File menu with your mouse. Then choose the Close All option and — thwoop! — all your open documents are closed.

Word still asks whether you want to save any unsaved documents before it closes them. See the section in Chapter 8 about saving a document to disk the first time.

Working with Other Document Formats

Believe it or not, Word isn't the only word processor in the world. It's not like Word is struggling for market dominance. Hey! It's there! Even so, other word processors exist as well as other document file formats. Occasionally, you may tangle with those file formats. When you do, you need to import their weird word-processing files into Word so that you can do something with them. Likewise, you can export your Word documents into weird word-processing formats. The following sections tell you how.

Loading an alien document

Prepare to welcome the intruder! Suppose that someone has sent you a text file, or a WordPerfect document, or a Web page, or some weirdo file that is in no way a Word document. No problem! Word can open and examine the document without so much as breaking an electronic sweat. Follow these steps:

1. **Do the Open command.**

2. **In the Files of Type drop-down box, select the file format.**

   If you know the format, choose it from the list. Here are some popular formats:

   - **Word Documents:** Any document created by Word.

   - **Web Pages and Web Archives:** HTML documents or Web pages that you've saved to disk.

   - **Rich Text Format (RTF):** A common file format for exchanging word processing documents between word processors.

   - **Text Files:** Plain, boring, text-only documents. No formatting. Blah, though this is a common file format. Also known as ASCII or MS-DOS Text.

   - **Recover Text From Any File:** A very handy option that lets Word extract text from any type of file. Use this one as a last resort.

   - **WordPerfect (various versions/platforms):** Used to read WordPerfect documents.

   - **Works (various versions/platforms):** Used to read in Microsoft Works documents.

   - **Word (various versions/platforms):** Reads in older Word documents and documents written on the Macintosh.

   When you choose a specific file format, Word displays in the Open dialog box only those files matching the format. Your next job is to find the file you want to open.

If you don't know the format, choose All Files from the drop-down list. Word then makes its best guess.

3. **Hunt down the text file you want to load.**

   Use the controls in the dialog box to find the file you want. See the section "Using Another Folder," earlier in this chapter, for more information.

4. **Click the text file's icon once with the mouse.**

5. **Click Open.**

   The alien file appears onscreen, ready for editing, just like any Word document.

✔ In some cases and with some file formats, you may need to fix the formatting.

✔ Word may display a File Conversion dialog box, allowing you to preview how the document appears. Generally speaking, clicking the OK button in this step is your best bet.

✔ If the Open dialog box doesn't display the file you're looking for — and you know that the file is there — try typing its name in the File name box and clicking the Open button.

✔ Word *remembers* the file type! When you go to use the Open dialog box again, it has the same file type chosen from the Files of type drop-down list. So, if you want to open a Word document after opening an HTML document, you *must* choose Word Documents from the list. Otherwise, Word may open documents in a manner that seems strange to you.

✔ Additional file types and conversion "filters" are available on the Word (or Office) CD. To install them, run the Setup program on the CD and choose to install only the new filters.

Saving a file in a horridly strange and unnatural format

Word is quite smart when it comes to saving files to disk. For example, when you open a WordPerfect document, Word automatically saves it back to disk in the WordPerfect format. Ditto for any other alien file format: Whichever format was used to open the document, Word chooses the same format for writing the document back to disk.

The secret, as with opening files of another type, is to check the Save as type drop-down list in the Save As dialog box. In fact, choosing a new item from that drop-down list is the only way to save a document in another format.

For example, if you need to save a document as a text file, choose Text Only from the Save as type drop-down list. Click the Save button and your document is saved. Ditto for the HTML format, RTF, or any other alien document format.

Word (or the Assistant) may explain that saving the document in alien format is, well, bad. Whatever. Click Yes to save the document.

✔ You can save a document to disk by using both the Word format as well as another format. First, save the file to disk as a Word document by selecting Word Document from the Save as type box. Then save the file to disk using another format, such as Plain Text.

✔ To save in HTML format, choose Web Page from the drop-down list.

✔ Be aware that Word remembers the format! If you notice that your documents are not being saved to disk the way you want them, the Save as type drop-down list is to blame! Always double-check it to ensure that you're saving documents to disk in the proper format.

Chapter 29

Modifying Word's Appearance

● ●

In This Chapter

▶ Understanding Word's menus

▶ Working with the toolbars

▶ Displaying toolbars

▶ Rearranging toolbars and floating palettes

▶ Adding a button to a toolbar

▶ Removing a button from a toolbar

▶ Using the Zoom command

▶ Tweaking Word

● ●

*I*sn't Word a little much? I mean, it's a word processor, right? The main purpose of which is processing words. Yet, look at the screen. It's a jet fighter cockpit of controls, menus, toolbars, and gizmos! All those buttons and whatnot surround the big, blank part in which you write. Don't let it all intimidate you! Believe it or not, you have a degree of control over how Word looks. You can change, rearrange, remove, mangle, spindle, fold, *and* mutilate to your heart's content. This chapter shows you what is customizable and how to customize it, plus a few other tidbits about Word's interface.

Menus Common and Everything

The wind that blows Windows sails puts her into some strange and interesting ports. Not that any of these territories is a final destination, but with each new stop, Windows and its applications seem to grow new ways of doing things. For example, Word's menus have two modes: Common and Everything.

In Common mode, Word's menus list only those commands you commonly use. The other commands remain hidden.

To show all the commands (Everything mode), you click on the "show more" arrows at the bottom of the menu. After they're visible, you can choose any command the menu sports, visible or not. If you choose a formerly invisible command, it becomes part of Common mode and you see it available the next time you visit that menu.

- You can also display all of a menu's items (Everything mode) by double-clicking the menu with the mouse.
- The official name for dual-mode menus is *personalized* menus.
- In Windows, you can turn the personalized menus on or off, but this option is not available in Word.

Retooling the Toolbars

Messing with the toolbars is one of the first things I do when I start using Word on a new computer. Word has dozens of toolbars. In fact, if you display them all, you end up with only a tiny little pigeonhole of window in which to write!

Fortunately, all Word's toolbars are optional. You can show or hide them, you can rearrange them, you can turn them into floating palettes, and you can add or remove buttons. It's all up to you — and I encourage you to play with the toolbars and really make them your own.

- The View menu is where you can control the items Word displays on the screen.
- The only items you cannot remove from the display are the menu bar and status bar.
- The ruler is not a toolbar, yet it's controlled through the View menu. To see or hide the ruler, choose View⇨Ruler.
- Word typically displays the Standard and Formatting toolbars. The Standard toolbar is the one with the New, Open and Save buttons on the left; the Formatting toolbar contains the Style, Font, and Point drop-down lists on the left.

- You can remove *everything* from the screen by choosing the View⇨Full Screen command. That gives you the entire screen on which to write. Click the Close Full Screen button (or press the Esc key) to switch back to non-Full Screen mode.

Looking at a toolbar

All toolbars are basically the same. They can sport buttons, some of which act like text fields, drop-down lists, menus, or some combination of each.

Additionally, you should pay attention to three gizmos on a toolbar: the grabber, the toolbar menu, and the toolbar show-more arrows.

 The grabber appears on the far left side of the toolbar. You use the grabber to move the toolbar. (Even the menu bar has a grabber, which means that it can be moved as well.)

The menu button appears as a downward-pointing triangle on the far right end of the toolbar. Clicking that triangle displays the toolbar's menu.

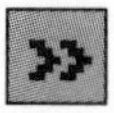

Toolbars also sport "show more" arrows, just like menus do, though the show-more arrows point to the right, as shown in the margin. When you click on this button, it displays a drop-down menu or list of the remaining buttons on the toolbar as well as any items in the toolbar's menu, as shown in Figure 29-1. You can choose a button from that menu or press Esc to hide the menu.

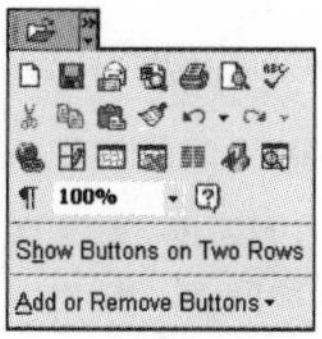

Figure 29-1:
A shortened
toolbar
displays the
rest of its
items.

To get rid of the toolbar's show-more arrows, you need to move the toolbar so that its entire length can be displayed at once. (Or, you can edit the toolbar to remove those buttons you don't often use.)

Toolbars need not be on the same line; you may find that Word comes out of the box with both the Standard and Formatting toolbars on the same line. To fix the problem, choose Show Buttons on Two Rows from either the Formatting or Standard toolbar's menu.

Refer to the "Moving and arranging toolbars" section, a little later in this chapter, for information on rearranging toolbars.

Where are the toolbars?

Though most toolbars appear when they're needed (such as the outlining toolbar when you enter Outlining mode), you can summon any toolbar you want by choosing it from the View➪Toolbars submenu, as shown in Figure 29-2. All Word's toolbars are listed on the submenu — even some toolbars you may have created yourself, such as the All Them Formatting Commands toolbar I created, shown near the bottom of the submenu shown in Figure 29-2.

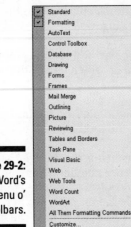

✓	Standard
✓	Formatting
	AutoText
	Control Toolbox
	Database
	Drawing
	Forms
	Frames
	Mail Merge
	Outlining
	Picture
	Reviewing
	Tables and Borders
	Task Pane
	Visual Basic
	Web
	Web Tools
	Word Count
	WordArt
	All Them Formatting Commands
	Customize...

Figure 29-2:
Word's
submenu o'
toolbars.

✔ A check mark appears by the toolbars that are already visible.

✔ To display a different toolbar, choose it from the submenu.

✔ To remove a toolbar, choose it from the submenu

✔ A quick way to get at the toolbars submenu is to right-click on any toolbar in Word. That action displays a pop-up toolbars submenu, from which you can switch various toolbars on or off.

Moving and arranging toolbars

You move a toolbar in Word by dragging it with its grabber, located on the far left side of the toolbar. When the mouse pointer changes into a four-way arrow thing (see margin), it means that you can drag the toolbar hither or thither to move the toolbar around.

Toolbars can also be dragged to floating palettes by using the grabber; just drag the toolbar into the document part of Word's window. There, it becomes a floating palette — a little mini-window that can hover over the top of all your other windows with its own Close button (the X in the upper-right corner), as shown in Figure 29-3.

Figure 29-3:
The
Standard
toolbar as a
floating
palette.

To convert a floating palette into a toolbar, drag the palette away from the document part of Word's window. When you find the sweet spot, the palette changes to a toolbar.

✔ Toolbars can exist above, below, or to the left or right of the document window. Yes, toolbars can live to the left or right of the document window, though it's uncommon.

✔ Sometimes it takes a while to position a toolbar properly. Be patient.

✔ The Standard and Formatting toolbars have a special menu item attached to them. You can choose the Show Buttons on Two Rows item to instantly arrange those two toolbars. Other toolbars do not have this menu, so you must arrange them solely by using the mouse.

✔ If you float and then accidentally close the Standard or Formatting toolbars, remember that you can resurrect them by using the View➪Toolbars submenu.

Adding common toolbar buttons

Nothing is sacred! You can customize any of Word's toolbars. After all, it's *your* word processor (no matter what the licensing agreement says!). Seriously, if you find yourself using one command quite often, why not make that command a button on the toolbar?

As an example, I use the Small Caps text format quite a bit, so a Small Caps text formatting button next to the Bold, Italics, and Underline buttons on the Formatting toolbar is really handy for me. To add that button, or any button to any toolbar, follow these steps:

1. **Display the toolbar's menu.**

   Click the down-arrow triangle thing at the far right end of the toolbar.

2. **Choose Add or Remove Buttons.**

   Another menu appears with two items. The first is related to the toolbar you've chosen. For example, the Formatting toolbar has a Formatting submenu, which lists all the various formatting commands. Very handy.

   The second menu item is Customize, which can be used to add any button to any toolbar or to create your own toolbar.

3. **Choose the named submenu.**

   For example, for the Standard toolbar, choose the Standard submenu. Figure 29-4 shows the submenu for the Formatting toolbar.

   Commands already appearing on the toolbar have check marks by them.

   Other common commands appear, which you can choose to automatically add to the toolbar.

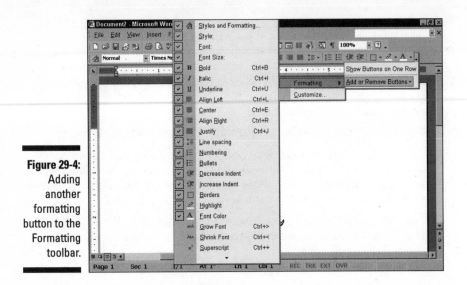

Figure 29-4:
Adding
another
formatting
button to the
Formatting
toolbar.

The last item on the menu is Reset Toolbar, which removes or adds buttons as necessary to restore the toolbar to the way it was originally
when Word came out of the box.

4. Choose the command to add.

Notice that the menu doesn't go away, thereby allowing you to add more
buttons as necessary.

5. Click in the document window when you're done.

This step makes the menu go away.

The buttons you added are placed on the far right side of the toolbar, which
may or may not be what you want. Don't worry — you can move them; see
the section "Removing or moving a toolbar button," later in this chapter.

Adding just about any button to a toolbar

Here is the best way to customize a toolbar, adding just about any command
in Word. Follow these steps:

1. Display the toolbar's menu.

2. Choose <u>A</u>dd or Remove Buttons⇨<u>C</u>ustomize.

The Customize/Commands dialog box appears, as shown in Figure 29-5.
(You can also summon this dialog box with the <u>T</u>ools⇨Customize
command.)

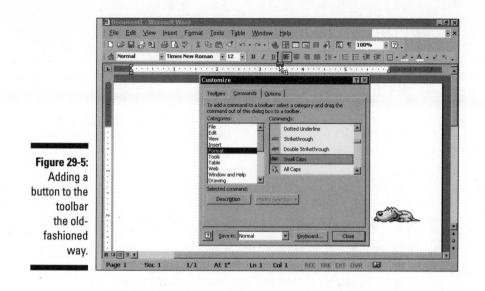

Figure 29-5:
Adding a
button to the
toolbar
the old-
fashioned
way.

Click the Commands tab if necessary; the dialog box should look like the one shown in Figure 29-5.

3. Locate the command you want to add.

The commands are organized like the Word menus. So, if you want to add a text format, select Format from the Categories list and then find the format command you want on the Commands list. All the commands are listed.

Some commands don't have cutesy little buttons. In that case, the command's text appears on the toolbar. Nothing wrong with that.

4. Drag the toolbar button you've found up onto the toolbar.

This is the tricky part, though Figure 29-5 should help. When you find the command you want, drag its icon from the Customize dialog box onto the toolbar. When the mouse is over the toolbar, a large *I* thing tells you where the command will be inserted. Release the mouse button to drop the command onto the toolbar.

5. Continue adding buttons, if you like.

Repeat Steps 3 and 4 as necessary.

6. Click Close to close the Customize dialog box.

Your new toolbar is awaiting its first use.

Removing or moving a toolbar button

The quick way to remove a button from a toolbar is to choose Add or Remove Buttons from the toolbar's menu. Then choose the toolbar's name submenu and click to remove whichever buttons you don't want there.

Alas, if you've added a button by using the Customize dialog box (as covered in the preceding section), you cannot use the toolbar's menu to remove the button. Instead, you need to return to the Customize dialog box. Here's how:

1. **Display the toolbar's menu.**

2. **Choose Add or Remove Buttons⇨Customize.**

   The Customize/Commands dialog box appears (refer to Figure 29-5).

3. **Drag any unwanted buttons off the toolbar.**

   Point the mouse at the toolbar button and drag it down to the document window. The button is "dropped" into empty space, which removes it from the toolbar.

   If you want to move any toolbar buttons, just drag them to a different spot on the toolbar. As long as the Customize dialog box is open, you can move, drag, or drop any button on any toolbar.

   The Modify button in the Customize/Commands dialog box can be used to further modify the button or to add separator items to the toolbar. (I don't have the space here to go into detail on the various commands on the Modify button's menu. Alas.)

4. **Close the Customize dialog box when you're done.**

Don't ever think that you can screw up here! Remember, it's *your* toolbar and you can move, delete, or add any items you like. And, if you ever think that you goofed the entire thing up, you can choose the Reset Toolbar command from the toolbar's menu to set things right again. Well, maybe not right, but back to the way Microsoft originally configured Word. See the section "Adding common toolbar buttons," earlier in this chapter, for information on getting to the Reset Toolbar command.

Zooming About

The Zoom command at the bottom of the View menu controls how big your document text looks. No, the command doesn't change the text size — that's done on the Font menu. Instead, the Zoom command controls how much of your text you see at once. Follow these steps for a quick demonstration:

1. **Choose View⇨Zoom.**

   The Zoom dialog box appears, looking much like the one depicted in Figure 29-6.

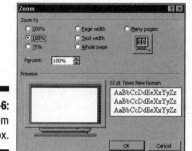

2. **Select a Zoom size.**

   For example, 200% makes your text look really big — ideal for Great Aunt Rebecca.

   The Page Width option sets the zoom so that you see your entire document from left to right margins.

   The Many pages item zooms you out into the next room, where you can see several pages on a single screen, which is good for writing only if you have 5/5 vision.

   You can set individual percent sizes using the Percent box.

3. **Click OK to view your document at a new size on-screen.**

   ✔ The Whole Page and Many Pages options in the Zoom dialog box are available only when you're in Page Layout view. Choose View⇨Page Layout and choose select the Zoom command to play, er, experiment with those options.

   ✔ When zooming takes you too far out, your text changes to shaded blocks, called *greeking*. Although not keen for editing, zooming out that far gives you a good idea of how your document looks on the page before printing.

   ✔ Way over on the right side of the Standard toolbar lives the Zoom drop-down list. Click it to set a Zoom size for your document quickly. Or, you can type an amount. For example, on my screen the documents look best at 125% zoom. (Funny, but I didn't need that magnification before I turned 40. . . .)

✔ If you have a Microsoft IntelliMouse (or any other wheel mouse), you can zoom by pressing the Ctrl key on your keyboard and rolling the wheel up or down. Rolling up zooms in; rolling down zooms out.

✔ Alas, you can zoom only in Word. The FreeCell game lacks a Zoom command.

Tweak Central

Further tweaking in Word happens in a busy place called the Options dialog box, as shown in Figure 29-7. You visit that place by choosing the Tools⇨Options command.

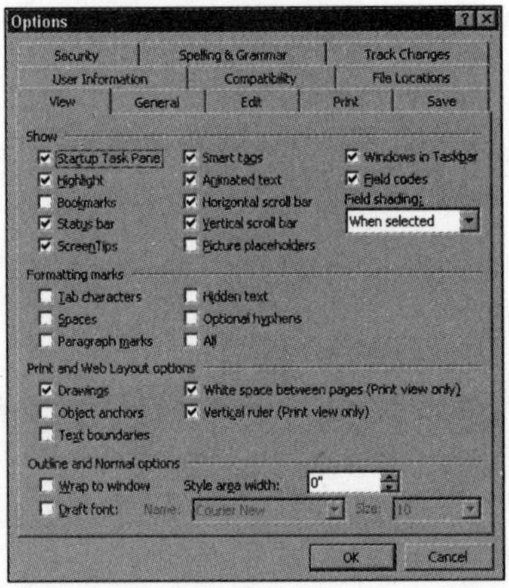

Figure 29-7:
The Options
dialog box.

Alas, there are just way too many options to go through the Options dialog box in its entirely. Most of the settings are familiar to anyone who has used Word for a few months. You can turn items on or off, such as the task pane at startup, shown in the upper-left area in Figure 29-7), as well as sound, animation, and other options that may annoy you. Remember, it's *your* copy of Word. Set it up the way you want.

Click the OK button when you're done changing the options.

Part V

Creating Lotsa Stuff in Word

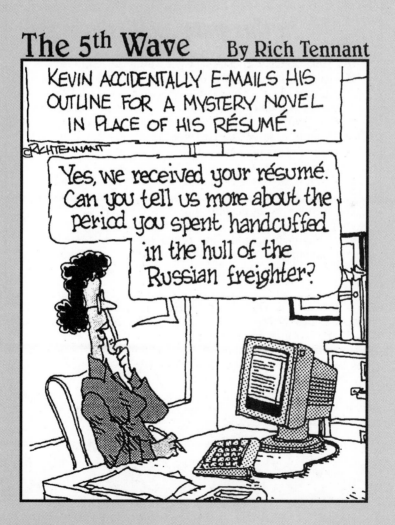

In this part . . .

It looks so easy, doesn't it? Ever watch those chefs on the early-morning TV shows? They just throw some ingredients together and *voilà!* There's a wonderful, tasty dish there, which the show's host salivates over. "I can do that too," you think, knowing darn well that what the chef creates and what you can do would look as dissimilar as sand and ice cream. Oh, well.

This part of the book is about getting that extra edge. It's a cookbook of sorts, showing you some interesting tricks and techniques for making your documents look really good without having to suffer through lots of learning. It's a fun, hands-on episode that, unlike the TV chef, will have you making great-tasting documents with a minimum of fuss. Go ahead. Salivate.

Chapter 30

Just Your Basic Letter and Envelope

● ●

In This Chapter

▶ Making a letter in Word

▶ Compose e-mail in Word

▶ Configuring Word to print envelopes

▶ Adding an envelope to a letter

▶ Printing an envelope on-the-fly

▶ Creating an envelope document

● ●

*U*sing Word to write a letter is kind of like using a jumbo jet to cross the street. Sure, it does the job, but it can be a little much. With all Word's features, it's easy to forget that most of the things people use a word processor for are really simple. Take the basic letter and envelope.

A few years back, doing a letter on a word processor was no big deal. But doing the envelope? That was not only a big deal, it was an ordeal. (Oh, a pun!) Anyway, this brief chapter gives you some tips and pointers on doing the basic letter and envelope in Word.

Writing a Silly Old Letter

Most letters start with two things right at the top: The date and the name and address of the recipient.

The date

To insert a date into any Word document, use the Insert➪Date and Time command. Choose the format for the date from the list in the Date and Time dialog box; then click OK.

✔ If you want the date to be current, always showing the current date rather than the date on which you created the letter, put a check mark in the Update automatically box. That inserts a date *field* into the document, which always reflects the current date. If you don't want a date field inserted, remove the check mark in the Date and Time dialog box.

✔ If you want the date shoved over to the right margin, press Ctrl+R after the date is inserted. Press the Enter key and then Ctrl+L to return to left-justify text in the next paragraph.

✔ You can also insert the date field code by pressing Alt+Shift+D.

The address

Two lines below the date (press the Enter key twice), most letter-writing folks place the recipient's address. I've no idea why we do this; we just do. Type the address, press Enter a couple times, and then type the salutation — something like

```
Wambooli Enterprises
P.O. Box 2697
Coeur d'Alene, ID 83816
To Whom It May Concern:
```

You may notice that most salutations, such as "To Whom It May Concern," are stored in Word as AutoText entries; you need to type only the first part and Word completes the rest if you press the Enter key. See Chapter 7 for more information.

The body of the letter

Typing the rest of the letter is up to you. Type away! La-la-la.

If the letter is longer than a page, consider adding page numbers. Use the Insert➪Page Numbers command for that.

Finally, end the letter with a signoff and your own name. You're done. The only thing left to do is add the envelope.

E-mailing your letter

If you want to e-mail the letter rather than print it, click the E-mail button on the Standard toolbar. This action displays in the document window the standard To, Cc, and Subject fields, plus a few familiar e-mail buttons, as shown in Figure 30-1.

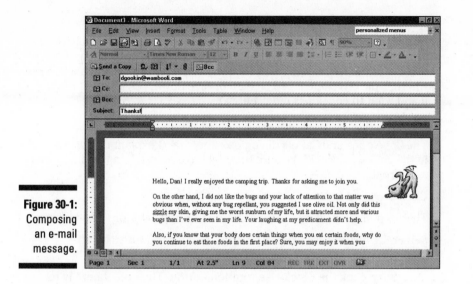

Figure 30-1:
Composing
an e-mail
message.

TIP

✔ To send the e-mail, click the Send a Copy button.

✔ In some cases, it may be necessary to be connected to the Internet *before* you try to send the e-mail in Word.

✔ The extra buttons visible in E-mail mode should be familiar to Outlook Express users. The buttons allow you to attach a document, use the address book, set the e-mail priority, and so on.

✔ You can also start a new e-mail message by choosing the Blank E-mail Message item on the New Document task pane.

All about Envelopes

To add an envelope to any document, you use Word's Envelopes and Labels command. It allows you to print an envelope on-the-fly or to "attach" an envelope to a letter so that they print one after the other. The following sections tell you everything you need to know.

Telling your printer to love an envelope

Each printer eats envelopes in a different manner. Some printers, why, they even have fancy envelope feeders. Other printers have envelope slots. Still other printers have a pop-out, manual-feeding tray that somehow can be used to feed in an envelope. The following steps show you how to configure Word to properly print an envelope on your printer:

1. **Locate the envelope feeder-slot on your printer.**

   Notice exactly how the envelope is inserted: An icon is probably printed or molded on the printer that tells you to insert the envelope in the middle, to the left, to the right, longways, or whatever. Also check to see whether the envelope is fed face up or face down. (Check the printer's manual for an *envelopes* index entry.)

2. **Choose Tools➪Letters and Mailings➪Envelopes and Labels.**

   The Envelopes and Labels dialog box appears. (I explain this dialog box in the next section.) Make sure that the Envelopes tab in the dialog box is up front.

3. **Click the Feed button.**

   This step displays the Envelope Options/Printing Options dialog box.

4. **Select the envelope's proper position and orientation.**

   Choose one of the six orientations. Choose Face up or Face down. And, if necessary, click the Clockwise rotation button. The object here is to match the way the envelope feeds into your printer. (So it's the printer that determines which options you select.)

5. **Click OK.**

   This step closes the Envelope Options dialog box.

Now you're ready to create or print an envelope, or you can click Cancel to return to your document. Word knows about your printer and can properly print an envelope the next time you demand one.

Adding an envelope to your letter

A quick way to print an envelope with every letter you create is to attach the envelope to the end of the letter. Here's how:

1. **Create your letter.**

   Refer to the sections at the beginning of this chapter for more information.

2. **Choose Tools➪Letters and Mailings➪Envelopes and Labels.**

   This step opens the Envelopes and Labels dialog box, as shown in Figure 30-2.

   If your document has a proper address in it, Word magically locates it and places it in the Delivery address box. Ta-da!

   If Word didn't automatically fill in the address, type it now.

   Optionally, you can also type your return address in the Return address area.

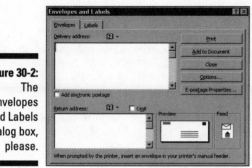

Figure 30-2:
The
Envelopes
and Labels
dialog box,
please.

3. **Click the Add to Document button.**

   The Envelopes and Labels dialog box goes away and you're returned to your document.

It may not be obvious on the screen, but the first page of your letter is now the envelope. (Choose File⇨Print Preview to see this wondrous thing.) When you're ready to print the letter, the envelope prints first and then the letter. All you have to do is stuff the letter into the envelope, seal it, and apply the outrageous postage.

✔ The letter and envelope are printed when you use the File⇨Print command for your letter (or press Ctrl+P or use the Print tool).

✔ Yes, you could create such an envelope-with-letter document as your main document in a mail merge. However, you're probably better off printing the envelopes all at the same time as opposed to feeding them in with every other page.

✔ Most printers prompt you to manually enter an envelope if that's what it wants you to do. After doing so, you may have to press the Ready, On-line, or Select button for the printer to continue. (My LaserJet just says "Me Feed!" and, for some reason, it knows when I insert the envelope because it just starts going!)

✔ Check the envelope to make sure that you didn't address the backside or put the address on upside down — as so often happens to me. This last step is important because you can just repeat the preceding steps to reprint your envelope if you goof.

✔ If you have trouble remembering how the envelope feeds into your printer, draw a picture of the proper way and tape it to the top of your laser printer for reference.

Printing an envelope on-the-fly

Whenever you need an envelope, for any reason, you can have Word whip one up for you. Follow these steps:

1. **Choose Tools➪Letters and Mailings➪Envelopes and Labels.**

2. **In the Envelopes and Labels dialog box, type the address you want on the envelope.**

   If you want to format the address, type it in the document first. Format it, select it, and then choose Tools➪Letters and Mailings➪Envelopes and Labels. Beware, though! Too much text may not fit on the envelope.

3. **Click the Print button.**

   Your printer may beep or otherwise prompt you to insert the envelope, or it may just print it right then and there.

If printing envelopes is something you plan on doing often, consider adding an Envelope button to Word's Standard toolbar. Refer to Chapter 29 for more information on how to do that.

The weird concept of envelopes as documents

An envelope is basically a sheet of paper, albeit folded and layered with the foulest-tasting glue known to man. But, bottom line — an envelope is merely a specialized piece of paper. As such, it's possible to configure Word to print a custom envelope as you would print any document. Follow these steps:

1. **Start a new document.**

   Word splashes a new document on the screen. You're going to transform it from a mere sheet of paper to an envelope.

2. **Ensure that you're in Print Layout view.**

   Choose View➪Print Layout if you're not. You can see things better in Print Layout view.

3. **Choose File➪Page Setup.**

4. **Click the Margins tab.**

5. **Set the margins to .5 all around.**

   Envelopes are small, and just about any printer can handle a half-inch margin all the way around: Enter **.5** in each of the Top, Bottom, Left, and Right boxes.

6. **Choose Landscape orientation.**

   Envelopes are wider than they are tall, but this move is made so that the printing on the envelope goes longways rather than on its side (which I hear bugs the post office).

7. **Click the Paper tab.**

8. **Choose the option** Envelope #10 4¹/₈ x 9¹/₂ in. **from the Paper size drop-down list.**

   Note the preview in the lower-right part of the dialog box. There's your envelope.

9. **Choose** Envelope Manual Feed **from both the First page and Other pages scrolling lists.**

   You want to be sure that the printer knows that it's eating an envelope and not that you've gone nutso in the Page Setup dialog box.

10. **Click OK.**

    The Page Setup dialog box goes bye-bye.

    In Print Layout view, you see the envelope floating in the document part of the window. It looks like an envelope! Wow.

11. **Type the return address.**

    Unlike using the Envelopes and Labels dialog box, you can apply style here, even add a graphic (as long as it's small enough not to offend the post office).

12. **Space down for the address.**

    Press the Enter key a few times until it's about even with the 1-inch marker on the left ruler. Or, just use your eyeball; you want the address to be roughly above center in the middle of the envelope.

13. **Indent the left margin 3 inches.**

    To indent the address, drag the Left indent gizmo on the ruler to the 3-inch position.

Left indent gizmo

14. **Type and format the address.**

    And there is your envelope.

If you need to add a memo to the envelope, restore the margin back to 0; drag the left indent gizmo back to the left margin. Then press Enter a few times until the toothpick cursor is near the lower-left edge of the envelope. There, you can type Attention: Mary in Marketing or whatever memo you like.

This method of creating an envelope as a document is far more versatile than using the Envelopes and Labels dialog box. Consider saving this document to disk and reusing it or saving it as a template for use over and over again. Refer to Chapter 17 for more information on creating templates.

Chapter 31

Brochures and Greeting Cards

- -

In This Chapter

▶ Planning a three-part brochure

▶ Designing various document titles

▶ Using the Drop Cap command

▶ Adding a floating text box

▶ Printing a three-part brochure

▶ Printing a greeting card

- -

*I*f you want to create something in Word that will just *dazzle* someone, you've come to the right chapter. The information here isn't secret, and it definitely isn't advanced. It's just a collection of information already offered in this book, but with a *purpose:* to create a threefold pamphlet or a greeting card. Go ahead. Amaze yourself!

Your Basic Three-Part Pamphlet

Some chores that you would think Word may utterly choke on, it can handle with ease. Take the typical threefold brochure, as shown in Figure 31-1.

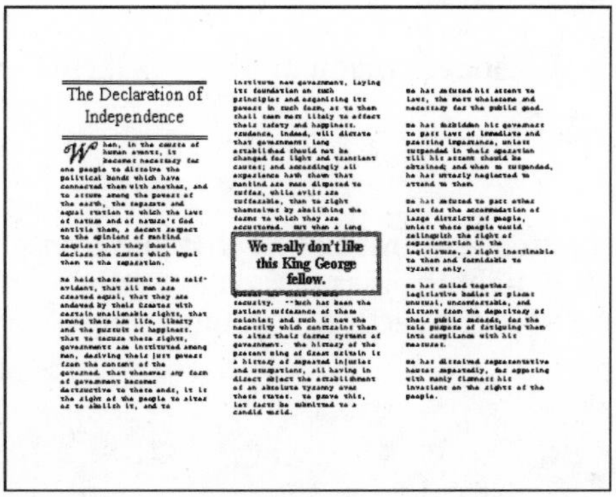

Figure 31-1: A typical threefold brochure is a cinch for Word to make.

Although Thomas Jefferson toiled away for days to pen the Declaration of Independence, Word and I whipped out a threefold brochure in about three minutes. In another few moments, the brochure could be flying out of my printer — provided the British don't storm my office before then.

Building the pamphlet

A *threefold* brochure is essentially a regular sheet of paper turned longways (landscape) and folded twice. In Word, you do this in two simple steps — *after* you write your text.

It's always best to work on the writing first and create the document later. Also, Word works faster when it's in normal (non-column) mode. If you need to edit later, fine.

To turn a document longways, follow these steps:

1. **Choose File⇨Page Setup.**

   The Page Setup dialog box appears.

2. **Click the Margins tab.**

3. **Select the Landscape option from the Orientation area.**

   Behold, your world is 90 degrees out of sync.

4. **Ensure that the Whole Document menu option is selected on the Apply To drop-down list.**

5. **Click OK.**

To make the three columns for the brochure, follow these steps:

1. **Choose Format⇨Columns.**

2. **Select Three from the Presets list.**

   It's at the top of the dialog box.

3. **Ensure that the Whole Document menu option is selected on the Apply To drop-down list.**

4. **Click OK.**

Now your document is formatted for three panels that fold over on a single page. To get your text to print on both sides of the page requires a few more tricks, all of which are covered in the section "Printing the brochure," later in this chapter.

Giving your brochure a title

The best way to create a title for a brochure is to draw a table. A table not only has built-in borders but also allows you to put bits of text to the right or left of the title without having to overly mess with Word's paragraph or tab formatting.

Use the table-drawing instructions from Chapter 20 to draw in the title part of the document, which is what I did in Figure 31-1. I then used the Format⇨Borders and Shading command to add the top and bottom borders. I could have used the Shading part of the Borders and Shading dialog box to add shading or color to the document title.

If you want to get fancier, draw in additional rows or columns of text. For example, create a 3-column title with the information in the left and right columns and the document title in the center. And don't forget that you can add graphics to a table easily.

Starting a paragraph with a big letter (a drop cap)

A *drop cap* is the first letter of a report, article, chapter, or story that appears in a larger and more interesting font than the other characters. Figure 31-1 shows an example. Here's how to add a drop cap to your brochure (or just any old document):

1. **Select the first character of the first word at the start of your text.**

   For example, select the *O* in "Once upon a time."

   It also helps if this paragraph is left justified and not indented with a tab or any of the tricky formatting discussed in Part II.

2. **Choose Format⇨Drop Cap.**

   The Drop Cap dialog box appears, as depicted in Figure 31-2.

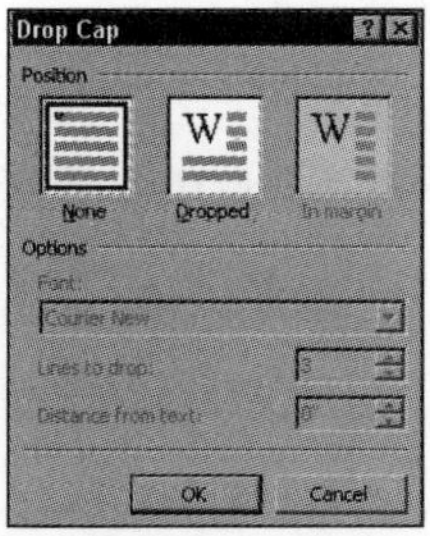

Figure 31-2:
The Drop Cap dialog box.

3. **Select a drop cap style.**

The first option, None, isn't a drop cap at all. The Dropped style is second, and the In Margin style is third. I prefer the Dropped style myself. Click in the box you prefer to select that style.

Select a font if you wish.

Oh, and you can mess around with the other options if you like. Especially if you're just starting a new novel, writer's block is a terrible thing. . . .

4. **Click OK.**

If you're not in Print Layout view, Word switches your document there so that you can see the drop cap in action.

The drop cap is highlighted and shown inside a hatched box with eight black handles — yes, astute reader, just like a pasted-in graphic image. (See Chapter 23.)

You may have to drag the drop cap/picture around, especially if you're using a table for the document title, as shown in Figure 31-1. Just point the mouse at the drop cap and drag when the mouse pointer changes to the 4-pointed arrow thing.

5. **Click the mouse in your text (not on the drop cap) and continue editing.**

You're free to go on with your work.

You can undo a drop cap by clicking its box and then choosing Format➪Drop Cap. In the Drop Cap dialog box, double-click the None position, and the drop cap vanishes.

Floating a box of text

Another fun element to add to the brochure is the floating text box. Basically, it works like a graphic image, floating in front of your text. The difference is that the "image" is really a chunk of text you can format and write. Here's how to add one to any document:

1. **Position the toothpick cursor to approximately the location where you want the text box.**

You can move the position later, but you need to start somewhere.

2. **Choose Insert➪Text Box.**

Four crazy things happen:

If you're in Normal view, you're instantly switched to Print Layout view.

A placeholder for the text box is inserted into your text. It's ugly: { SHAPE * MERGEFORMAT }. Ugh. Live with it for now.

The Drawing toolbar appears.

The mouse pointer changes to crosshairs, which you use to drag and draw the text box.

3. **Drag the mouse to create the text box.**

   Drag from the upper-left corner down to the lower-right to create the box. When you release the mouse button, you see the text box floating over your text, as shown in Figure 31-3.

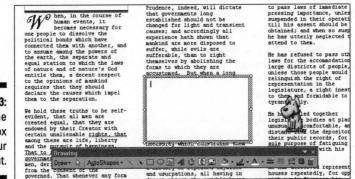

Figure 31-3: Drawing the text box in your document.

4. **Type and format the text inside the box.**

   You can use all your basic text writing and formatting skills inside the box, just as you would type text outside the box. You can choose fonts, styles, bold, center, and indent. You can even turn the text sideways.

   You can resize the box by dragging its edges or corners in or out.

   Move the text box by pointing the mouse at it until the mouse pointer changes to the 4-pointed arrow thing. Then drag the box hither, thither, or yon.

   Use the Line Style button on the Drawing toolbar to set the border style for the box. Other buttons on the toolbar affect the box as well; experiment with them in your free time.

5. **Click the mouse back in your document when you're done.**

   This step leaves text box mode and returns you to the document's regular text for editing and whatnot. (You may need to manually close the Drawing toolbar; click its X, or Close, button.)

You can return to the text box for editing by simply clicking the mouse inside.

Printing the brochure

Printing brochures is something best done by Kinko's or Insty-Prints or some other printing professional. But, if you're on a budget, you can do them yourself.

First, print a sample brochure just to get the process down. Then you can print a bunch of brochures in batches.

To print a sample brochure, follow these steps:

1. **Get the printer ready to print.**

2. **Choose File➪Print from the menu.**

3. **Select the Odd Pages option from the Print drop-down list.**

   The Print drop-down list can be found in the lower-left corner of the Print dialog box. What you're doing is printing the front side of the brochure first — the odd pages.

4. **Click OK.**

The odd pages of your brochure print. If you have a 1-page brochure, only one page spews forth from the printer. Otherwise, you get only pages 1, 3, 5, and so on.

Now, the tricky part:

Gather those pages and put them back in your printer's feed tray *upside down*. You want to print on their backside. This may take a few steps. You need to ensure that the odd-numbered printed pages are oriented in the paper tray so that the even-numbered pages are printed properly. Don't be discouraged if this takes you a few tries. (And don't feel reluctant to use a Sharpie and write *UP* on one side of the paper tray.)

After you reload the paper, follow these steps to print the even pages:

1. **Choose File➪Print from the menu.**

2. **Select the Even Pages menu option from the Print drop-down list.**

3. **Click OK.**

Check your results. If you have to try again, do so.

Another conundrum you may notice: The brochure may not fold the way you want it to. Don't worry! Use the Columns dialog box to adjust the width and spacing of the columns. Or, use the Page Setup/Margins dialog box to move the margins in or out.

When you're ready to mass-produce, simply repeat the preceding steps, but in the Print dialog box enter **50** in the Number of copies box. That way, you're printing 50 copies of the brochure, front and back, each time. (Any more than 50 and you may run out of paper.)

Do-It-Yourself Greeting Cards

Greeting cards are simply a variation of the brochure example shown earlier in this chapter — with one special exception.

To set up Word to create a greeting card from a single sheet of standard letter-size paper, follow these steps:

1. **Choose File⇨Page Setup.**

2. **Click the Margins tab.**

3. **Select the Landscape option in the Orientation area.**

4. **Choose** 2 pages per sheet **from the Multiple pages drop-down list.**

    This option tells Word to vertically split each page down the middle, creating (aha! — you guessed it) a greeting card.

5. **Click OK.**

Now your document is properly formatted. All that remains is for you to fill in the greeting card with text and maybe a few graphics. But there's a special way you need to do it!

The greeting card must be four pages long: two pages on the inside and two pages on the outside. (Only one sheet of paper is used, two "pages" per sheet.) Here's how the various pages shape up:

✔ **Page 1** is the inside left-hand page. Usually, this page is left blank. So, in your document, you can press Ctrl+Enter to create a hard page break and leave that page blank.

✔ **Page 2** is the inside right-hand page. This page is where you put your sappy message — maybe a graphic.

✔ **Page 3** is the outside "back" cover. This page can be blank, or you can put at the bottom some wee, tiny text boasting of your word-processing prowess or that the card would have cost $3.95 ($5.95 Canadian) had you bought it at Hallmark.

✔ **Page 4** ends up being the *cover* for the greeting card. Put a graphic or flowery text here.

Got it? If not, trust me — it all works out.

Fill in your greeting card accordingly.

To print the greeting card, you need to be tricky. Follow these steps:

1. **Choose File⇨Print.**

2. **Type 1-2 in the Pages box.**

   You want to print only pages 1 and 2 the first time.

3. **Click OK.**

   Take the page out of the printer and put it back into the printer tray. Ensure that the page is in the printer tray *upside down* so that the next page prints on the backside. (This may take a few tries, so be patient.)

Now, print the backside:

1. **Choose File⇨Print.**

2. **Type 3-4 in the Pages box.**

   You want to print only pages 3 and 4 this time.

3. **Click OK.**

   If everything goes well, you should be able to fold the paper down the middle and — voilà! — you have a greeting card.

- ✔ If you're into elaborate greeting-card formatting, consider using section breaks to divide the greeting card and not just the hard page breaks you get by pressing Ctrl+Enter.

- ✔ Watch out for fancy, thick paper. It tends to jam most laser printers. (If your laser printer has a single-sheet feed and a pass-through slot out the back, printing on thick paper may work.) Greeting-card stock is difficult as all heck to get through an inkjet printer, too!

Chapter 32

Making Some Labels

In This Chapter

▶ Understanding labels

▶ Printing a sheet of labels

*O*ne of Word's most esoteric duties is printing labels. Now, this task isn't too far out of the realm of word processing. The first time I printed up my own return labels was with WordPerfect 4.0, back in the dark ages of DOS. Unlike WordPerfect 4.0, however, Word has its own Label command and many exciting label options. This chapter discusses how to put them to use.

All about Labels

Because my handwriting is so darn lousy, I print labels with my return address on them and stick those on my bills and whatnot. I do it as a favor to the overworked men and women of the U.S. Postal Service. Of course, labels can be used for more than addressing envelopes.

If you're curious about what types of labels are available, visit your local office-supply store (or megawarehouse). You can find all sorts of ingenious labels there, from the mundane "Hello, my name is" to labels you can use in creating your own CDs.

Ensure that you buy labels compatible with your printer. Laser printers need special laser printer labels. Some inkjet printers require special, high-quality labels to hold the image. Impact printers need tractor-feed labels.

Transparent labels are also available, but if you have a laser printer, watch out! Transparent labels must be made specifically for a laser printer; otherwise, the heat inside the laser printer may melt the labels and you'll have a serious mess on your hands.

Of all the label brands available, I recommend Avery. Its stock numbers are standard for almost all computer programs. So, if you buy Avery stock number 5160 or something similar, your software and printer know which type of label you have and in which format it is.

Printing a Sheet of Identical Labels

Here are the instructions for printing an entire sheet of labels in Word, such as your name and address for return mailing labels:

1. **Choose Tools➪Letters and Mailings➪Envelopes and Labels.**

2. **Click the Labels tab.**

   What you see on your screen should look like Figure 32-1.

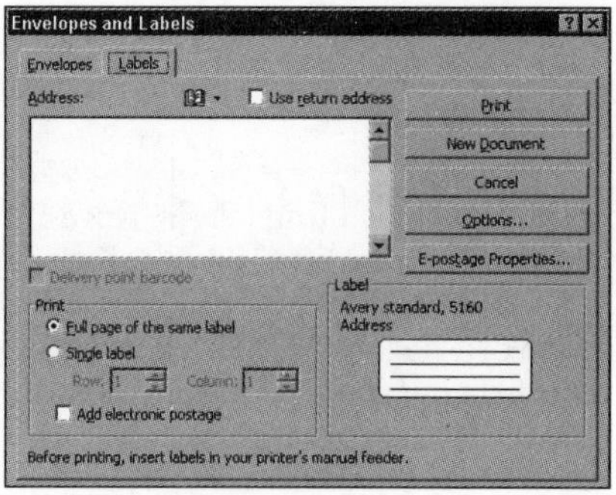

Figure 32-1:
The Labels side of the Envelopes and Labels dialog box.

3. **Choose the type of label you're printing on.**

   Confirm that the stock number in the lower-right corner of the dialog box matches the labels on which you're printing.

   If the numbers don't match up, click the Options button to display the Label Options dialog box. Locate the correct Avery stock number in the Label Options dialog box's scrolling list. Select it; then click OK.

4. **Type in the Address box what you want printed on the label.**

   Keep in mind that you have only so many lines for each label and that each label is only so wide. Alas, you cannot format the label here. (But you can in Step 6.)

   Press the Enter key at the end of each line.

5. **Click the New Document button.**

   Ha! I bet that you thought you'd click the Print button. No way! The labels are typically more ugly than you think, and you may want the chance to spiff them up a bit before you print.

   The labels appear as a table in your Word document. From this point on, you can work with the labels in your document just as you work with a table. (Refer to Chapter 20 for more information on working with tables.)

Be careful not to adjust the table's columns and rows! Everything is formatted just so. If you change something, the labels may not print properly.

6. **Format the labels (if you like).**

Press Ctrl+A to select the entire document (it's only a page long), and then change the font to something more pleasing. Refer to Chapter 11 for more information.

Don't mess with the margins or paragraph formatting. This is all carefully tuned to print on the labels you specified.

You can edit the labels. Sure, they all look the same, but if you like, you can type a few new names or other information in several of the little boxes.

7. **Print the document.**

Make sure that your printer is on and ready to print and that you have the proper type of label-printing material in the printer, right side up and all that. Then print your document as you normally would. Click the li'l Print button and the labels soon unfurl from your printer, ready for lickin' and stickin'.

✔ You do not have to save this document to disk, unless you just like the labels and want to keep them around. Press Ctrl+W to close the document and press **N** for *no* save.

✔ Avery, the Label People, make a software program called LabelPro, which I use instead of Word to manage and print labels. Recommended.

✔ It's also possible to print labels from a database of labels using Word's Mail Merge feature. Alas, this complex and detailed process lies in the realm of Advanced Word Tricks. It works best if you've created a database (shown in Chapter 27) or use Microsoft Outlook to maintain a contacts list. Even with all that work done, you still have a massive amount of formatting and other hoops to jump through, making the operation more toil than trick.

Part VI
The Part of Tens

In this part . . .

Welcome to the trivia part of the book. It's The Part of Tens, where I list various things about Word by ten items each. Maybe not the top ten, but just ten. This is the kind of trivia I love: "What are the ten most beautiful lakes in the world?" or "Ten fun freebies you can find in Vegas" or "Ten rock formations that bear a striking resemblance to Margaret Thatcher." It's that sort of fun stuff that makes the world go 'round.

The chapters in this part contain lists of ten things. Here you'll find some tips, comments, suggestions, things to avoid, and things to remember. It's the traditional way to end a *For Dummies* book. And in keeping with tradition, be warned that not every chapter has exactly ten items. Some have more, some less. After all, if there is an eleventh rock formation that bears a resemblance to the Iron Lady, why not list it too?

Chapter 33

The Ten Commandments of Word

Moses was probably the first guy to come up with a well-known list of ten. Not only that — it's the only list of ten anything that's had several films made about it. That film about *The 10 Worst Days on the Stock Market* just doesn't have the same gravity as, well, Charlton Heston bifurcating the Red Sea.

This chapter contains the ten commandments of word processing, specific to Word, but you can apply these tips to other word processors as well (just don't tell). These are the rules and suggestions I make throughout this book, condensed into one handy little chapter — much lighter than two of those tablet things Charlton Heston had to lug down that papier-mâché mountain.

Thou Shalt Not Use Spaces Unnecessarily

Generally speaking, you should never find more than one space anywhere in a Word document. Whenever you have more than one space in a row in your document, you should probably be using the Tab key instead. Use the

Spacebar to separate words and to end a sentence. If you align lists of information, use the Tab key. If you want to organize information into rows and columns, use the Table command (see Chapter 20).

A special note to all high school typing teachers: Please do not insist that your students continue the arcane habit of typing two spaces at the end of a sentence. With a word processor, that's unnecessary. And I doubt that any of your students will be employed using a typewriter in the near future, so continuing this practice is a waste of time.

Thou Shalt Not Press Enter at the End of Each Line

Word automatically wraps your text down to the next line as you approach the right margin. You have no need to press Enter, except when you want to start a new paragraph. (Of course, if your paragraph is only a line long, that's okay.)

If you don't want to start a new paragraph but need to start a new line, use Shift+Enter, the *soft* return command.

Thou Shalt Not Neglect Thy Keyboard

Word is Windows, and Windows is mousy. You can get lots done with the mouse, but some things are faster with the keyboard. For example, when I'm working on several documents at once, I switch between them with Alt+Tab. And stabbing the Ctrl+S key combo to quickly save a document or Ctrl+P to print works better than fumbling for the mouse. You don't have to learn all the keyboard commands, but knowing those few outlined in this book helps.

Thou Shalt Not Reset or Turn Off Thy PC until Thou Quittest Word and Windows

Always exit properly from Word and especially from Windows. Shut off or reset your computer only when you see the "It's now okey-dokey to turn off this PC" type of onscreen prompt — never when you're running Word or have Windows active. Believeth me, if ye do, ye are asking for mucho trouble, yea, verily, woe.

Thou Shalt Not Manually Number Thy Pages

Word has an automatic page-numbering command. Refer to the section in Chapter 14 that talks about where to stick the page number.

Thou Shalt Not Use the Enter Key to Start a New Page

Sure, it works: Brazenly press the Enter key a couple of dozen times, and you're on a new page. But that's not the proper way, and you mess up your new page if you go back and re-edit text. Besides, pressing Ctrl+Enter is quicker. Doing so inserts a *hard page break* into your document.

For the details, refer to the section in Chapter 14 about starting a new page.

Thou Shalt Not Quit without Saving First

Save your document to disk before you quit. Shift+F12 is the key combo to remember. Or, Ctrl+S is the one you don't even have to remember because it's so sensible. If only all of life — no, forget life — if only all of Word were so sensible.

Thou Shalt Not Click OK Too Quickly

Word has many Yes/No/OK-type questions. If you click OK without thinking about it (or press Enter accidentally), you can delete text, delete files, or perform a bad replace operation without meaning to. Always read your screen before you click OK.

Some dialog boxes have a Close button rather than an OK button. These buttons are typically used when you make some choice or reset some option and you don't want to continue with the command. For example, you can change printers in the Print dialog box and then click the Close button to continue without printing.

And don't forget your handy undo key, Ctrl+Z!

Thou Shalt Not Forget to Turn On Thy Printer

The biggest printing problem anyone has is telling Word to print something when the printer isn't on. Verify that your printer is on, healthy, and ready to print before you tell Word to print something.

Never (or at least try not to) keep using the Print command over and over when a document doesn't print. Word tries to print once every time you use the Print command. Somewhere and sometime, those documents will print, unless you do something about it.

Thou Shalt Remember to Save Thy Work

Save! Save! Save! Always save your stuff. Whenever your mind wanders, have your fingers wander to the Ctrl+S keyboard shortcut. Honor thy documents. Savest thine work.

Chapter 34

Ten Truly Bizarre Things

*E*verything in this program is bizarre, but some things are more bizarre than others. Below are listed what I feel are the ten most bizarre things, in no particular order. Read on. If you dare.

Using the Options Dialog Box

Choosing the Tools⇨Options command accesses the Options dialog box. What you get in this dialog box is 11 — count 'em, 11 — panels of various things Word does. The settings in the panels control how Word behaves.

The Options dialog box doesn't really contain any hints or secrets. In fact, you've probably been here a few times if you clicked any Options button in the various Word dialog boxes — no big deal, just, well, bizarre. Review the panels every so often as you use Word. Maybe you'll discover something useful.

The Unbreakables

The two weird keys on your keyboard are the Spacebar and the hyphen. They're weird because Word uses both to split a line of text: The space splits a line between two words and the hyphen splits a line between two word chunks.

There are times, however, when you don't want a line to be split by a space or a hyphen. For example, splitting a phone number is bad — you want the phone number to stay together. And spaces can be annoying as well. Suppose that you work for the firm of Bandini, Lambert, and Locke and, by golly, Mr. Locke doesn't like to be left on a line by himself. If so, insert a nonbreaking (hard) space between each name to make sure that they're always together.

To prevent the space character from breaking a line, press the key combination Ctrl+Shift+Spacebar rather than the Spacebar by itself. That inserts a non-breaking space between two words.

To prevent the hyphen character from breaking a line, press Ctrl+Shift+- (hyphen) rather than the hyphen by itself. If you type the first three digits of the number and then press Ctrl+Shift+-, the phone number doesn't split between two lines.

The Document Map

I suppose that the Document Map feature is there to help you see the big picture, especially if you use Word's Heading styles. Choose View➪Document Map and a "pane" opens to one side of your document, listing a quick summary.

A scary, weird thing you should avoid at all costs

Over many years of using Word, I've discovered one of the most annoying commands in the history of word processing. It's the terrifying menu item remover, something you may stumble over accidentally someday. (I hope you don't.)

If you press Ctrl+Alt+- (hyphen) in Word, the mouse pointer changes to a thick, horizontal line. That line is the menu item removal cursor. Just choose any menu item and — thwoop! —

it's gone, deleted, zapped, dead. And there's no way to get that menu item back, either. Deadly! Scary! Not even Rod Serling could dream up something that bizarre.

If you do accidentally press Ctrl+Alt+-, quickly press the Esc key to cancel that mode. Yikes! What kind of sick mind thought up that trick, huh?

This feature can be useful. In fact, because I use the Heading styles, the Document Map gives me a quick overview of how my document is laid out — like a mini-outline view. It's just a *bizarre* feature, which is why it's in this chapter.

Choose View⇨Document Map a second time to close it.

Hyphenation

Hyphenation is an automatic feature that splits long words at the end of a line to make the text fit better on the page. Most people leave it turned off because hyphenated words tend to slow down the pace at which people read. However, if you want to hyphenate a document, choose Tools⇨Language⇨Hyphenation. Continuously jab the F1 key when you need help.

Math

Did it ever dawn upon the Word people that math and English are two separate subjects for a reason? The math and English parts of the SAT scores are separate. Math and English are always taught as separate courses. So who needs a math function in a word processor? I don't know. Even if you do, it's still easier to calculate the numbers by using your desk calculator and typing them manually.

To use the Math command, you must first place your data in a table. Then highlight the row or column you want computed. Choose Table⇨Formula. Word suggests a formula type, or you can tell Word what you want done with the numbers. On second thought, I guess that this woulda been kinda handy during algebra class. Anyway, Word puts the answer wherever you left the blinking toothpick cursor.

Macros

Macros are beyond the scope of this book.

Making a Cross-Reference

The Insert⇨Reference⇨Cross-Reference command allows you to insert a "Refer to Chapter 99, Section Z" type of thing into your document. This feature works because you've taken the Krell brain-booster and now have an IQ that can be expressed only in scientific notation. Fortunately, you may have also used the Heading style to mark in your document some text you want to cross-reference. Using the Heading style means that the Insert⇨Reference⇨ Cross-Reference command works and sticks a "Refer to Chapter 99, Section Z" type of thing in your document — complete with an updated reference to that page in case you overhaul your document.

Fixing Word

Word is a part of the Microsoft Office suite of applications, which is a part of Microsoft's new attempt to prevent you from using software developed by any other company. Understanding your loyalty, Microsoft has built into Office (and Word) the ability to fix itself when needed. So, at random moments, you may see the Optimize program running. Don't let it freak you out.

A feature of the Optimizer is the Help⇨Detect and Repair command in Word. This command is used to fix any bugs or boo-boos that may creep into Word. So I suppose that if Word is starting to behave like, well, like every other Microsoft program written, it would be a good idea to run that command.

Understanding Smart Tags

Word guesses at who's who in your document. When Word believes that it has found someone, it wiggles a dotted purple underline beneath that person's name. To Word, that person is a contact. And the purple underline is a sign that Word has attached a *smart tag* to the name.

If you point the mouse at the smart tag, the Smart Tag icon appears, as shown in the margin. Click that icon to display the Smart Tag menu, which works only if you have Microsoft Outlook (not Outlook Express) on your computer and it's all set up and ready to use as your contacts database.

To disable smart tags, choose Tools⇨AutoCorrect Options and click the Smart Tag tab. Remove the check mark by the option Label text with smart tags. Click OK.

What the Heck Is a "Digital Signature?"

Word 2002 introduces the concept of digital signatures to your documents. A *digital signature* is a widely accepted method of guaranteeing that something has not been modified since the original creator "signed" that something. It's used mostly for creating Word macros (which this book does not cover); by digitally signing the macro, you can guarantee to others that it is your original work and has not been modified or hacked without your permission. Weird stuff.

Chapter 35

Ten Cool Tricks

Determining what's a cool trick (and what's not) is purely subjective. I'm sure that people who formerly numbered their pages manually think that Word's Page Numbers command is a cool trick. I think AutoCorrect is a great trick. And repeating "Dan Gookin" over and over, only to have the speech-recognition feature believe me to be uttering "tan cool can" — now, *that's* a cool trick.

This chapter explains some of the neater Word tricks — mostly obscure stuff I may not have mentioned elsewhere in this book. Some are simple and straightforward; some take a little longer for the human mind to grasp.

Typing Strange Characters

You can use the Insert⇨Symbol command to stick odd and wonderful characters into your document. Quite a few Windows fonts have a few weird and wonderful characters in them. The Symbol font is full of neat stuff; the Wingdings font has all sorts of fun doodads; even the normal font, Times New Roman, has several cool characters in it.

To insert any of a number of weird and wonderful characters, follow these steps:

1. Choose <u>I</u>nsert⇨<u>S</u>ymbol.

The exciting Symbol dialog box appears, as shown in Figure 35-1.

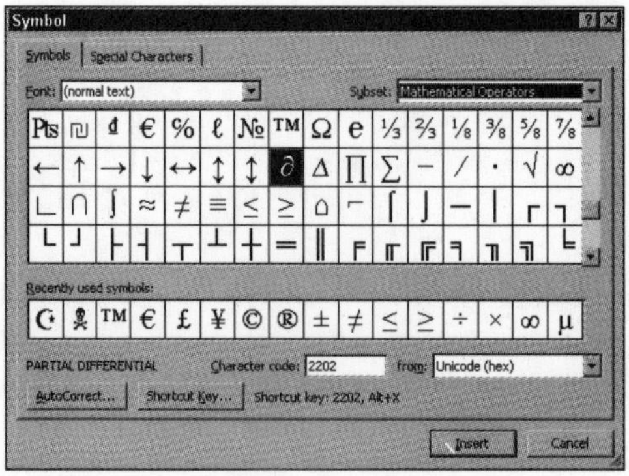

Figure 35-1:
The Symbol
dialog box.

2. Choose a font.

Some fonts are designed for fun, such as the Symbol, Webdings, and Wingdings fonts. Choose them from the Font drop-down list and you'll see their various characters displayed.

To see a smattering of all sorts of cool characters, choose (normal text) from the top of the Font drop-down list. Unlike in some fonts, those characters are available to anyone who uses Windows. (They're not specific fonts tied to specific computers.) Furthermore, you can choose which type of "normal" symbol you want by using the Subset drop-down list. In Figure 35-1, the Mathematical Operators subset is chosen. That merely scrolls the list of cool characters down to the math-like ones, such as the fractions you see in the figure.

3. Choose the character you want to insert.

The character is highlighted.

4. Click the <u>I</u>nsert button.

This step inserts the character in your document.

5. Click the Cancel button when you're done.

Some interesting symbols to consider inserting: the multiplication symbol × rather than X, and the division symbol ÷ rather than /. I typically use this command to insert the left, right, up, and down arrows for use when I write about, oh, word processing!

✔ You have to click the Insert button once for each symbol you want inserted. If you're putting three Σ (sigma) symbols into your document, you must locate that symbol in the grid and then click the Insert button three times.

✔ Note that some symbols have shortcut keys. These appear at the bottom of the Symbol dialog box. For example, the shortcut for the degree symbol (°) is Ctrl+@, Space, which means to type Ctrl+@ (actually, Ctrl+Shift+2) and then type a space. Doing so gives you the degree symbol.

✔ In addition to choosing them from the Symbol dialog box, many foreign language characters can be produced by using special key combinations. See the section "Typing Characters Such as Ü, Ç, and Ñ," later in this chapter.

✔ Some characters, such as ☺ or © or ™, can be inserted by using AutoText. See Chapter 7.

✔ It's possible to insert symbols by typing the symbol's code and then pressing the Alt+X key combination. For example, the code for Σ (sigma) is 2211: type **2211** in your document and then press Alt+X. The 2211 is magically transformed into the Σ character.

✔ Also note the Recently used symbols list near the bottom of the dialog box. Very handy.

Creating Fractions

The Symbol dialog box contains many handy fractions you can insert into your document (see the preceding section). And, if you have AutoCorrect on, Word automatically converts these three fractions for you. Otherwise, you need to build your own fractions using the superscript command. Here's how:

1. **Press Ctrl+Shift+= (the equal sign).**

   This is the keyboard shortcut for the superscript command.

2. **Type the numerator — the top part of the fraction.**

   For example, **4** for ⅘.

3. **Press Ctrl+Shift+= again to turn off superscript.**

4. **Type the slash.**

5. **Press Ctrl+= to turn on subscript.**

6. **Type the denominator — the bottom part of the fraction.**

7. **Press Ctrl+= to turn off subscript.**

There's your fraction.

Super- and Subscript Buttons on the Toolbar

If you plan on typing lots of fractions or the idea of super- and subscript text appeals to you, why not add those buttons to the Formatting toolbar?

Click the downward-pointing triangle at the toolbar's far-right end. Choose Add or Remove Buttons⇨Formatting and a huge menu appears. Near the bottom are commands for Superscript and Subscript. Choose each one and then press the Esc key.

The superscript (x^2) and subscript (x_2) buttons are added to the toolbar for you.

Typing Characters Such as Ü, Ç, and Ñ

Word has all sorts of nifty tricks for typing foreign language characters with *diacriticals*. Those are the tiny commas, apostrophes, and various accent marks that appear over vowels and other characters in various and sundry tongues. For example, you could be dull and type resume or be spiffy and type r♫sum♫. It's cinchy, after you figure out how Word thinks.

Most diacriticals are created using special prefix keys. You type the prefix key and then the corresponding letter to create a diacritical. And, lucky for you, the prefix keys sort of make sense. They're shown in Table 35-1.

Table 35-1	Typing Those Pesky Foreign Language Characters
Column 1	*Column 2*
Ctrl+'	á é í ó ú ý
Ctrl+´	à è ì ò ù
Ctrl+,	ç
Ctrl+@	å
Ctrl+:	ä ë ï ö ü
Ctrl+^	â ê î ô û
Ctrl+~	ã õ ñ
Ctrl+/	ø

Just follow the prefix key with the vowel (or *N* or *C*) to get the accent mark. For example, to get an é into your document, type Ctrl+' and then the letter *E*. Uppercase *E* gives you É, and lowercase *e* gives you é. And that makes sense because the ' (apostrophe) is essentially the character you're adding to the vowel.

Ctrl+' followed by a D equals Đ (or ð).

Be sure to note the difference between the apostrophe (or *tick*) and back tick, or *accent grave*. The apostrophe (') is by your keyboard's Enter key. The back tick (`) is below the Esc key.

For the Ctrl+@, Ctrl+:, Ctrl+^, and Ctrl+~ key combinations, you also need to press the Shift key, which is required anyway to get the @, :, ^, or ~ symbols on your keyboard. Therefore, Ctrl+~ is really Ctrl+Shift+`. Keep that in mind.

If this trick doesn't work, then it doesn't work. For example, if you type Ctrl+' and then a D to put a back tick over a D and nothing happens, well, then, it doesn't work! You have to use the Symbol dialog box (discussed earlier in this chapter) to see whether you can find that particular symbol.

Lugging Blocks Around

Here's a weird trick: Select a paragraph of text, or any old chunk of text. To move that text up one paragraph at a time, use Alt+Shift+↑. Every time you press Alt+Shift+↑, the block moves up one paragraph.

The Alt+Shift+↓ shortcut moves the selected block down one paragraph. Interesting, no?

I believe that you may find these keyboard shortcuts handy for moving chunks of text that would take the mouse a while to master.

AutoSummarize

In the category of "How the heck did they do that?" comes the AutoSummarize tool. Just like those prehighlighted, used textbooks in college, this tool takes any document and immediately fishes out all the relevant points, highlighting them on the screen. I have no idea how this tool works, but it's pretty keen — for Word, that is.

To AutoSummarize your document, choose the Tools⇨AutoSummarize command. Heed the steps on the screen. In a few minutes (longer if the computer is unplugged), the AutoSummarize dialog box appears. Click OK. (You can peruse the options in the AutoSummarize dialog box on your own, if you like; clicking the OK button generally does what you want it to do.)

Splat! Your document then appears on the screen with relevant parts highlighted in yellow. Also visible is an AutoSummarize floating palette, which I have yet to figure out.

To return to normal editing mode, click the Close button on the AutoSummarize palette.

No, it's the AutoSummerize tool that makes it bright and sunny outside.

Select All

There are times when you want to block the whole shooting match; highlight everything from top to bottom and from beginning to end; select the entire document. When you want to do so, click the mouse three times in your document's left margin. Click, click, zowie! There it is.

Oh, and you can hold down the Ctrl key and press the 5 key on the number keypad. Zap, zowie! There you go.

Oh, and you also can press F8 (the Extended Text key) five times. Zap, zap, zap, zap, zowie! There you go again.

Oh, and the Edit⇨Select All command does the same thing. Press Ctrl+A. Zowie!

Inserting the Date

Word's date command is named Date and Time and hangs under the Insert menu. Selecting this option displays a dialog box full of date and time formats, one of which you're bound to favor. Click OK to insert the current date or time or both.

You can quickly insert the date field by pressing Alt+Shift+D. Remember to right-click the field and choose Toggle Field Codes to switch between the ugly field and the actual date.

Sorting

Sorting is one of Word's better tricks. After you understand it, you go looking for places to use it. You can use the Sort command to arrange text alphabetically or numerically. You can sort paragraphs, table rows, and columns in cell tables and tables created by using tabs.

Always save your document before sorting.

Sorting is not that difficult. First arrange what needs to be sorted into several rows of text, such as

```
Dopey
Sneezy
Sleepy
Doc
Happy
Grumpy
Bashful
```

Word sorts by the first item in each line, so just select all the lines as a block and then choose Table⇨Sort. The Sort Text dialog box appears. (Yes, the Sort command is on the Table menu, though your text need not be in a table.)

Mess around in the dialog box if you need to, but as Word tosses it up on the screen, the dialog box is set to sort your text alphabetically. Just click OK to do so.

Automatic Save

When the AutoSave feature is active, your document is periodically saved to disk. This isn't the same as pressing Ctrl+S to save your document. Instead, Word makes a secret backup copy every so often. In the event of a crash, you can recover your work from the backup copy — even if you never saved the document to disk.

To turn on AutoSave, choose Tools⇨Options. Click the Save tab. Put a check mark by the Save AutoRecover info every option. Then enter the backup interval in the Minutes text box. For example, I type **10** to have Word back up my documents every ten minutes. If the power is unstable at your home or office, enter **5**, **3**, **2**, or even **1** minute as the backup interval. Press Enter to return to your document.

With Automatic Save, you don't recover your document in case of a mishap, but you get most of it back.

Chapter 36

Ten Things Worth Remembering

*T*here's nothing like finishing a book with a few heartening words of good cheer. As a Word user, you need this kind of encouragement and motivation. Word can be an unforgiving, but not necessarily evil, place to work. This book shows you that having lots of fun with Word and still getting your work done is possible. To help send you on your way, here are a few things worth remembering.

Let Word Do the Work

There's so much Word can do. Even so, some stubborn people still insist on doing things their way because, well, that's just the way things get done around here. Wrong! You can use a handy Word command to do just about anything, and you'll never remember the commands if you're afraid to try them.

Keep Printer Paper, Toner, and Supplies Handy

When you buy paper, buy a box. When you buy a toner cartridge or printer ribbon, buy two or three. Also keep a good stock of pens, paper, staples, paper clips, and all the other office supplies handy.

If you want to back up your work, use floppy disks, super disks (LS-120), or Zip disks. These removable disks can be used to hold a copy of your data, which you can store in a safe place. (I put my Zip disk backups into a fire safe.) Use Windows to copy your Word document files to the removable disk; see *PCs For Dummies* (published by Hungry Minds, Inc.) for more information on copying files to a removable disk.

Keep References Handy

Word is a writing tool. As such, you need to be familiar with and obey the grammatical rules of your language. If that language just happens to be English, you have a big job ahead of you. Even though a dictionary and a the-saurus are an electronic part of Word, I recommend that you keep these books handy. Strunk and White's *Elements of Style* (Allyn & Bacon) is also a great book for finding out where apostrophes and commas go. If you lack these books, visit the reference section of your local bookstore and plan on paying about $50 to stock up on quality references.

Keep Your Files Organized

Use folders on your hard drive for storing your document files. Keep related documents together in the same subdirectory.

Remember the Ctrl+Z Key!

The Ctrl+Z key is your undo key. If you're typing away in Word, press it to undelete any text you mistakenly deleted. This command works for individual letters, sentences, paragraphs, pages, and large chunks of text.

Save Your Document Often!

Save your document to disk as soon as you get a few meaningful words down on the screen. Then save every so often after that. Even if you're using the AutoSave feature (discussed in Chapter 35), continue to manually save your document to disk: Ctrl+S.

Take Advantage of Multiple Windows

Each document in Word appears as its own window on the screen. It's possible to have dozens of them open at once. Typically, when I write a book, I have an outline open in one window, the current chapter in another, and maybe some other chapters, references, or appendixes open in other windows. I use the buttons on the taskbar, or the Alt+Tab key combination, to switch between these windows.

Use AutoText for Often-Typed Stuff

To quickly insert things you type over and over, like your name and address, use an AutoText entry. Type your entry once, and then define it as a glossary entry under the Edit menu. Then use the shortcut key to zap it in whenever you need it. See Chapter 7 for more about AutoText.

Use Clever, Memorable Filenames

A file named LETTER is certainly descriptive, but what does it tell you? A file named LETTER TO MOM is even more descriptive but still lacking some information. A file LETTER TO MOM, APRIL 23 is even better. If you want to be brief, try 4-23 MOM LETTER. (Or just throw them all into a MOM folder.) You get the idea here: Use creative and informative filenames.

Don't Take It All Too Seriously

Computers are really about having fun. Too many people panic too quickly when they use a computer. Don't let it get to you! And please, please, don't reinstall Word to fix a minor problem. Anything that goes wrong has a solution. If the solution is not in this book, consult with your guru. Someone is bound to be able to help you out.

Index

• *Y* •

• *Z* •

Notes

Notes